THE THEATF

M000316920

Alan Nadel is William T. Bryan Chair of America Literature and Culture at the University of Kentucky. In addition to several books on postwar American literature and media, including *Invisible Criticism: Ralph Ellison and the American Canon* (1988) and *Television in Black-and-White America: Race and National Identity* (2006), he is the editor/contributor for two volumes of essays on the drama of August Wilson: *May All Your Fences Have Gates: Essays on the Drama of August Wilson* (1994) and *August Wilson: Completing the Twentieth-Century Cycle* (2010). His poetry has appeared in numerous journals, including *Georgia Review, Partisan Review, Paris Review,* and *Shenandoah.*

For a full listing, please visit www.bloomsbury.com/series/critical-companions/

THE THEATRE OF AUGUST WILSON

Alan Nadel

Series Editors: Patrick Lonergan and Kevin J. Wetmore, Jr.

methuen | drama

LONDON • NEW YORK • OXFORD • NEW DELHI • SYDNEY

METHUEN DRAMA
Bloomsbury Publishing Plc
50 Bedford Square, London, WC1B 3DP, UK

BLOOMSBURY, METHUEN DRAMA and the Methuen Drama logo are
trademarks of Bloomsbury Publishing Plc

First published in Great Britain 2018
This paperback edition published 2020

Cover design: Adriana Brioso
Cover image © Nobby Clark/ArenaPAL

A catalogue record for this book is available from the British Library.

Library of Congress Cataloging-in-Publication Data
Names: Nadel, Alan, 1947- author.
Title: The theatre of August Wilson / Alan Nadel.
Description: London ; New York : Bloomsbury Methuen Drama, 2019. | Series:
Critical companions | Includes bibliographical references and index.
Identifiers: LCCN 2017040931| ISBN 9781472534439 (pb) | ISBN 9781472530486 (hb)
Subjects: LCSH: Wilson, August—Criticism and interpretation.
Classification: LCC PS3573.I45677 Z79 2019 | DDC 812/.54--dc23 LC record
available at https://lccn.loc.gov/2017040931

ISBN: HB: 978-1-4725-3048-6
PB: 978-1-4725-3443-9
ePDF: 978-1-4725-2764-6
eBook: 978-1-4725-2832-2

Series: Critical Companions

Typeset by Deanta Global Publishing Services, Chennai, India

To find out more about our authors and books visit www.bloomsbury.com
and sign up for our newsletters.

This book is dedicated to the very fond memories of:

Martha Black (1927–1999)

Rosalind Green (1927–2004)

Sharon Anderson-Gold (1947–2011)

CONTENTS

ACKNOWLEDGMENTS

Even working in isolation, one never works alone. This book is indebted not only to the plays of August Wilson, but to the numerous actors, directors, and production people who brought those plays to life in the twenty productions that I have seen, and to the students in the graduate seminars devoted to Wilson's canon that I have taught at the University of Kentucky, and especially, to terrific graduate students at L'Orientale University in Naples, where I spent a Fulbright semester learning about the rich international relevance of Wilson's work. The fifty students and scholars who attended the 2008 August Wilson Conference in Lexington, Kentucky, all helped invigorate my thinking and shape my thought, and my research assistants over the past two years, Matthew Bryant-Cheney and Kate Gooch, were invaluable in helping me get this manuscript into shape. Emily Kretschmer, who was August Wilson's assistant when I was working on Wilson's plays and who arranged my first meeting with Wilson, has over many years provided me with invaluable insights about him and his work. Portions of the contents have been previously published and appear here with permission:

Alan Nadel, "Beginning Again, Again: Business in the Street in *Jitney* and *Gem of the Ocean*," in *August Wilson: Completing the Twentieth-Century Cycle* © 2010 University of Iowa Press. Used with permission of the University of Iowa Press.

Alan Nadel, "*Ma Rainey's Black Bottom*: Cutting the Historical Record, Dramatizing a Blues CD," in *The Cambridge Companion to August Wilson* © 2007 by Cambridge University Press. Used with permission of Cambridge University Press.

Alan Nadel, "Boundaries, Logistics, and Identity: The Property of Metaphor in *Fences* and *Joe Turner's Come and Gone*," in *May All Your Fences Have Gates: Essays on the Drama of August Wilson* © 1994 by the University of Iowa Press. Used with permission of the University of Iowa Press.

Donald E. Pease, "August Wilson's Lazarus Complex," in *August Wilson: Completing the Twentieth-Century Cycle* © 2010 by the University of Iowa Press. Used with permission of the University of Iowa Press.

INTRODUCTION

August Wilson had perhaps the most accomplished twenty-year span in the history of American theatre, writing ten plays of remarkable quality, comprising a coherent cycle—one play for each decade—that represented African American life in the twentieth century. There are no weak works in the cycle and several masterpieces. The plays, which won numerous awards,[1] furthermore, were the product of the last twenty-two years of Wilson's life. He was born in 1945 and his first play reached Broadway in 1984. Although drafts of some of the plays had been written in the early 1980s, and a version of *Jitney* had been produced regionally in the late 1970s, Wilson seemed to explode into theatrical consciousness in the mid-1980s and, until his death in 2005 at age sixty, he was the dominant playwright of American mainstage theatre.

After *Fences* became the most lucrative drama in the history of American theatre, it naturally became a very hot film prospect, but Wilson's insistence that the film have a black director led to public debate and film industry complications that, in effect, delayed the film of *Fences* for almost thirty years. The controversy exposed many cherished Hollywood prejudices, not just about racial bias but also about studio politics and executive egos. Talking about his dealings with Hollywood, Wilson told me:

> They try to seduce you by giving you things so that you get used to having them. Then they start to take them away *and they have you. . . .* So they would tell me they would reserve a suite for me at the Ritz Carlton, and I'd say, "That's OK, I'll just get a motel." And they would say they would have a limo waiting at the airport, and I'd say, "No, I'll just take a cab. I'll get receipt and you can reimburse me." It makes them crazy. They don't know what do with me.

He similarly challenged the theatre establishment. Although he was determined to get full recognition on the American mainstage, the place where plays became eligible for Tony Awards and Pulitzer Prizes, he delivered a keynote speech to the Theater Communications Group decrying the underfunding of black regional theatres. And despite advocating for African Americans on stage and backstage, he argued against the practice of colorblind casting. Just as he had punctured the sense of "magnanimity" in which Hollywood executives took pride, he thus exposed the sense of liberal self-satisfaction with which Broadway distributed (rationed?) roles to ethnic minorities. In both instances, at great personal expense, Wilson exposed the invisible hierarchy and privilege that tacitly instantiated American whiteness.

This theme runs through Wilson's cycle, for although it may be possible to deracialize privilege, history has shown that in twentieth-century America, it has been impossible to deprivilege race. Or at least history has shown that to the people represented by Wilson's characters, so that Wilson's plays attempt to show it to everyone else. The minimum task of this volume, therefore, is to underscore—in the same way that Wilson's public stances did—the dimensions of privilege that have transparently enveloped America during what has been called "The American Century."

One aspect of the plays that I foreground is that America has always suffered from a profound confusion of human rights with property rights. In that regard especially, and in many others as well, the law has been an instrument of privilege rather than an agent of justice. Those deprived of the law's judicious instrumentality have found themselves improvising in a world dependent upon extralegal negotiations in liminal spaces. In a nation traditionally dedicated to principles of renewal and reinvention, African Americans were often forced to construct artistic, rather than juridical or institutional, sites of innovation. These sites can generically be called the extralegal, unruly, improvisational world of the blues, as a musical form and lyrical rendition, as a philosophy and sensibility. In the blues Wilson found his entry into history and the means by which it spoke to him as the musical inscription of American racial privilege. The blues, Wilson demonstrates, offered American culture a psychic tableau of disrupted dreams and displaced passions, of violence and aspiration, of infinite possibility. Each of his plays, therefore, engages some form of cancelled contract, some broken promise along with its potential—achieved or failed—for transcendence.

My discussion tries, as well, to put Wilson's plays in the context of the chronological story they tell about his development as an artist and the chronological story he tells about African Americans and the conditions of the twentieth century with which African American life had to cope. Wilson, as the adage goes—and as his Hollywood encounters demonstrated—did not suffer fools well, a trait he shared with almost all of his characters as they turned the foolish privileges and vicious hierarchies of the American Century into myriad solos in a blues symphony.

CHAPTER 1
BECOMING AUGUST WILSON

August Wilson was a wonderful raconteur. In the same way that Wilson loved the way the blues consolidated, disseminated, and retained African American oral history, one has to love how Wilson's own storytelling—as a body of lore and a mode of performance—did the same thing. When Wilson was writing *Two Trains Running*, he learned that whenever he was lost he could find his way by asking a character a question. Since these characters, by definition, lived not just in his imagination but in his historical past, this questioning—a walk into the unknown—was also how Wilson produced knowledge. In this way, his work presents "the past as present," to quote the apt title of Harry Elam Jr.'s award-winning book on Wilson's drama.

To put it another way, his plays do not enact past events—in the tradition of historical drama or fiction, steeped in the researched details of another time and place—but rather become our present experience, just as does a blues song resung or the acting out of trauma. This kind of retelling has the authenticity of origins and the urgency of gossip. In Wilson's ten-play cycle, we are not born to the past but instead encounter its becoming; we enter his theatre like newborns, unto whom the past is delivered. As individuals and as a culture, we starve the past or nurse it, we let it run wild or we discipline it, we encourage its unruly outbursts or we teach it to be respectable.

A requisite task of a culture, a community, a family, or an individual, therefore, is to organize experience into the stories that become its past. Without such stories, cultures cannot exist, communities cannot cohere, families dissolve into the inchoate stuff of DNA patterns, and individuals succumb to advanced dementia. In the spirit of the fabric of this cultural retelling, in the vitality of cultural narrative, Wilson's cycle was inseminated. Speech became plays, became a cycle, became a century, became national and ethnic history.

So too, Frederick August Kittel's stories became the past of August Wilson, the name that consolidates the stories of Kittel/Wilson's history. The point that I am making is that the biography of August Wilson is the story of becoming the man consolidated under that name, in the same way that making the plays consolidates the identity of playwright August Wilson, which replicates the making of the African American history that the plays consolidate. Since it was Wilson's words that produced his identity, it seems both fitting and accurate to explain the history of Frederick August Kittel's becoming August Wilson in his own words. Although what follows is written in the third person, it combines much quotation and extensive paraphrase from Wilson's interviews, mixing, as such dialogues are prone to, fact and lore, record and interpretation.

Frederick Kittel

Frederick August Kittel, or Freddie, as he was known, was born on April 27, 1945, to Daisy Wilson, an African American woman from South Carolina who lived at the time with her three daughters in a two-room apartment in the Pittsburgh's Bedford Hills section. His father, also Frederick August Kittel, a German baker, did not live with the family, drank heavily, and was an erratic presence in their lives. His mother, with only a sixth-grade education, was a very good reader who taught Freddie and his five siblings to read.[1] Freddie started reading at four years old. When he was twelve, he discovered the Negro section of the library and by fourteen had read "all the books. . . . There were only about thirty or forty books there" (*Conversations*, 47).

The family lived in a mixed neighborhood—mostly Syrians, Jews, and blacks. Their street constituted a community of people, and Freddie remembered, when coming home from school, seeing all the parents "sitting on the stoops, talking and exchanging recipes, talking about what they were cooking for dinner, talking about their kids. That was a nice neighborhood in the sense that anyone in the neighborhood was your social parent" (*Conversations*, 41–42). His parents' generation sheltered the children from many indignities. "I think it's wrong," he explained, "but there are some things you don't want to tell your kids. . . . You can go to Woolworth's and buy something, but they won't give blacks a paper bag." Now, he gets a bag for everything. If he buys a pack of gum, he asks for a bag. "I'm making up for all the bags I didn't get" (*Conversations*, 42).

Freddie's mother was a profound influence on his values, his sense of integrity, and what he would later, as August Wilson, call his warrior spirit. One story that exemplifies Daisy's integrity relates to a radio contest that promised a new Speed Queen washer to the first listener who identified the product associated with the slogan "When it rains, it pours." At the time, Daisy was washing clothes on a scrub board, and she had to heat up the water because they didn't have hot water. She recognized the phrase as the new Morton Salt slogan and sent her daughter to the store with a dime to call in the answer. Although she was the first caller, when they found out who Daisy was, they wanted to give her a certificate to go to the Salvation Army for a used machine. They wouldn't give her a new washing machine, which she had legitimately won, because she was black. "In so many words," Wilson explained, "she told them what they could do with their certificate" (*Conversations*, 73).

It wasn't until two or three years later that they got a brand new Speed Queen from Herb Glickman, a white man who would buy appliances on credit, because he could get it, and sell to black people on credit plans. "He would buy merchandise for $39 and sell it to blacks for $49, because he was willing to take the risk of you paying him. He was willing to come every week to get his $2, so he earned every dime of that extra he charged, and were it not for him, a whole lot of blacks would have had nothing" (*Conversations*, 47–48).

When Freddie entered adolescence, the family moved to a rented house in Hazelwood, a white working-class neighborhood where many people were employed by the local steel mill. When the family moved in, someone threw a brick through the window with a note that said "Nigger Stay Out." They had just started letting blacks into the parochial school Freddie attended, and he was the only black in his eighth-grade class. His grade school in the Hill District, like the neighborhood, was very mixed, racially and ethnically, so at fourteen, when Freddie went from there to Central Catholic, it was the first time he confronted anything like overt racism. Every morning there was a note on his desk that said "Go home, nigger," which he would pick up, like clockwork, and throw away. White students constantly instigated him, and he got into many fights. One particular day, because around forty kids were waiting outside after school for him, the principal had to send him home in a cab. The conditions became so impossible that he left Central Catholic and entered a trade school, where he spent half the day "doing fifth grade work" and the other half making tin cups in a sheet metal shop.

In the middle of the year, at age fifteen, he transferred to a public high school. His tenth-grade history teacher "was one of those black teachers who did not like black people" (*Conversations*, 43). When Freddie handed in a term paper on Napoleon, the teacher asked to see him after school.

He wrote "A+," and then he wrote "E." And then he said "I'm going to give you one of these two grades." . . . He began flipping through the paper, and he asked me where I did my research, and I said "Well, I've got a bibliography here." And he said, "Well—you have some older sisters, don't you?" I said, "Yeah, I have three of them." "Well—is it possible that *they* could have written this paper?" I said, "To be honest, I write *their* papers." . . . He drew a circle around the "E" . . . I tore [the paper] up, threw it in the trash, and walked out. (*Conversations*, 44)

Freddie never attended school again. "The next morning I got up and played basketball right underneath the principal's window. . . . I wanted him to come and say, 'Why aren't you in school?' so I could tell someone. And he never came out" (*Conversations*, 67).

Based on his experience, Wilson developed a low opinion of formal education:

The schools are horrible and don't teach anybody anything. From about fifth grade on, I was always butting heads with my teachers. I would ask them a question and they would say "Shut up. Sit down," because they didn't know the answers. So I'd go to the library to find out. When I quit school . . . I didn't want my mother to know, so I'd get up and go to the library and stay there until three o'clock . . . . In the library for the first time in my life I felt free. I could read whole books on subjects that interested me. (*Conversations*, 207)

By the time Freddie left the library, he thought, "Okay, I'm ready. I know a lot of stuff. It always amazed me that libraries were free" (*Conversations*, 207).

At nineteen, Freddie moved into a basement apartment (in the Hill District) with a group of writers and painters. One of them, Rob Penny, exposed him to tapes by Malcolm X. Freddie bought a record player that only played 78 rpm records. "I used to go to this place that had stacks and stacks of 78s. I'd buy them ten at a time—give the man fifty cents and I'm gone" (*Conversations*, 84). One day he heard a Bessie Smith recording for the first time. "I listened to it twenty-two straight times, and I became aware that this stuff was my own. . . . There was an immediate emotional response. It was someone speaking directly to me. I felt this was mine" (*Conversations*, 84). At the time, Wilson was living in a Pittsburgh rooming house. "After I discovered the blues, I began to look at the people in the house a little differently than I had before. I began to see the value in their lives that I hadn't seen before. I discovered a beauty and nobility in their struggle to survive. . . . The mere fact that they were all able to make this music was a testament to the resiliency of their spirit" (*Conversations*, 64).

August Wilson

When Freddie was twenty, his father, Frederick August Kittel, died, and Freddie, adopting his mother's maiden name, called himself "August Wilson" and started writing poetry under that name. He also wrote a term paper for his sister, who was attending Fordham University. With the $20 she gave him, he bought a second-hand typewriter. "I sat right down and typed up a couple of poems. And this was work, because it took, like, a half-hour to type five lines, because I didn't know where the keys were" (*Conversations*, 49).

In 1967, Wilson and some other black artists and writers put out a magazine called *Connection*, of which Wilson was the poetry editor, and they founded the Center Avenue Theater Poets' Workshop, which featured poetry readings and gallery jazz sessions. This led to the formation, in 1968, of the Black Horizons Theater. He founded the theatre troupe with Rob Penny in order "to politicize the community" (*Conversations*, 14). He was interested in art and literature and felt the arts could alter the relationship between blacks and society. "There was an explosion of black theater in the late sixties—theater was a way of . . . raising the consciousness of the people" (*Conversations*, 21). At that point, he wasn't writing plays. "I was directing—I mean I didn't know how to do that either; I'd never even seen a play" (*Conversations*, 14), so he went to the library and got books out on how to direct.

At age twenty-four, Wilson married for the first time. Although the marriage produced a daughter in 1970, the union was short-lived, dissolving because of religious differences. Wilson's wife, Brenda Burton, was a Muslim. During that period, Wilson describes himself as "just hanging around writing poetry and stories and that" (*Conversations*, 15). Something happened, however, in 1976, when Wilson saw *Sizwe Bansi Is Dead* at the Pittsburgh Public Theater. "Most of the plays I have seen are Fugard plays, so he's probably had an influence on me without my knowing it" (*Conversations*, 23). That influence, apparently, had started to work its way into his poetry, because when his friend, Claude Purdy, read a series of his poems about the mythic Western figure Black Bart, Purdy asked Wilson to turn the poems into a stage production for the Penumbra Theater in

St. Paul. "He called me from there and said, why don't you come out and rewrite this script?" and he offered to pay Wilson's way (*Conversations*, 16). "I thought 'A free trip to St. Paul, what the hell?' so I went out there and did a quick rewrite of the play" (*Conversations*, 22). It was called *Black Bart and the Sacred Hills*—a musical satire. In January 1978, the Inner City Theater in Los Angeles did a staged reading of it, and in 1981 it was produced at the Penumbra Theater.

In 1965, when Wilson had started writing poetry, he read "anything and everything that was out there," and, as a result, he felt that it took him many years to find his own voice. "It took me until 1973 before I could write a poem that was *my* poem" (*Conversations*, 23). Therefore, when Wilson started writing plays in earnest in 1979, he did not want to read the body of Western theatre. Instead, he decided, "I will just do it my way—I will just say this is my idea of a play" (*Conversations*, 103).

When he went to St. Paul, Wilson also decided that "this is a nice place, I should move up here" (*Conversations*, 16), and he did. Ten years later, when the mayor proclaimed an "August Wilson Day," Wilson said he had "found a city that encourages dreams" (*Conversations*, 39). By moving to Minneapolis-St. Paul, Wilson went from a neighborhood of 55,000 blacks to a state in which there were only 35,000. "This was a tremendous change. In Pittsburgh it was a question of not being able to see the forest for the trees. The reason I couldn't write dialogue was because I didn't respect the way blacks talked."[2] He thought that he had to change black speech to make art out of it: "I was always trying to mold it into some European sensibility of what language should be" (*Conversations*, 183).

His ability to recognize the artistry inherent in black speech was enlightening.

> I have stood around in Pat's Cigar Store in Pittsburgh and watched these guys using Aristotle's Poetics much better than some university students because theirs is an intuitive sense. Some of the stories were absolutely incredible—incredible, too, in the way in which they were told. The story is basically simple but it is the telling and the structure of the story that is fascinating. (Bigsby, 209)

His love of this speech merged with a love of blues, cultivated much earlier. "I knew very little about jazz, and I wanted to find out something about it, so I started at the very beginning. I got as far as Jelly Roll Morton and I got bogged down" (*Conversations*, 17). The blues informed him that there was nobility to the lives of blacks in America which I didn't always see. . . . After I discovered the blues, I looked at the lives of the people in the [boarding house where I lived] a little differently . . . I began to understand . . . that the avenues for participation in society were closed to these people and that their ambitions had been thwarted. . . . That they were able to make this music was a testament to the resiliency of their spirit. (*Conversations*, 63–64)

We are not a people with a long history of writing things out. . . . In order for information to survive, you have to tell it in such a way that it's memorable—so that someone else hearing the story will want to go and tell someone else. That's a way of ensuring survival. One way to make information memorable is to put it into music. Music provides an emotional reference to the content of the song. (*Conversations*, 58)

This is one of the reasons why the blues is important to Wilson and his work: "The blues is the core. All American music . . . is influenced by the blues. This is one contribution that everyone admits that Africans have made. . . . The music is ours, since it contains our soul, so to speak—it contains all our ideas and responses to the world" (*Conversations*, 37). "[The musician's] expression has been so highly developed, and it has been one expression of African American life. It's like culture is in the music. And the writers are way behind the music. So I'm trying to close the gap" (*Conversations*, 152). "My assumption would be that music is cross-cultural. One of the driving things of any black aesthetic is improvisation or the idea of improving. It's the thing that enabled us to survive" (*Conversations*, 252).

This August Wilson, self-schooled in public libraries, coming of age as a Black Nationalist activist, laboring as a Black Arts poet, burdened by the heft of the Western poetic tradition, exposed to Athol Fugard's plays and the patter of restaurants, barber shops, bars, and sidewalks, directing plays out of necessity rather than expertise, who at the request of a friend converted a series of poems, never intended for the stage, into a play; this man, renamed August Wilson, with little money and no income, about to turn thirty-three, embarking on a new career in a new city, in an overwhelmingly white state, was half a decade away from commencing a career as one of the most successful, and arguably the greatest, of American playwrights.

Shortly after arriving in Minneapolis, Wilson got a job writing children's plays for the Science Museum of Minneapolis. "I would dramatize the tales of Northwest Indians . . . I did a series of Profiles in Science, one on Margaret Mead, one on William Harvey" (*Conversations*, 16). Wilson quit that job to devote more time to writing, for two-and-a-half years working as a staff cook for a social service organization called Little Brothers of the Poor. The job paid only $88 a week, but the schedule was flexible and he worked only four hours per day, which gave him the time to write *Ma Rainey.*

Wilson had actually started *Ma Rainey* in 1976:

> I wrote a one-act play called *The Homecoming*, which dealt with economic exploitation. It took place in an abandoned train station. These two black guys encounter two recruiting scouts from the record companies. Then I started working on *Ma Rainey's Black Bottom,* which is about the economic exploitation of early black performers. I planned a third play about Otis Redding and so *Ma Rainey* fitted naturally into this trilogy that I was calling *Dangerous Music.* (Bigsby, 207)

At that time, Wilson joined the Playwright's Center of Minneapolis and got a grant from the Jerome Foundation, and he began submitting plays to the O'Neill Conference, five of which were rejected before they accepted *Ma Rainey.* There, Wilson "learned to respect the stage and trust that it will carry your ideas. The intensity of the O'Neill process—working in four days, working fast—was also good experience. It comes down to problem solving. But there's no one correct solution" (*Conversations*, 24).

The problem solving involved in writing *Ma Rainey* was replicated in the play. Each of the characters, faced with a specific set of problems, had to wrestle with possible solutions, in the same way that Wilson had to wrestle with the options for expressing their dilemmas and with choosing the language that comprised their options and choices. The play, about human rights, artistic rights, and copyrights, pitted several characters against one another, as each had to decide what was his or hers, what was essential and what was negotiable, what one right was worth in exchange for another. Unifying the spectrum of rights is the figure of Ma Rainey, who, knowing she must ultimately sign her artistic rights away, leverages to the greatest extent possible the value she can exact for the exchange. The centrality of her worth, however transient, impacts in different ways the use value and exchange value of all those in her orbit, from the cab driver with whom she has a minor collision to her piano player, who pays with his life for the devaluation her actions inflict on the trumpeter and on his art.

In a way both ironic and iconic, the value of the play *Ma Rainey* put Wilson in the same position as his characters (which was the same position he put himself in by trying to articulate their options and choices). After the O'Neill Conference, Wilson was given the option to have the play produced at the Yale Repertory, under the direction of Lloyd Richards, with whom he had worked at the conference and who was then the Dean of the Yale School of Drama. But that option was in competition with a much more lucrative offer from Broadway producers, who, it turns out, wanted to make a musical out of the play:

> They sent me a contract, just a terrible contract. They had the rights to bring in other writers. . . . I called one of the guys up . . . and he said "Listen, it doesn't matter what the contract says. The important thing is for you to sign it and get to work. A lot of things in this business are done on faith." I said, "Okay, if it doesn't matter what the contract says, let's make it say what I want it to say." Whereupon I was met with silence. (*Conversations*, 135)

The Yale Rep, where Wilson brought *Ma Rainey* instead of signing it away, "is a great place to work. We do the work necessary for the play to realize its potential without any regard to what may happen to it after we finish. . . . We don't work with Broadway in mind" (*Conversations*, 51). There, Wilson learned from Richards to "respect [the stage] and realize that what you put up there is important, and that you have a responsibility for what you put up there, and that everyone of those words on the page are going to get said, and they'd better be the words you want said" (*Conversations*, 52).

Playwright August Wilson

In the crucible of the Yale Rep, Wilson polished *Ma Rainey* into the production that could move to Broadway on his terms, where it won the Drama Critic's Circle Award. While *Ma Rainey* was in rehearsals, *Fences* had already been drafted. After telling people that he knew how to write a more conventional play, focused on one central character, Wilson asked himself, "do I really know how to write that kind of a play? So I wrote *Fences* in answer to the challenge I'd given myself" (*Conversations*, 88). The play, which opened on Broadway in 1987, won Wilson another Drama Critics' Circle Award, as well as the Tony for best play and the Pulitzer Prize. And it grossed $12 million in one year, making it the most financially successful drama in American history.

During this same period, two plays that Wilson had written earlier, *Jitney* and *Joe Turner's Come and Gone*, were finding regional productions. *Joe Turner*, after being workshopped at the O'Neill Conference in 1984 and being staged at the Yale Rep in 1986 and the Arena Stage in Washington in 1987, premiered on Broadway in 1988, winning Wilson yet another Drama Critics' Circle Award. By this time, *The Piano Lesson*, which would win Wilson his second Pulitzer Prize, was going from the O'Neill Conference to regional production.

The purposefulness with which Wilson wrote, revised, and brought to Broadway these plays reflected how he insisted on envisioning his work as part of a greater product. In the largest sense, that was a political project.

> All art is political. It serves a purpose. All of my plays are political but I try not to make them didactic or polemical. . . . I hope my art serves the masses of blacks in America who are in desperate need of a solid and sure identity. I hope my plays make people understand that these are African people, that this is why they do what they do. (*Conversations*, 37)

But to participate in his political agenda, he needed to situate himself in a large artistic project, of which each work was only a part. For that reason, he could never complete a play until he knew the setting and the first lines of his next play. The idea of a ten-play cycle, organized according to African American life in the twentieth century, was a heuristic to guarantee that sense of purpose, one that emerged out of a reflection on his first plays:

> I wrote a play called *Jitney!* that was set in 1971, and then I wrote a play called *Fullerton Street* (ultimately omitted from the cycle) that was set in 1941, and then I wrote *Ma Rainey's Black Bottom* which was set in 1927. And I said, well, I have written plays set in three different decades; why don't I continue to do that. It gave me an agenda, a focus, something to hone in on, so that I never had to worry about what the next play would be about. (*Conversations*, 102)

Ma Rainey's Black Bottom, which in effect commenced Wilson's career as a playwright, opened at the Repertory in April 1984 and had its Broadway opening in October 1984. Wilson had written other plays earlier. One of them, *Jitney*, eventually became part of the cycle, and first drafts of two others, *Joe Turner* and *Fences*, were also written before *Ma Rainey*'s premiere, but in many ways it seems prophetic that it initiated his Broadway career. The process by which it went to Yale, as I have noted, involved Wilson's refusing to sign away his rights to producers in a situation that echoes Ma Rainey's experience in the play. Then, when an album was recorded based on the play, a similar situation occurred. Although the terms of the contract with the record company included Wilson's writing the liner notes, after the recording session, he was informed that someone else had been hired to write the liner notes.

> I said, "I don't believe this. Now I'm Levee—Mr. Sturdyvant, you said you'd let me record them songs." And he says, "Mort's going to say some nice things about you." I looked at him like he was crazy. . . . I called my lawyer and said—I hadn't signed the contract at that time. And I said, ". . . I am not signing the contract." (*Conversations*, 139)

Playwright August Wilson's one story

Yet in another way, he has argued that all his plays are about the same thing: "I once wrote this short story called 'The Best Blues Singer in the World', and it went like this: 'The streets that Balboa walked was his own private ocean, and Balboa was drowning.' End of story. . . . Since then I've been writing the same story over and over again. All my plays are rewriting that same story" (*Conversations*, 211).

In whatever sense the "story" is the same, Wilson got the core of each play's historical uniqueness from the blues. "I listen to the music of the particular period I'm working on. Inside the music are clues to what is happening with the people" (*Conversations*, 62). When he was writing *Ma Rainey*, for example, he didn't want to know anything about the singer. "I figured what I needed to know I'd get out of her music" (*Conversations*, 238).

Wilson wrote in bars and restaurants. "At the start of the day I take out my tablet and go out and search for a play. I get some coffee and sit down. If I feel like writing something I do" (*Conversations*, 26). He starts with a line of dialogue instead of any concept of what the play is about.

> Someone says something and they're talking to someone else. I don't know all the time who's talking or who they are talking to, but you take the line of dialogue and it starts from there. The next thing you know is you've gotten four pages of dialogue, and after a while

you say, "Well, let me name this guy; let's give him a name. Who's talking?" And in the process of him talking you find out things about him. So the more the characters talk, the more you know about them. (*Conversations*, 224)

Sometimes Wilson has trouble shutting his characters up, and he gets so immersed in the world that he's also becoming a part of it. "You discover that you're walking down this landscape of the self, and you have to be willing to confront whatever it is that you discover there" (*Conversations*, 78). Nevertheless, Wilson considers the foundation of his playwriting to be poetry: "Not so much in terms of the language but the concept . . . I try to find a metaphor to carry the work" (*Conversations*, 23).

His process of discovery continues through the stages of production, initially at the O'Neill Theater Center's National Playwrights Conference, where the two staged readings give Wilson "ideas about how [he] could make the play better" (*Conversations*, 113), such that he can create a draft suitable for going into rehearsal, followed by a production at the Yale Repertory Theater, where "we do not open it in the spirit that this is an incomplete or unfinished work" (*Conversations*, 113). Nevertheless, as the play is performed in other cities, he continues to "watch the performance and continue to revise" (*Conversations*, 113). His initial experience workshopping *Ma Rainey* at the O'Neill was crucial to his developing this process. "About *Ma Rainey* I felt I was growing as a playwright and moving toward learning more about the craft and how to articulate my ideas dramatically" (*Conversations*, 6).

All of Wilson's plays, from the 1982 reading of *Ma Rainey* at the O'Neill Conference to the 1987 reading of *The Piano Lesson*, went through this initial production process: *Fences* (O'Neill, 1983; Yale, 1985), *Joe Turner* (O'Neill, 1984; Yale, 1986), *The Piano Lesson* (O'Neill, 1987; Yale, 1987). *Two Trains* opened at Yale in 1990, skipping the O'Neill Conference, and *Seven Guitars* was the first Wilson play in the cycle to go directly to regional theatre (the Goodman, in Chicago), bypassing both the O'Neill Conference and the Yale Repertory. The same is true of *Jitney*, the revised version of which opened at the Pittsburgh Public Theater in 1996, as did *King Hedley II* in 2000. The last two plays, *Gem of the Ocean*, which initiates the cycle's chronology, and *Radio Golf*, which concludes the chronology and also serves as a direct sequel to the *Gem*, draw on Wilson's earlier production process: *Gem* had a reading at the 2002 O'Neill Conference, and *Radio Golf* premiered in 2005 at Yale.

His first six plays were directed by Lloyd Richards, who first mentored Wilson at the O'Neill Conference and saw *Ma Rainey* from its reading there, through its Yale production and its regional performances, to its Broadway premiere. Wilson's relationship with Richards was such that many people started treating Wilson's plays as a virtual collaboration. Wilson's sense of authority as a playwright and, eventually, as a producer seems, however, to have made a split with Richards inevitable. For the director of his seventh play, the 1996 revised version of *Jitney*, Wilson chose Marion McClinton. "Wilson may have lost a kind of father in his split with Richards," John Lahr explains, "but in McClinton he gained a brother" (Bigsby, 46). McClinton also directed Wilson's next play, *King Hedley II*, and he directed the initial regional production of *Gem* in 2003, although the version that reached Broadway in 2004 was directed by Kenny Leon.

CHAPTER 2
HISTORY AND/AS PERFORMANCE: THE DRAMA OF AFRICAN AMERICAN HISTORIOGRAPHY

In an essay on the African American writer John A. Williams, I once wrote that History is an intersection of time and place at which an accident is happening. I go on in that essay to elaborate some of the issues at stake in such an intersection and accident, especially those concerning who gets to write the accident report, for, as I have argued elsewhere, History belongs to whoever owns the erasers.[1] That is to say, we cannot construct a history until we clear away all the irrelevancy, all the opaqueness, all the confusion and chaos out of which accidents occur. And, in our culture, we cannot resolve the accident until we impose narratives of cause and effect; in other words, until we extract from the accident its accidentalness, its unpredictability, and until we identify the victims and determine the conditions of culpability and liability. In this context, we could say that all historians are ambulance-chasers. But some people never get an ambulance; they remain the unaccounted casualties of history or, to put it another way, the causalities of historiography, the process of writing history. In this sense, history performs acts of inclusion and exclusion that have profound social consequences.

History, in other words, can be regarded as a constative discourse, that is, a way of *describing* a set of conditions, or it can be regarded as a performative discourse, that is, a way of *creating* a set of conditions.[2] If we consider one of the classic examples of performative speech, the promise, we can see that when one makes a promise one is doing more than simply describing an intention; one is also entering into a social contract, creating a set of expectations for, and implicit agreements with, the listener. Performative discourse serves a function, and it alters the extant state of things. Although they are simply speech, performative speech acts have material implications in that they affect the way people behave in the material world, and hence how they reorganize that world.

Although it may be convenient to treat History as though it were merely a record or an analysis of phenomena, as though it had no opportunity to change the things it describes, History is always and necessarily performative; it always and necessarily creates History rather than describes events. First, to use the metaphor with which I started, it determines what constitutes an accident, distinguishing, for example, a pedestrian hit by a car from the insect splattered on that car's windshield; it also cordons off the accident site, thus marking what falls outside the margin of the accident's impact; it identifies who may be considered a witness and under what conditions that witness may be considered reliable. Having done all of this social engineering, History then produces narratives that not only treat these prior conditions as "fact" and the recording of them as "method" but also contribute to the sense of time and place within which its audience, in other words, the historical subject, lives.

History, passing, and fences

Lest this seem too abstract, let us consider the following. At the end of *Fences*, Cory arrives for his father's funeral dressed in an army uniform. Instead of having gotten a football scholarship and gone to college, he has joined the armed service. Several historical conditions inform this moment. The first is that Cory was prevented from playing football in his senior year of high school and thus of getting a football scholarship because of his father Troy's sense of history. History, for Troy, is a form of rationalization. When his friend Bono explains why Troy, despite his immense talents, was unable to play major league baseball, Bono says to Troy "You just come along too early" (9), meaning before the major leagues were integrated. When Troy angrily rejects Bono's explanation: "There ought not never have been no time called too early" (9), he subsequently explains, "I'm talking about if you could play ball then they ought to have let you play. Don't care what color you were. Come telling me I come along too early. If you could play . . . then they ought to have let you play" (9).

History is thus an enabling fiction to rationalize retrospectively racial discrimination in professional baseball. History records as an accident of time and place that Troy could not play, when it was not accidental at all. The same historical methodology that could create this invisible timeline for baseball would not apply, for example, to some privileged histories of science and technology, in which progress is *defined* by the talent of the scientist or inventor. The Wright Brothers did not come along too early for the age of aviation; rather, the age of aviation was initiated by their talents. They came along at exactly the right historical moment, *by definition*.

Troy is thus noting the way in which Bono's iteration of a historical cliché performs an act of racial discrimination rather than describing a condition of necessity. He has caught Bono in a moment, so to speak, of passing, that is, of living inside the reality of a narrative that excludes him. In Wilson's work, we find many phrases for and instances of such passing. In *Joe Turner's Come and Gone*, for example, it's called losing (or having someone steal) your song; it's meeting the conditions of a recording company, as Ma Rainey does, or trying to, as Levee does; in *The Piano Lesson*, it's attempting to exorcise the ghosts of the slave holders by substituting Christian ritual for ancestral power. The car service in *Jitney* is passing for a taxi service, despite the fact that urban renewal has excised the site of its existence. The problem of being a legitimate business in a space that has been delegitimized informs *Two Trains Running* as well, where the same urban renewal program is about to condemn Memphis Lee's restaurant. Although Memphis says that if he knows the rules he can play by them, because the rules emanate from a narrative that excludes him, in the same way that the baseball narrative excluded Troy Maxson, Memphis has two deeds to two properties from which he is excluded.

Both Hambone in *Two Trains* and Hedley in *Seven Guitars* assert—to the point of derangement—their rights to property that they never will receive, never *can* receive, because their assertions have no standing in the dominant narrative; they are asserting rights while standing outside the narrative to which those rights accrue. The bookend plays of Wilson's cycle, *Gem of the Ocean* and *Radio Golf*, examine the history of the twentieth century through a legacy of passing initiated by Caesar Wilkes, whose distance—temporal as well as logistic—from his grandson, from his family, and from his community exists more or less explicitly on racial grounds.

At the same time that Troy exposes Bono's historiographic error, in mistaking performative history for constative, Troy is also acknowledging the performative power of history. Although there "ought not never have been no time called too early," Troy is also accepting that the consequences of such historical constructions are unalterable.[3] Troy will continue to tell the story that white history says it is too early until it's too late for Cory. In this way, Troy articulates his own version of history, which, within the limits of his own home and property line, has the same performative power that the history he rejects has in the larger spaces of American society. From

Cory's perspective, it's about time that Troy gave up his historical premises, and from Troy's, it's about time Cory faced reality, and from Wilson's it always is, as we shall see, all about time.

History, time, and performance

Time has three dimensions: frequency, duration, and tempo, all of which are also dynamics of historiography. The writing of history creates temporal periods, gives the pace to the events that fill them, and marks the patterns of repetition that give shape to those events. The stuttering Sylvester in *Ma Rainey* speaks at an unusual tempo, while Levee wants to change the tempo of the musical arrangements in order to accommodate the changing times. Like baseball, music has its own history, which operates according to timelines related to, but also independent from, the timelines of politics, of war, or of poetry. Because Wilson's characters live outside the sanctioned timeframes of the dominant culture, the temporal discord of their situations becomes intrinsic to the dramatic situation. Boy Willie in *The Piano Lesson*, for example, wants to sell the piano in time for him to buy the land on which his ancestors worked as slaves. In one sense, time may be short for Boy Willie, who has a small window in which to raise the necessary money, but given that his family's labor gave value to the land, the opportunity to buy it is long overdue.

In *Seven Guitars*, Floyd Barton needs to get his guitar out of the pawn shop in time to make a recording date in Chicago, while Ruby has to find a father for her child before her time is due. Hedley has been waiting for the money he believes he will receive from Buddy Bolden, but because he is suffering from tuberculosis, Hedley's time to receive the money is nearly up. When Hedley comes along at the wrong time and mistakes Floyd's money for Buddy Bolden's, it turns out that Floyd's time is up. *Radio Golf* starts with the recognition that it is time for Pittsburgh to have a black mayor and ends with the realization that this time is only possible at the expense of the history that enabled it.[4]

Thus, all these events fall outside of historical time, as unreported accidents, in the same way as did Troy's baseball records. For this reason, both Troy and Cory cannot describe things as they are. While the dominant historical narrative subordinates the demands of the game to the social limitations of its chief audience, Troy's historical narrative not only ignores the changes that have become part of the history of baseball, but also conflates the history of all professional sports in the United States. Football, Cory's sport, had been integrated long before baseball, and it afforded black athletes many opportunities—although even today with noteworthy limitations—to rise to the top. Cory is thus caught in a conflict between versions of History, with each version having a different performative power at a different site. His choice to join the military may at first seem to resolve the conflict by rejecting his father's historiography; instead, Cory has pledged loyalty and allegiance to the historical narratives of the dominant white society. Given the options available to a young black man in Corey's situation, joining the peacetime army seems to be, the numbers have shown, a credible option. But the play ends in 1964, and from our historical perspective we can assume, when we see a black man in the regular army in 1964, that his next tour of duty will be Vietnam.

One reason for this situation was that President Lyndon Johnson had— unlike, for example, George Bush or Donald Trump—a strong sense of history, and his sense of history told him that if he pulled out of Vietnam he would be the first American president to lose a war. He believed this because the American textbooks he studied said that America had fought the War of 1812 to keep the British Navy from impressing American sailors. To whatever extent that war succeeded in that goal, there can be no doubt that the American "War of 1812" failed to win one of its chief goals, at least according to Canadian history texts: America's annexation of Canada. One can only wonder, in other words, how many fewer black men would have died in Vietnam had President Johnson read Canadian instead of American history books.

We have no reason to expect that he should have done so, or to expect that if he had, he would have accepted the Canadian version over the American. But that underscores the basic point: History is performative; that is, it iterates narratives to the point at which they acquire referential cogency. Witnessing their sundry performances in myriad contexts, we refer to them as though they were true, believe they define the accidental collisions of time and place in which we are situated, adopt them as our sense of past and our source of identity. We do this in terms of familial identity as well as national, ethnic as well as sexual, institutional as well as cultural. Located within that matrix of historical references, moreover, we act as historical subjects, for only by remembering the accumulation of historical narratives that have been performed for us can we find historical dimensions to our actions.

In this regard, we can say, at least figuratively, that History is theatre; that is, it is the process of assigning roles and of selecting, highlighting, foregrounding, and framing events so as to make them theatrical: people *perform* on the *stage* of history; battles occurred in the European *theatre* of operations; specific events and figures *occupy the public spotlight*; we recognize *acts* of great moment and consequence; we say that a person's ability to *act* presidential contributes to his *performance* in office; those who fill the *role* of "the nobility" ought to *act* . . . well, "noble." Especially in contemporary America, when so much of what we consider historical occurs in the same public space that provides hundreds of hours of drama each week, that is, the television screen, often in formats that erode generic boundaries between the fictive and the historical, it is hard to ignore the ways in which History depends on its own theatricality.

To put it another way, if we learn history from being exposed to its repeated performance, then we learn how to read history from our experience of theatre. In the Western tradition of mainstage drama (and classical Hollywood cinema), this means that we focus on the goals of individuals whom we see as better than ourselves; they exist in an implicitly hierarchical relation to surroundings, so that we can tell immediately whose goals are important and whose are marginal, and thus what kind of resolution constitutes a satisfactory ending. Within this paradigm, the concepts of rising action, complication, reversal, climax, and denouement are possible. This sets the necessary conditions for the performance of acts that lead to a successful climax and a definitive conclusion.

History, too, as a narrative enterprise, participates in the same literary conventions, replete with stars and minor players, acts of dramatic moment and consequence, greater goals and necessary effects. One need only think of the way that Saddam Hussein twice achieved status as a major antagonist in the melodramatics of contemporary American history, while the leaders of the genocide in Rwanda have, at the most, served as extras in a background motif of global turbulence, the deaths of hundreds of thousands of Rwandans drawing far less official attention and concern in America than the outcome of several reality television competitions. On talk radio, in nightly news, newspapers, pop magazines, and more subtly throughout the full spectrum of popular culture, the concerns of the globe's six billion people are frequently reduced to a small bushel of personalities and motives. History books, too, rely upon tropic distillation, wherein the mass of events and non-events that comprise activity on the planet, the entropic lump of lost act and utterance, are replaced by language whose authority—the claim that it is factual—relies on everything it has necessarily omitted, on everything that has had to be discarded so that History can be represented coherently. As Michel de Certeau reminds us, of all the things that happen, how few get written down.[5]

History and historiography

It is, of course, in History's disciplinary interest that it establish a method for this omission, a scientific selection process, a mode of representation that claims to be accurate rather than imaginative. In this way, historiography can be seen as a rational process marshaled against the fear that the processes it represents—that of all past human activity, that which we refer to generically as History—may admit to no reasonable description at all.

Late in Ralph Ellison's *Invisible Man*, the nameless protagonist, in a state of shock after witnessing Tod Clifton's murder by New York policemen, has a moment of revelation when he sees three young black men walking toward him on a subway station: "It was as though I'd never seen their like before: Walking slowly, their shoulders swaying, their legs swinging from their hips. . . ."[6] He is noting their sense of (1940s) fashion outside of the style of the dominant culture, antithetical to any sense of a melting pot. He sees them as dancers participating in a secret ritual, and yet, distinctive as they are, he wonders whether anyone can see them, for, as he says, "they were men outside of historical time,"[7] by which he means the timelines established by the official constructions of history, those constructions of history in which the idea that a Troy Maxson came along too early could make sense. From his contemplation of their performance, the invisible man constructs an alternative understanding of history: "But who knew," he wonders,

but that they were the saviors, the true leaders, the bearers of something precious? The stewards of something uncomfortable, burdensome, which they hated because, living outside the realm of history, there was no one to applaud their value, and they themselves failed to understand it. What if Brother Jack were wrong? What if history were a gambler, instead of a force in laboratory experiment, and the boys his ace in the hole? What if history was not a reasonable citizen, but a madman full of paranoid guile and these boys his agents, his big surprise! His own revenge! For they were outside in the dark . . . ."[8]

At stake here is the selection process by which historiography establishes its authority for representing the past, and thus the method by which it performs narratives of the past, the ways in which it creates the stage and the audience for history. From the perspective of an invisible man, that is, any of those whose names fall outside of History's *dramatis personae*, Ellison is suggesting that historiography's selection process may seem neither rational nor fair. It may be blind to alternative modes through which the matrix of accident and event were recorded, the ways in which clothing, motion, music, and idiom have their own historicity.

These boys, in other words, occupy a status similar to that of the piano in *The Piano Lesson*, in that they represent the history of their family and, by extension, of their community through the unique inscription of nonverbal stylization. The piano in the play was traded to Robert Sutter for the grandfather and great-grandmother of the siblings Berniece and Boy Willie, whose 1936 argument about the disposition of the piano focuses the play. Because Sutter's wife missed the slaves whom Sutter gave up for the piano, Sutter asked Berniece and Boy Willie's great-grandfather, Willie Boy, an accomplished woodworker, to carve into the piano the images of his wife and son, whom Sutter had traded away. Willie Boy did this and much more, decorating the piano's entire surface with *his* family's images and scenes from *his* family's history.

The piano thus exists in several contexts. It is the property of the Sutter family, in that the family legally exchanged valuable property—that is, two slaves—in order to obtain it. It is the property of Boy Willie and Berniece, in that it was *their* ancestors who were exchanged for it. It is a mechanical instrument, the product of European technology and Euro-American craftsmanship. It is a work of art, attributable to the unique talents of the slave, Willie Boy, steeped in the artistic traditions of African culture. It is also a historical document, recording iconographically the images and experiences of people who otherwise might be invisible to History.

In addition to *being* a historical record, this object also *has* a history, in that it was stolen in 1911 from Sutter's grandson by Bernice and Boy Willie's father, Boy Charles. As a result, he was killed in a railroad car set afire apparently by the younger Sutter, the sheriff, and some of his friends. The piano thus exists for its inheritors—like all historical phenomena, if we revisit the site of the accident—in a mire of ambivalence. It contains the only permanent record of the family; that is, the conclusive proof that they were once treated as less than human. It also stands as a record of all the suffering and death that constitute their history, the object worth dying for.

For these reasons, it constitutes an impasse in the lives of Boy Willie and Berniece. Seeing it only in terms of its market value, Boy Willie wants to sell the piano so that he can purchase the Sutter farm on which his family worked as slaves. Seeing it only as history, and therefore as something to be escaped, Berniece does not want to deal with it at all, refusing equally to play it or to sell it. In economic terms, we can say that she is denying both its use value and its exchange value. She is denying, in other words, the basic conditions of property value, in that it was exactly the belief in property value, in the priority of ownership, that made slavery possible, that allowed the conditions under which her family experienced the painful history in which the piano was so instrumental both as a commodity and as a record of human commodification. In refusing, in this sense, to *own* the piano, however, she becomes owned by it, a slave now not to men but to their history.

To state the tension in the play differently, we can say that the conflict is between Boy Willie's belief in the value of property—that is, the value system that made slavery possible—and Berniece's belief in the value of History—that is, the system that makes slavery a fact and renders its victims virtually invisible. We can approach this impasse, however, by asking, with Ellison's invisible man, what if History is "not a reasonable citizen, but a madman full of paranoid guile?" In other words, we can argue that Berniece has mistaken for History the form and version of history performed by the dominant culture, or, to use the distinctions I have been developing, that the performative power of dominant versions of History has tainted Berniece's relationship to the piano, so that the piano as machine and as decoration remains an instrument of the white slaveholders, a legacy of domination rather than of resistance to that domination.

The same dynamic holds true of Aunt Ester's house, set for demolition in *Radio Golf* in the ostensive interests of renewing a community whose history must be ignored in order to justify the demolition. Aunt Ester's life spanned 366 years, marking African American history from the initiation of American slavery to Emancipation to Jim Crow to the civil rights movement to the era of White Flight and "Urban Renewal." The sanctioned history of cities sanctioned the illegal appropriation of Aunt Ester's home, which neither the legal owner nor the illegitimate recipient of the property is able to reverse. Thus, the tortuous history of Aunt Ester, of her property, and of her legacy is not only obscured but, in its erasure, obscures the same truth that obtains to *The Piano Lesson*'s piano: that we are talking about stolen property, and thus about the evidence of a crime. It is, however, not clear who is the victim of that crime. Although the piano was stolen from Sutter by Boy Charles, it was purchased by Sutter's grandfather with stolen goods. As with the illegal auctioning off of Aunt Ester's house for non-payment of taxes, the issue is not about theft but about when one starts keeping records, because only after the accident report becomes official can we ascribe liability, but History belongs to whoever owns the erasers. Nor can we retrieve the artifact from its history of usurpation and appropriation; we cannot forget that the community's renewal, in the interest of which Aunt Ester's house was acquired, enhanced corporate banking interests more than the interest of the community its demolition was supposed to renew. In the same way, it is important to remember that the piano's decorations were made to please Miss Ophelia, that for the better part of a century its appearance as well as its sound entertained Sutter's white guests with white music. Some of that white music, however—like some of the white guests, I suspect—had a genealogy with strains and traits that were not openly acknowledged.

History and the whiteness of public space

If there is no way of purifying the piano, of extracting its defiant art and transparent historiography from its material history of pain and violence, there is no way, equally, to establish the white purity of the musical and social culture in which it played a part. No amount of denial, repression, or urban renewal, finally, will escape the pervasive evidence that American culture is hybrid, and, as a friend of mine reminded me, "hybridity" may be an awkward word, but it's the only game in town.

This does not mean that it is a fair game. The history of American slavery, like the history of American baseball or the history of American urban planning, was governed by numerous rules that, obviously (in spite of what films like *Gone with the Wind* or *Field of Dreams* tell you), did not distribute their burdens and benefits equally. In regard to the traders and owners, in fact, in regard to the entire national legal system of antebellum America, for the institution of slavery to *have* a fair game, Africans had to *be* fair game, fair game to be hunted, shipped—virtually by the pound—and sold at fair market price.

This is a game, moreover, central to the legal structure of antebellum America and to the tacit assumptions of its history, for the Union was not just a constituted body but also a performing organism, constantly expanding and reshaping its borders, altering and reconfiguring its populations, articulating and disarticulating its venues and avenues of commerce. Even antedating the inception of an independent nation, the bonds of commercial traffic were inextricably linked to traffic in human bondage because the establishment of a colony with affluent self-sufficiency required an abundance of free labor, just as the fabric of the British industrial revolution—grounded in textile production—required a prolific and inexpensive source of cotton fiber. So extensively was the economic material of American capitalism woven with the threads of slave labor that, by the mid-nineteenth century, its preservation became a material part of antebellum American jurisprudence, which repeatedly favored property rights over human rights, as the mobility of private property was essential to defining the parameters of a union and, therefore, to facilitating its limitless expansion. So strong was the power of property over the demands of humanity that even a civil war could not fully rectify its inequities; as history has shown, the Thirteenth, Fourteenth, and Fifteenth Amendments served only to modify, rather than eliminate, America's race-based economic caste system. This is in large part what happened in nineteenth-century America, and from what we can glean from the unofficial reports, it was no accident.

In 1996, Wilson delivered a now-famous (for some infamous) speech at the Theatre Communications Group National Conference, which pertains directly to the asymmetric historical conditions that inform the dominant version of hybridity.[9] Specifically, Wilson addressed the notion of black culture in relation to American culture regarding the funding for black theatre, and regarding "colorblind casting," asserting that "We do not need colorblind casting; we need theaters."[10] The term "African American," he stated, "not only denotes a race. It connotes a condition."[11] It constitutes, in other words, the formal way in which we act and the conditions under which our actions are interpreted, what Wilson accurately identified as the "notions of common sense": what appears "natural" or comes "naturally."

Although race is based, as Wilson pointed out, on reference to a gene pool, what moves the inheritors of a gene pool into a social category is perception, perception colored by national and dominant cultural assumptions. Thus, when Wilson argued that in America, race "most influences your perception of yourself and it is the [category of identification] to which others . . . most respond,"[12] he was joining a chorus of thinkers who view race as socially constructed. The political and social imperatives of race thus derive from a complex network of perspectives. Although there is no way to measure precisely the network of racial perception, for many Americans it may be, as

Wilson said, the perceptual category most pervasively employed in shaping their sense of themselves and of others, more delimiting even than religion or gender.

In this arena of perception, issues of theatre become particularly cogent, for theatre recreates and deploys codes of identification. Like all American life, theatre in American life is marked by issues of race, of how racial narratives are to be performed or ignored, and where, and with what audience assumptions. These issues are as germane to the launching of a Broadway production or the funding of regional theatres as they are to nightly news coverage. For this reason, Wilson rightfully critiques the idea that funding agencies have started using sociological criteria instead of aesthetic criteria, as if art were not a function of society, as if public venues could exist a-socially. Sociology examines the specific conditions that circumscribe the distribution of space, power, and performance, in other words, the conditions of theatre. To oppose sociology to art is to imagine that there could be art outside of the society that produced it. The funding of art, the production of performances, the assembling of audiences, the designating of recognizable public sites and social practices are the mark and emblem of a society. It is impossible to exempt theatre from its performative social power, from being scrutinized as a part of society, or from participating in cogent social narratives. This absurdity, moreover, is a symptom of the tacit assumption that in America, neutral public space, like the normative site of history, is to be construed as white.

And yet, theatre funding is only one small example of the ways in which—from the initial framing of the Constitution through to the social engineering of housing policy after the Second World War and more recent Supreme Court decisions decrying "reverse discrimination"—America accepts its whiteness with neutrality. So, when Wilson called attention to the "overwhelming abundance of institutions that preserve, promote, perpetuate white culture,"[13] he was attacking the idea that the neutral space is implicitly white and that white culture, all things being equal, does not depend on being perpetuated, only on being protected from defilement, assault, and dilution.

Of course, all things being equal, Wilson is wrong. *But all things are not equal, and that is exactly his point.* For those not forced to live at the margin, the temptation to confuse equilibrium with equality remains comfortingly strong, but the equilibrium of race relations in America (to the extent that there is equilibrium) exists by virtue of a publically fostered suspended animation. Far from being natural, that suspended animation required bolstering from the very start, first from the Fugitive

Slave clause of the Constitution, then through a systematic series of court decisions, official Congressional "compromises," and supplementary laws. After Emancipation, the neutrality of white space was promoted by a stilted Reconstruction, followed by the Tilden-Hayes compromise, which led to what Ralph Ellison called the counterrevolution of 1876. But even there the equilibrium threatened to dissolve under the heft of equality's weighty promises. More bolstering was necessary: lynchings, castrations, crossburnings, Jim Crow laws, actual and de facto segregation. To give official sanction to the whiteness of public policy, at the end of the nineteenth century, the Supreme Court declared that separate but equal was not unequal. In the centennial year of that decision, Wilson's speech reminds us once more how unnatural the constitution of white neutrality has been and also how expensive, for surely no equilibrium required more unnatural support, no scales of justice more invidious props and weighty thumbs to keep the needle ostensibly centered.

From this perspective, American history itself is fair game, in that it is based not on facts in general, but on those facts emerging out of the privileged assumptions of specific interests. The hybridity of our legal system, in other words, can be seen in its disposition of mute parties, in the unarticulated interests in a contract, or in the whole system of contract law or liability law. We thus return once more to the image of historian as ambulance-chaser, with the knowledge that there is an invisible man chasing the ambulance-chaser, armed not with law books or history but with the blues.

Blues historiography

What I mean by this is that the blues emerges out of the imaginary seams in the official version; it plays with authority, revealing what Ellison called infinite possibilities; it sees all history, especially its own, as something to be played, played with, played upon; it relishes complexity and variation; it thrives on the unpredictable patterns that emerge from the combined effort of an implicit community. And, perhaps most significant for this discussion, it is unremittingly revisionist, seeing History as a lived and performed act of the imagination, not as a set of scientifically inscribed verities. "One of the driving things of any black aesthetic," Wilson has said, "is improvisation or the idea of improvising. It's the thing that enabled us to survive, to think on our feet" (*Conversations*, 252). "The thing with the blues is that there's an entire philosophical system at work. And I've found that whatever you want to know about the black experience in America is contained in the blues" (*Conversations*, 58). "I think what's contained in the blues is the African American's response to the world. . . . One way to make that information memorable is to put it in a song" (*Conversations*, 58).

In several ways, Wilson's plays, therefore, are about History as blues performance rather than as official record. The first is that they are all concerned in one way or another with how origins are lost or distorted. I have discussed the conflict over the origin of the piano's value in *The Piano Lesson*. Similarly, the original version of Ma Rainey's voice conflicts with the commercial and technological processes that will reduce it to a standard version, one that can be reproduced and distributed by those who own the rights to that reproduction; her vocals conflict as well with the original direction in which Levee wants to take the music, which itself conflicts with its own origins. If Ma Rainey is thus an original source of the musical style that her band plays and of the sounds that come from her throat, Wilson's play captures a moment when both of these are about to become history. It is important to note, therefore, that this historical moment depends in every direction on performance: Ma Rainey's style is the consolidation of the styles that have influenced her, that is, of the way the blues has been performed before her. Her style too will be performed, because of the recording, as a stabilized norm that can then serve as a node in plotting the history of the blues, or of American music. But within the very moment at which the performance is about to acquire its normative form, we see the elements that mark not its emergence but its superannuation. Even the violent end to which the band will come cannot alter our sense of another, even more extreme violence in the substitution of the standardized recording for the live performance, the authority of the record company for the authority of the performer.

In the sense that we can extrapolate from this play a lesson about how history is made, it shows the violence at work in the historiographic enterprise, violence made explicit by Levee's killing of Toledo, but implicit in this killing is the way in which both men are the victims of historical marginalization. "I think Levee has a warrior spirit," Wilson explained. "He does a terrible disservice to blacks by killing Toledo, because he's killing the only one who can read, he's killing the intellectual in the group. That's a loss we have to make up. We have to raise up another one to take Toledo's place. But I still salute Levee's warrior spirit. It's a progression to the wrong target, but I salute his willingness to battle, even to the death" (*Conversations*, 79).

By cutting the record, moreover, Levee, Toledo, and all the other members of the band have participated without consent in that process of marginalization. From Ma Rainey's mouth at the structural center, the play ripples out like the concentric circles on a record's surface spinning around the imprimatur that gives the sound a label. A record's surface, of course, is not really made of concentric ripples. The groove is actually a straight line that has gotten wrapped up in itself several hundred times. Here again, we have a play about the making of a historical record. The original sound emanating from Ma Rainey's mouth is a wave, a series of concentric ripples, many of which fall outside the range of the microphone and go unrecorded. And when the record is played in numerous places, its sound again makes ripples that trail faintly away into a world of unrecorded effects. Between the places of performance and reception—these two sites of ripple and echo—the historical record keeps the needle in the official groove, from which so much has been removed in the cutting of the record.

The violence that official history performs on originary freedoms also informs *Joe Turner's Come and Gone*, a play motivated by the search for the dubious site of origin: Herald Loomis is looking for his start. The start in this play is linked to an anachronism, in that the black visitors who come to the Pittsburgh boarding house in 1911 are identified as "the sons and daughters of newly freed African slaves," although it is nearly half a century since the end of the Civil War. The start toward freedom, in other words, has taken a long time to get started, and Loomis is thus caught in a time warp—a man wandering forward so that he can find his beginning. The anachronism that imaginatively conflates several decades of freed slaves and their offspring is thus the anachronism of History itself, as performed by the invisible Joe Turner. Turner simply steals black men and puts them in forced labor for seven years. Joe Turner's comings and goings thus form a cycle of eternal return to the origins of slavery, a time warp as relentless as Loomis's, albeit its mirror opposite.

In this model, Joe Turner is the historiographer and Loomis is the man who disappears from the accident report. Or, to put it another way, Loomis is in search of History. In the play, Bynam figures Loomis's search as the search for his song. His song—Herald Loomis's blues—like Berniece and Boy Willie's piano, thus marks the accident of history, the moment of theft in which History itself has been stolen, and the return that Loomis seeks is the return to the point at which he, not Joe Turner, controls his song, just as the resolution of *The Piano Lesson* brings us to the moment when Berniece, not Sutter's ghost, plays the piano. The more tragic *Ma Rainey's*

Black Bottom takes us to the moment when Ma Rainey loses her song; *Seven Guitars* marks the moment when Floyd Barton will be prevented from recording his song, and *Two Trains Running* the moment when Hambone can no longer repeat his chant. *Jitney*, *King Hedley II*, and *Radio Golf* mark moments when the neighborhood and the community that defines it are destroyed under the official historical rubric of "renewal." These are all moments of blues history, marked with the double inscription of pain and triumph, through a revision only possible in the context of the ensemble community. Thus, in *Fences*, we can understand as a form of historical resolution the moment when Raynel and Cory sing Troy's blues together.

In this way, the blues emphasizes the performative aspects of history, for empowerment, the plays make clear, derives from performance, in that performance is the only defense against possession. This theme is expressed most explicitly at the end of *The Piano Lesson*. Although the play seems to be structured around the conflict between Boy Willie and Berniece about their joint ownership of the piano, it becomes clear that the piano is still possessed by its historical owner, Sutter, and that he cannot be exorcised permanently, nor can he be exorcised even temporarily by traditional Christian ritual alone. Berniece can keep the piano that bears her family's history free from its historical owner only by performing on it, so that Berniece must control the performative aspects of her history, lest she continue to be possessed by them. She must, in other words, avoid the trap into which Ma Rainey, despite her struggle, fell.

For possession is not only nine-tenths of the law; it is also the basic premise of slavery, the historical contract that placed property rights over human rights. And the struggle over possession in all of Wilson's plays is ultimately over the possession of History itself, with the mode of repossession being blues performance, by which I mean a recognition that performance can not just revive but revise, and that these revisions constitute, always and necessarily, struggles with ghosts and with the fear of being possessed. In this light, we can understand Ma Rainey's belligerence at the recording session, and we can read the purpose of Troy Maxson's fences, his pledge to struggle with death, his refusal to let Cory be the slave of a sport or a scholarship, in other words the source of his heroics, as representing his refusal to be possessed, however painful the consequences. Vera in *Seven Guitars* only agrees to go to Chicago with Floyd because she is keeping in her shoe a one-way ticket back to Pittsburgh, good for a year; she is thus refusing to be possessed by Floyd or by a prescribed gender role. Similarly, both King Hedley I and King Hedley II killed men rather than be denied what they felt were their proper names; in this way, they were refusing the historical condition of subordination, whereby the master possessed the power to name the slave.

History, possession, and repossession

The invisible Sutter and the invisible Joe Turner thus play a common historical role, that of repossessing the victims of slavery, of circumscribing their freedom with material needs, of orchestrating their comings and goings, of delimiting their performance, just as do the record producers in *Ma Rainey's Black Bottom* or Lutz, the owner of the meat market in *Two Trains Running*, who refused to pay Hambone the ham he had promised. Hambone, possessed by the specter of Lutz, is reduced for nine years to his unrelenting chant—"I want my ham"—orchestrated by Lutz's comings and goings. Although there may be two trains running, the characters in that play have gotten sidetracked by the relentless commodification of their existence. There is hardly a moment in *Two Trains* when someone is not calculating the cost or value of something, the relationship of self-possession to material possession, the expense of living and of dying: playing numbers or running them, buying property or selling it, working or stealing, making contributions or giving charity. In this sense, the somewhat deranged Hambone is not the aberrant character but the logical extension of all the characters who, in 1969, remain possessed by the same principles that underwrote slavery.

Holloway, the chronicler and historian of the group, explains their dilemma when he distinguishes between riches and luck. In the play, the magical figure of Aunt Ester, a woman as old as the existence of slavery in America, changes people's luck by having them throw their money into the river, for in African American history, the equation of wealth with luck, the privileging of property rights over human rights, has provided the conceptual rationale for slavery and rendered the fugitive slave or the migrant worker or the black laborer the vulnerable transgressor in the historical systems of legal inequity and iniquity. Although, as Memphis points out, Hambone's problem is that he made a deal in which he let Lutz decide what to pay him for his work, Holloway argues that Hambone might have more sense than all the rest of them, in that he is not going to accept less than his labor is worth. When calculated by the hour, Hambone has indeed not used his time profitably, but when calculated in terms of his sense of himself as historical subject, he has separated value from money, in that he is unwilling to live in the historical narrative written by Lutz, even if it means stopping dead in his tracks, refusing to utter one more word than the last line in the narrative of which he was the author. In this way, he has not gotten sidetracked in the way that, for instance, Memphis had. Memphis, the owner of the Pittsburgh restaurant where the play's action takes place, had been run off his land in Jackson. Mississippi, when the law declared his deed null and void, and he is still fixated on returning. "All I got to do is find my way down to the train depot," he points out. "They got two trains running everyday."[14]

Like the piano in *The Piano Lesson*, the railroad tracks play an important and conflicted role in African American history, for the railroad stands, as Holloway so cogently explains in *Two Trains*, as one more instrument of Western technology that contributes to the history of white Western progress built out of an unequal relationship with black labor: "If it wasn't for you the white man would be poor. Every little bit he got he got standing on top of you. That's why he could reach so high. He give you three dollars a day for six months and he got him a railroad for the next hundred years."[15] And yet, very much like the piano, the railroad became an important instrument of black history. In *The Piano Lesson*, Berniece's uncle, Doaker, was one of the day laborers to whom Holloway was referring: "I'm cooking now, but I used to line track. I pieced together the Yellow Dog stitch by stitch. Rail by Rail. Line track all up around there."

But Doaker understands that, like the piano, the railroad is an instrument that can be made to perform a variety of tasks, liberating as well as constricting, despite its rigid parameters:

See you got North. You got West. You look over here you got South. Over there you got East. Now you can start from anywhere. Don't care where you at. You got to go one of them four ways. And whichever way you decide to go, they got a railroad that will take you there. Now that's something simple. You think anybody would be able to understand that. But you'd be surprised how many people trying to go North get on a train going West. They think the train's supposed to go where they going rather than where it's going.

Within the rigidity, however, is the counter-possibility, that of freedom: "They got so many trains out there they have a hard time keeping them from running into each other. Got trains going every whichway." The crisscrossing of train lines thus forms what Houston Baker has called a blues matrix, a cross grid of infinite possibility. As Doaker explains, "if the train stays on track: it's going to get where it's going. It might not be where you going. But if it ain't, then all you got to do is sit and wait cause the train's coming back to get you. It'll come back every time."[16]

This is another way of saying about history that what goes around comes around, that the chickens come home to roost, that the same terrain can take one in many different directions, that the industries that enslaved laborers at the same time provided them with the means to escape that enslavement, just as the legal system that sanctified that enslavement, that made Joe Turner legitimate by nullifying the rights of Loomis or the deeds of Memphis, thus helped sanction the rails by which Memphis can return to his land or maintained the highways by which Boy Willie can drive to it.

But in Wilson's work, the instruments of Western culture provide the means not only for material return but for spiritual or magical, if by magic we mean any system of causes that has not gotten visible respect. The term "mythology" is often used in common parlance to mean a religion of which the practitioners no longer have any political heft—as in "Greek mythology" or "Norse mythology"—and "folklore" is the term used to refer to the religion of people who *never* had any political heft—as in "native American folklore" or "African folklore." In this light, magic could mean non-Western religion, or what some people call the occult, or what constitutes the hidden mechanics practiced by those entertainers we commonly call magicians, or it could be what Coltrane does to Richard Rogers's "My Favorite Things" or to King Henry VIII's "Greensleeves" or more basically to our understanding of the magic latent in the mechanics of a soprano sax. The distinction between the ways these forms of magic are performed is merely historical.

And thus, we can see one more way in which Wilson's plays engage history, in that they blend and equate the forms of magic with the means by which those forms acquire historical cogency. The same Yellow Dog for which Doaker lined the tracks returns to Doaker's home to confront Sutter's ghost, not just the men—including Boy Charles—burned to death in the boxcar by Sutter and company, but the train itself. For like the piano, or, we might say, like Loomis, the instrument and its ghost have become one, and the magic of invisible causes performs the act of bringing that union into the light of history, and thus makes history perform its mysteries.

Wilson's ten-play cycle owes much to one initial train ride that took place outside the scope of that century, the ride in 1892 of Homer Plessy, an

American of one-eighth Negro descent going north in Louisiana, who was denied the right to sit in the white sections of the train. Plessy's multifaceted argument before the Supreme Court in part entailed the claim that a train conductor was not qualified to make fine racial distinctions, distinctions for which visible evidence was to most eyes nonexistent. The Court, voting seven to one, nevertheless upheld the conductor's power to do so, making the famous pronouncement that separate but equal is not unequal. The *right* of the state to separate based on race was thus privileged over its *ability* to do so. The principle of segregation took precedence over the actual status of the facts. Regardless of whether the conductor discerned correctly in principle, he was never wrong, and History, being a principled enterprise, records the facts as the conductor sees them. Thus, History performs the act of segregating even when the conductor fails to, is blind to the history of his passengers. Who is this nameless and interchangeable conductor who sorted through the genetic and cultural history of race so that he could perform the crucial sorting out where two trains were running every day? Invested with the power of the Supreme Court, he organized the riders on the train but, as Doaker and Memphis and August Wilson point out, not the inevitable direction of that train.

CHAPTER 3
CUTTING THE HISTORICAL RECORD, RECORDING THE BLUES: *MA RAINEY'S BLACK BOTTOM*

Production history

Ma Rainey's Black Bottom opened on April 6, 1984, at the Yale Repertory in New Haven, Connecticut, directed by Lloyd Richards, with Theresa Merritt in the title role and Charles Dutton playing Levee. Under the same direction, and with the same cast in principal and featured roles, it opened at the Cort Theatre on Broadway on October 11, 1984, where it ran for 276 performances.

Cut one: *Ma Rainey's Black Bottom*

In the context of Wilson's historiographic enterprise, what is his "cycle"? In dedicating himself to this ten-play project, Wilson was not constructing a ten-play serial, following specific people or their families through several generations, or historicizing a specific place, even though as a group the plays at specific moments do all of those things.[1] We see members of the Wilkes family in 1903 and in 1996. We meet Sterling in 1969, and he returns in 1996. Ruby appears in both *Seven Guitars* and *King Hedley II*, as does Canewell, although in the latter play, he is known as Stool Pigeon.

Unseen characters, such as Stovall, the abusive landowner who, we hear in the *Piano Lesson*, had tried to make Lymon an indentured servant, we learn in *Two Trains*, had also driven Memphis off his land. Patchneck Red is a legendary figure mentioned in both *The Piano Lesson* and *Two Trains Running*. In addition to being the central character in *Gem of the Ocean*, Aunt Ester functions as an unseen but crucially active presence in four of the plays, one of which announces her death and another takes place a decade after it.

Only *Ma Rainey* has no overlap with any other play, although Chicago as a site for recording blues records is as important a presence in *Seven Guitars* as it is in *Ma Rainey*. And Bedford Hills locales populate the other nine plays.[2] Logan Street, a Hill venue filled with pushcart vendors, is mentioned in seven of Wilson's plays, as is the Crawford Grill in both *Fences* and *King Hedley*. West's Funeral Home is a site in two plays, with the owner, West, appearing as a significant figure in one of them, and the Ellis Hotel is mentioned as the site of offstage encounters in three. An important recounted event in *King Hedley II* takes place in Irv's Bar, a place also mentioned in three other plays. The Workmen's Civic Club is mentioned in four.

Many more details, explicit or inferential, connect the plays in the cycle, but there is no narrative thread that takes us from the beginning of the century to the end. Nor can the cycle properly be called a series, any more than its ten component plays can be called historical dramas. In many ways, the plays ignore some of the major historical features of the times in which they are set. Wilson, for example, specifically omits mention of the Great Depression in *The Piano Lesson*; although the play takes place in the heart of the Depression, it is no more a factor in the play than the crack epidemic of the 1980s is in *King Hedley II*.

Call it a wrap

By the same token, the ten plays are not just a random set of plays that happen to take place in different decades. Rather, I want to suggest, they should be regarded as ten cuts on an album (or CD) surveying twentieth-century African American blues. From this perspective, we can see Wilson's plays as orchestrations, arranged according to the blues style and blues themes of specific periods. Each play can be productively viewed, therefore, as a blues cut, performed by an improvisational jazz combo with one to three female singers. Even though, ultimately, only a recorded version will be noteworthy, even the recorded version will be only a footnote to history, because the historical record is always a revision, a chronicle of change. In that sense, whether we arrange the ten-play cycle according to the chronology of the plays' writing or of the decades they depict, we see that although the elements may remain relatively constant, the arrangements continue to be radically different.

As in jazz performance, moreover, what is very important to understanding Wilson's drama is the role of community in determining the outcomes. Although the decisions are never communal, Wilson continually makes us aware of the ways in which each member of the community affects the historical record by creating conditions and introducing factors that inflect and delimit the choices of others.

Ma Rainey's Black Bottom deals with this very explicitly by showing how Ma Rainey manipulates the record company for which she ostensibly works. The various arrangements—what musical version, who does the introduction, how they are paid, even whether they will record before they have a bottle of Coke—are thus metaphors for all the unrecorded arrangements that allow the production of musical records and of historical records. These include interpersonal arrangements, business arrangements, and musical arrangements. The record, in other words, like all of Wilson's plays, like all musical and social gatherings, is a community arrangement. *Ma Rainey's Black Bottom* (1984), Kim Pereira points out,

> resembles a jazz composition . . . [each musician's story at the outset] is like a solo performance in a jazz quartet that, though it possesses the characteristics of a 'set piece', is related to the major themes on an imagistic and emotional level. . . . As the play moves along easily, its improvisatory cadences contain ever-quickening impulses that gather force toward a cataclysmic ending, like a shattering crescendo.[3]

Pereira's description, however, applies not only to *Ma Rainey* but, more generally, to Wilson's approach to drama. As I have written elsewhere, because his plays resemble

> a jazz set as much as they do a Euro-American play, we are confronted not with protagonist and antagonists, but rather with the tension of interpretive energy, as a community of players play off one another's solos. If they tend at times to play variations on recognizable themes, the synergy of the interaction creates unexpected and exciting results. These interactions are exciting not in the way that a tragic death is but in the way that a Duke Ellington or a John Coltrane finale is.[4]

Nor is it only a matter of style. Wilson's use of the blues instantiates an alternative form of historiography, so that a blues rendition can have the same status for African American culture as a history text. "The thing about the blues," Wilson has said, "is that there's an entire philosophical system at work. And whatever you want to know about the black experience in America is contained in the blues" (*Conversations*, 58). If Wilson's drama is fundamentally structured by blues performance, his ten-play cycle can be thought of as a record (or CD) album that orchestrates and arranges the American twentieth century as ten versions of African American blues, played by a combo with one to three singers.

The early Wilson combo includes the warrior, the historian, the earnest young man, the trickster, the pragmatist, and the man-not-quite-right-in-the-head. With the addition, in *Joe Turner's Come and Gone* (1986), of the magician/healer and a spectrum of female soloists, the full array of Wilson's styles and arrangements becomes evident, providing a blues history and a history of the blues that reconciles the styles of African American blues to the events and traditions that produced them. At the same time, the variegated forms of the blues delimit the possibilities for reconfiguring the community produced by those historical and aesthetic conditions.

In this context, it is useful to think of Wilson's characters as figuratively forming a band throughout his cycle in the same way as they do literally in *Ma Rainey*. The debate over competing arrangements is thus a debate over who will solo, and when, and for how long. It is also a debate over the set of relationships that will be acceptable to the general public. This is a question of history in two ways: It is not only a chronicle of changing styles and fashions but also a chronicle of power, that is, of who gets to decide what comprises the general public or to determine the parameters of public taste.

The paradigmatic band

Although we can see the blues community, the members of the band, in all of Wilson's plays, from *Jitney* to *Radio Golf*, *Ma Rainey's Black Bottom* serves as a useful introduction, since Wilson has acknowledged that in *Ma Rainey*, the characters are metaphorically identified with their instruments: "I tried to make Levee's voice be a trumpet. I was conscious when I was writing the dialogue that this is the bass player talking, this is the trombonist playing" (*Conversations*, 25). Thus, in the play we have a template for the basic combo that performs the twentieth century, in its sundry arrangements. The historian, a figure in every Wilson play, is Toledo, whose part will be played, for example, by Holloway in *Two Trains Running*, Canewell in *King Hedley*, Doaker in *The Piano Lesson*, Turnbo in *Jitney*, and Old Joe in *Radio Golf*. We also have Cutler, the pragmatist, whose part is taken by Seth Holly in the arrangement of *Joe Turner's Come and Gone*, Memphis in *Two Trains Running*, Becker in *Jitney*, or Mame in *Radio Golf*. Levee plays the warrior, a man driven equally by demons and dreams; we can hear his tones in Booster (*Jitney*), Boy Willie (*The Piano Lesson*), Troy Maxson (*Fences*), Solly Two Kings (*Gem of the Ocean*), and King Hedley, and Slow Drag, like Bono in *Fences* or Doub in *Jitney*, is one of Wilson's accommodators. And then we have the singers: Ma Rainey, of course, but also consider Rose's blues solo in *Fences*, Tonya's in *King Hedley II*, or the duo of Molly and Mattie in *Joe Turner's Come and Gone*.

After *Ma Rainey*, Wilson increased the size of the group, adding the earnest young man, such as Jeremy in *Joe Turner's Come and Gone* or Lymon in *The Piano Lesson*, the man not-quite-right-in-the-head, such as Hambone in *Two Trains Running*, Hedley in *Seven Guitars*, Gabriel in *Fences*. (Arguably, *Jitney*'s alcoholic, Fielding, is a precursor, just as *Jitney*'s Youngblood is an earlier version of the earnest young man.) With *Joe Turner's Come and Gone*, the Wilson arrangements broaden to include the harmonics of the shaman, a part played sometimes in conjunction with the obsessed man (Hedley), the historian (Bynum), or the lead singer (Aunt Ester in *Gem of the Ocean*).

This sketchy list is not meant to suggest that Wilson reuses the same characters from play to play or that these types comprise rigid categories. I am arguing, in fact, exactly the opposite. These types do not represent themes but rather, instruments arranged and rearranged to play the blues in its infinite variations. Thus, in the arrangement in *Joe Turner*, the character of Loomis combines the warrior and the crazed man, just as the magician and the historian are combined in the character of Bynum. In this context, one way to read *Gem of the Ocean*, for example, is as the story of how the Great Migration converts Citizen Barlow from the earnest young man into the warrior. (In keeping with this paradigm for understanding the Wilson cycle, my discussion of each of the other plays will be preceded by a speculative discussion of the play's musical "character arrangement.")

Rather than reduce the plays to a game of trivia and puzzle parts, however, I want to make a larger point, suggested by this quick taxonomy: the structure, development, and resolution in each play and in the entire cycle has to be understood as those terms work in music, not as they apply to traditional—especially Aristotelian—drama.[5] History, despite the implications of some traditions of historiography, is *not* the work of a handful of privileged people, for whom the rest of the world serves as "sidekicks" and "extras." The energies of communities, or of societies, or of nations are always the product of that large mass, that critical mass necessary for a body to be recognized as a community or a society or a nation. And that mass is not a fixed unit, a painted backdrop for the stage of history. Rather, it is the ever-changing set of arrangements and rearrangements, of melody, and harmony, and rhythm.

From this perspective, *Ma Rainey's Black Bottom* becomes the paradigmatic play in the Wilson canon by openly identifying his dramatic structure with the arrangements of a blues band and the kinds of characters instrumental in those arrangements. The play takes place during an afternoon recording session in 1927. First, three members of Ma Rainey's band, Toledo, Cutler, and Slow Drag, arrive, then the fourth, Levee, a belligerent, cocky trumpeter who is proud of his expensive new shoes and what he thinks may be the possibility of securing a recording contract. Eventually, Ma Rainey arrives with her friend Dussie Mae and her stuttering nephew Sylvester. The recording session is delayed several times while Ma Rainey exerts her prerogatives and the members of the band verbally spar with one another. After the session and the resolution of a dispute over payment, Levee learns that instead of offering him a contract the recording studio will simply buy the rights to his songs at five dollars apiece. When Toledo accidentally steps on Levee's new shoes, that trivial incident becomes the focus for Levee's frustration, disappointment, and rejection; in a furious and self-defeating attempt to assert his self-worth, he stabs Toledo fatally. Thus, the play ends in a tragedy that never finds its way out of the rehearsal room and on to the stage of history. In a very literal way, the band becomes the embodiment of the blues.

While not all Wilson's plays end in tragic deaths, in *Ma Rainey's Black Bottom*, as in all his plays, his blues orchestrations reconfigure the notes, the time, and the key of the dominant society to produce a blues variation. Dependent on orchestration rather than crisis and resolution, the play establishes the community as the locus of dramatic action, recognizing that a community constitutes a critical mass that is not a fixed unit or a painted backdrop on the stage of history. For Wilson, a community is an ever-changing set or series of arrangements and rearrangements of melody and time.

For the record

In 1982, after the Eugene O'Neill Theater Center's Playwrights Conference workshopped *Ma Rainey*, Wilson, I noted earlier, was offered $25,000 to take the play to Broadway. At the time, since he was still making only $88 a week as a cook, the offer seemed tempting compared with Lloyd Richards's more modest offer to produce the play at the Yale Repertory Theatre. Because the Broadway contract gave control of the script to the producers, Wilson ended the negotiations and brought the play back to Richards, who did produce the play at Yale before taking it to Broadway. The fact that history (as this anecdote illustrates) might have been very different informs all of Wilson's works, which manifest an acute awareness of the plasticity of the official record. Consider, for example, the role in *Fences* (1985) of the home-run records "earned" by white baseball players who did not have to face black pitchers, the historical record inscribed on the surface of the piano in *The Piano Lesson* (1987), and the criminal records of so many of Wilson's characters, including Floyd Barton, Troy Maxson, Herald Loomis, Sterling Johnson, Lymon, and Levee. Records, Wilson makes clear, are not facts but interpretations. In *The Piano Lesson*, for example, Lymon had been given an exorbitant fine for not working, so he fled rather than allow that fine to turn him into an indentured servant. Whereas his official criminal record means that he is a fugitive from justice, from his and from Boy Willie's perspective, it means that he is a fugitive from injustice. The meaning of Lymon's criminal record, in other words, is determined by the record keepers; but History, as I have pointed out, belongs to whoever owns the erasers.

This point is made early in *Ma Rainey's Black Bottom* when Toledo wins a bet with Levee about the spelling of the word "music" but cannot collect because everyone else is illiterate. "I done won the dollar," he states, in a way that articulates the problem that Troy Maxson has with baseball records, which is the quintessential problem of black history: "But if don't nobody know but me, how am I gonna prove it to you?" (29). The problem of history, in other words, is how the record is produced, whose voices it includes, what arrangements it uses, and who has the rights to control its distribution and accrue its revenues. Although the historical record is being cut and recut in all Wilson's plays, that process provides the explicit content of *Ma Rainey*. If, as many have noted, the play is about recording the blues,[6] it is also about versions of the blues and the conditions that produce them.

Changing the notes

For Wilson, the blues thus comprise an alternative history encoding the African American experience ignored by official historical documentation.

As Ma Rainey points out, "White folks don't understand the blues. They hear it come out, but they don't know how it got there. They don't understand that's life's way of talking" (82). "Life's way of talking," of course, is a vernacular name for history, a vernacular name for vernacular history, and Ma Rainey is acutely aware that she does the work of the historiographer: "This be an empty world without the blues. I take that emptiness and try to fill it up with something" (83). Exactly because she regards the blues as history, Ma Rainey understands that she is necessarily as much its inheritor as its producer. "They say I started it," she explains, "but I didn't. I just helped it out" (83).

In this moment, she is footnoting herself as purveyor of history in a play replete with historical footnotes. Toledo, the piano player—who is the only literate member of the band—constantly attempts to create historical contexts. When the bass player, Slow Drag, and the guitarist, Cutler, bond through naming, he explains that they are performing an African ancestral retention ritual, a bond of kinship. Calling attention to the diasporic aspects of African American culture, he insists, "We done sold Africa for the price of tomatoes" (94). Toledo's role in the band, in other words, is to supply the notes, not just the melody; he retrieves the historical circumstances that have brought Ma Rainey, her band, and her entourage to this time and this place.

The tragedy Ma Rainey foregrounds, however, is that although the band can supply the notes, none of them, not even Ma Rainey at the peak of her power, can control the record. For the record to be produced, in fact, Ma Rainey must sign away her voice. The play thus pivots around the historical moment when her song, in its unique moment of production, becomes the property of the white company. As the play represents it, that moment comes in such a way as to reduce "art" to "labor," in that Ma Rainey is paid a fee for the session rather than receiving contractual residuals. This effacement of her labor, by reducing it to merely labor, makes her song ahistorical. In other words, it is the history of its own production. The unavoidable self-consciousness with which Ma Rainey and her band participate in this moment of erasure renders that moment an unmistakable site for the blues.

Thus, Wilson's conflict with the Broadway producer over the meaning of the contract to produce *Ma Rainey's Black Bottom* replicated the conflict in the play between establishing a recording of Ma Rainey's art and transferring the rights from the maker of the music to the producers of the recording. In both instances, the official record is circumscribed by the historical conditions that give it meaning, that is, that multiply its meanings.

In the short term, Ma Rainey's authority prevails, because nothing can progress until she makes the recording and until she records her signature relinquishing her rights to that recording. In that interim, her song and signature comprise a form of extortion, empowering her to control the music's orchestration and even to make the studio accommodate her stuttering nephew, who, she insists, must not only introduce her but also be paid for his performance commensurate with the amount paid to the other members of the band.

In the long run, however, the contract will be more powerful than the signatory, and the control of the physical record will merge with the control of the artistic record and the historical record. In that process, the rest of the play's events will be omitted, so that the events and the black people who enact them will be what Toledo calls "leftovers":

> The colored man is the leftovers. Now, what's the colored man gonna do with himself? That's what we waiting to find out. But first we gotta know we the leftovers. Now, who knows that? You find me a nigger that knows that and I'll turn any whichway you want me to. . . . The problem ain't the white man. The white man knows you just a leftover. 'Cause he the one that done the eating and he know what he done ate. But we don't know that we been took and made history out of. (*Ma Rainey*, 57)

In this sense, *Ma Rainey's Black Bottom* not only explicitly articulates the position of the historical subject in general, and of the African American historical subject in particular, but also plays out the fate of the leftovers in direct contrast to those who make and keep the records. Inverting the hierarchy of power that official history demands, Wilson's play foregrounds those most marginalized by the process, playing out an arrangement in the time measure of those in the margins.

The only performance of the song "Black Bottom" that the audience hears, moreover, is the unofficial version, because the play skips the actual recording session, moving directly from the failed attempts to the moment when the lights come up in the studio as "the last bars of the last song of the session are dying out" (*Ma Rainey*, 100). Wilson intentionally dramatizes what preceded and followed the dying of the music, that is, everything the session did not resolve: the conflict over Ma Rainey's withheld signature, over the band's delayed payment, over Levee's delayed rejection first by Ma Rainey and then by the studio, and finally the delayed confrontation between Toledo and Levee, ostensibly over Toledo's stepping on Levee's shoes, but more basically about the accuracy of Toledo's sense of history as the instrument that steps on Levee's aspirations. In this sense, the play culminates in the moments when Levee has run out of time, when Toledo's time is up, and when Ma Rainey's time has passed.

Changing the tempo

From both a musical and a historical perspective, therefore, it is not surprising that so much of *Ma Rainey's Black Bottom* deals with time and who controls it. Sandra G. Shannon and Sandra Adell have both noted the importance of waiting in the play.[7] For Shannon, the waiting is crucial to the play's structural tensions. It gives meaning to the multiple conclusions of the play: the completion of the session, the completion of the compensation negotiations, the recording of Ma Rainey's signature, the culmination of Levee's employment in Ma Rainey's band, the (unsatisfactory) conclusion of Levee's negotiation with Sturdyvant to record his own songs in his own style, the conclusion of Toledo's life at the point of Levee's knife. For Adell, the waiting comprises the presence of Ma Rainey, a presence that is at odds with the action of the play, in that the recording session is precisely designed to replace the real woman with a mechanical reproduction. Paradoxically, Wilson creates a play in which the very vibrancy of the central character serves to underscore the process of her elimination, as her talent, her cultural truth, is appropriated by a white world that understands little and cares less about her or the world she embodies and expresses.

When the play opens, two white men, Ma Rainey's agent, Irvin, and the director of the recording studio, Sturdyvant, are preparing for the session and implicitly preparing the audience for the problems they foresee with Ma Rainey and the future of her style of blues. Even before the band arrives, Sturdyvant tells Ma Rainey's manager that he is worried Ma Rainey will not be on time, that the session will take too long. Because Sturdyvant thinks that Ma Rainey wastes his time, the only way she can refute him is to make him wait for her, in other words to demonstrate that, despite his claims to the contrary, he thinks her recordings are worth the time it takes.

This is the first of numerous occasions in which scenes of waiting organize the time. Next, the four members of the band arrive and kill time while they wait for Ma Rainey, who, it turns out, has been detained by a policeman after a melee following a car accident. The band then wait for Irvin to cajole (and bribe) the officer; then, they wait in the band room to rehearse. At the same time, Ma Rainey waits in the studio to begin the recording session. More waiting is necessary, however, while Ma Rainey disputes the song list and the arrangements. Not until the second act, in fact, does the session actually start, but this turns into a false start, because Ma Rainey insists that, despite his stutter, her nephew, Sylvester, introduce the song "Black Bottom," and when he fails to do so without faltering, she makes everyone wait again while Sylvester and the bassist, Slow Drag, go out to get her a Coca-Cola. As Ma Rainey waits for her Coke, and the producers, the band, and the audience wait for Ma Rainey, the trumpeter, Levee, seduces Ma Rainey's friend Dussie Mae in the band room. Even after the Coke arrives, however, and the recording session resumes, we wait through several more starts before Sylvester can complete the brief introduction without stumbling on the words.

This dispute over time is manifest not only in the procrastination effected by Ma Rainey's refusing to record until someone buys her a bottle of Coca-Cola, but also by Sylvester, who challenges authorized time in several ways. As a stutterer, he speaks his words according to his own time and rhythm, not those of his audience. Each time he stutters in the introduction, moreover, means one more time that the recording has to be made. It also means additional delays while the band or the producers argue over whether Sylvester can be used on the record. "He don't stutter all the time," Ma Rainey insists, to which Irvin replies, "Ma, we don't have time" (*Ma Rainey*, 85).

Irvin, of course, is right. People do not have time; time has them, and they make of that condition what they can. To put it another way, the historical record is what people make out of our captivity by time. Within the parameters of that captivity, everyone is a slave, and slavery thus is the definitive historical condition. From this perspective, Toledo is wrong: the black man is not the leftover but the quintessence. Thus, Ma Rainey states an irrefutable truth when she responds to Irvin, "If you wanna make a record, you gonna find time" (*Ma Rainey*, 74).

But even after Sylvester finally makes the introduction smoothly, and we hear Ma Rainey sing her song according to her arrangement, the producers discover that, because of a mechanical failure, they have to start again. If Sturdyvant and Irvin have to make time for Ma Rainey, she has to make time for the recording because the mechanical device wields more authority over the song than she does, reducing her excessive displays of power to a meaningless performance in the face of the official record and all its attendant apparatus.

Learning the blues

Because the play is about people who are waiting for their lives to be put on the record, only to find out that the record will render those lives superfluous, it is structured around the ways that people tell the stories of their lives while they are waiting for the significant moments. In this sense, it can be viewed as an initiation rite, one that focuses especially on Levee, the warrior turned killer, and Toledo, the historian reduced to fatal victim.

Levee has, as Wilson puts it, a warrior spirit; that is, he refuses to accept the limitations society imposes. Because, for African Americans, this constitutes rejection not just of personal circumstances but of history itself, his assault on Toledo is, in one sense, inevitable and, in another sense, self-defeating. Levee, Wilson points out, "does a tremendous disservice to blacks by killing Toledo, because he's killing the only one who can read, he's killing the intellectual in the group. That's a loss we have to make up. . . . It's a progression towards the wrong target, but I salute [Levee's] willingness to battle, even to death" (*Conversations*, 78). What is at stake, in many ways, is change, which is simultaneously necessary and threatening. These characters and their music are the carriers of the past, and in that sense, cultural historians, recorders of past sufferings and the transmutation of those sufferings into art. Yet, they are also aware that the times are changing and that certain changes are necessary, not simply for their survival but also for their growth. It is the tension between those conflicting necessities that constitutes Wilson's drama, as it was those tensions that he registered in the world he set himself to capture.

In *Ma Rainey's Black Bottom*, there is a tension between Ma Rainey's voice and those who record it, as there is a tension between Levee's materialism and Toledo's literacy, and we become aware of this, and of the centrality of change as an issue, even before Ma Rainey and her entourage arrive or Levee and Toledo engage in an argument. When Levee complains about changes in the rehearsal room, Toledo notes that everything is changing all the time, to which Levee responds, "I ain't talking about no skin and air. I'm talking about something I can see!" (*Ma Rainey*, 24). In a sense, both men have a vested interest in the given, in the world that has shaped them and the music they play, but they also have an interest in change, their social and artistic positions putting them in thrall to the white world. It is precisely this paradox that drives the play. Levee wants to change his music, and thereby his life, but can do so only by undermining Ma Rainey's authority and appealing to the white record producers. As Toledo warns him, "As long as the colored man look to white folks to put the crown on what he say . . . as long as he looks to white folks for approval . . . then he's never gonna find out who he is and what he's about. He's gonna find out what white folks want him to be about" (*Ma Rainey*, 37).

The inevitable collision between Levee and Toledo results from a musical, historical, and ontological conflict about the nature of change, but they are also at odds when it comes to language, Toledo favoring metaphor, Levee the immediate, the material. When Toledo remarks to Levee, "Things change. The air and everything. Now you gonna say you was saying it. You gonna fit two propositions on the same track . . . run them into each other, and because they crash, you gonna say it's the same train," Levee replies, "Now the nigger talking about trains! We done went from the air to the skin to the door . . . and now trains" (*Ma Rainey*, 25).

One of the play's ironies, though, lies in the fact that however much of a materialist he seems to be, Levee, too, sees the world in symbolic terms. He has bought a pair of new shoes, shoes that will prove the source of contention between himself and Toledo, a seemingly trivial dispute, which nonetheless leads to Toledo's murder. These shoes have come to be a sign of Levee's ambition, a mark of his self-esteem, a symbol of his hope for an expansive future in which his life will be transformed. When Toledo accidentally scuffs them, it is a minor incident but one, to Levee, which seems to bear on his sense of himself. An assault on his property is an attack on him, and property, in its various guises, turns out to be crucial in *Ma Rainey's Black Bottom*. Beyond that, indeed, it has also been crucial to the African American experience, to a people who were themselves once regarded as property and whose access to property was subsequently curtailed, not least because property rights have always been intertwined with human rights. Thus, when Ma Rainey deals with efforts to control her art and her life and, through both, the history which that art and that life embodied, she is enacting the same struggle as did Wilson's mother when she won a new washing machine in the radio give-away competition, but was denied a new one when they discovered she was black. Refusing the used machine, she got no prize at all, but "she didn't want no used washing machine because she was due a brand new machine" (*Conversations*, 47). Forced to choose, Wilson's mother showed that she considered the figurative value of her human rights more important than tangible property.

This is the same struggle enacted by Ma Rainey as she deals with efforts to control her art and her life, and, through both, the history that life and that art embodied. No matter how she asserts her rights, however, in the end she cannot prevent herself becoming a commodity for sale in a competitive market that has distant echoes of the slave auction block, except that the slave had no voice and she does. To be sure, on one level, that voice is appropriated, but on another, it captures all those conflicting emotions that we see as the various musicians come together to create an art that finally resists co-option. To the white record company, she is property and her music no more or less than a piece of entertainment. For Wilson, she contains and expresses the history of the African American, a history that provides the context for music rooted in the black community. Her song is her life, as it is the life of that community, often divided in its vision of the future but united in a common sensibility and apprehension of the past.

Wilson's characters figuratively form a band throughout his cycle in the same way as they do literally in *Ma Rainey's Black Bottom*. The musicians are individuals with their own distinctive ways of playing, their own voices, their own dreams, and there are moments in which they dominate the stage, play their solos. But when they play together, no matter how briefly, they express what is shared rather than what divides, and in the end, as in *Ma Rainey*, it is the black musicians, real and symbolic, not the whites who exploit them, who demand and receive his and our attention.

The pragmatist, the earnest neophyte, the trickster, the magician, the madman, the maternal nurturer, the independent woman, and the dependent woman, each discrete, with their own personal histories, needs, and urgencies, all come together to express a community, which is an expression of history but which is something more than a simple product of that history. In *Ma Rainey's Black Bottom*, Wilson orchestrates those individual artists, as he does in all ten of the plays in his cycle. In *Ma Rainey*, the music is literal, as it is on occasion in some of the other plays. But, literal or symbolic, what he creates is a dramatic blues, in doing so laying explicit claim to the significance of lives excluded from the American Dream but not from their own dreams of becoming. Each voice is clear and distinctive, but, taken together, they tell a story of the struggles, defeats, and victories that have defined the experiences of those invited to live on the margins of American life but who have done so much more than merely survive.

CHAPTER 4
BEGINNING AGAIN, AGAIN:
GEM OF THE OCEAN AND *JITNEY*

Jitney

Performance history

The first publically performed version of *Jitney* took place at the Allegheny Repertory Theater in Pittsburgh, in October 1982 and in 1985 at the Penumbra Theater in St. Paul, Minnesota. A version rewritten for inclusion in the cycle was first performed under the direction of Marion McClinton at the Pittsburgh Public Theater in 1996, followed by numerous regional productions over the course of the following five years. It premiered in New York at the Second Stage—an off-Broadway venue—on April 25, 2000, and had its first Broadway production, under the direction of Ruben Santiago-Hudson, on January 19, 2017.

Arrangement

As the earliest play that Wilson drafted, *Jitney* has fewer character-instruments than his later plays. Central to this one is the *pragmatist-entrepreneur*, Becker, who runs the jitney station. Doub is the *accommodator*, and Youngblood is the *earnest young man*. Shealy, the numbers runner, is the *hustler*, and Becker's son, just released from prison, is a classic Wilson *warrior*. Turnbo is the *historian*, and like most Wilson historians, he is a curmudgeon, in fact perhaps the most curmudgeonly of all Wilson's historians. Rena, the *female singer*, has a relatively small part, with no strong solo of the sort that Wilson will later write, for example, for Rose (*Fences*) or Tonya (*King Hedley II*). Perhaps what differentiates the arrangement of parts in this play from later Wilson works is the degree to which orchestration is more thematic than harmonic: although there are elements of the warrior in Youngblood, for the most part the characters do not perform harmonic combinations of character types.

The Theatre of August Wilson

Gem of the Ocean

Performance history

Gem of the Ocean was first performed at the Goodman Theater in Chicago on April 28, 2003. It was directed by Marion McClinton and featured Kenny Leon as Citizen Barlow and Greta Oglesby as Aunt Ester. There were subsequent productions in Los Angeles and Boston, during which time Kenny Leon replaced McClinton as director, and there were significant cast changes, most notably: Phylicia Rashad assumed the role of Aunt Ester, John Earl Jelks played Citizen Barlow, and Ruben Santiago-Hudson played Caesar. That production of the play had its December 6, 2004, Broadway premiere at the Walter Kerr Theater, where it ran for seventy-two performances.

Arrangement

A very late Wilson work, *Gem* has a rich, complex blues orchestration. It is the only play in the cycle that foregrounds the female singer, with the band backing her up. Although this is the power arrangement of the characters in *Ma Rainey*, it is not how the play as performed is scored. In the intricate harmonics of the play, only Eli—the *accommodator*—plays his single role consistently. Three people—Aunt Ester, Solly Two Kings, and Caesar Wilks—all combine *historian* with their other roles, so much so, and so competitively so, that the play could be read as Wilson's introducing the twentieth century in the form of a competition for control of history between the warrior (Solly), the pragmatist-entrepreneur (Caesar), and the shaman (Ester). If so, this competition is performed in counterpoint with the direct themes produced by the earnest young man (Barlow) and the backup singer (Black Mary), in such a way as to make them the audience at whom the historical harmonies are directed, to which end, we learn in *Radio Golf*, Barlow opts for warrior by taking Solly's place, and Black Mary opts for shaman, eventually assuming the role of Aunt Ester.

Looking for a start

The foreboding presence of Herald Loomis that haunts *Joe Turner's Come and Gone* is explained, finally, in terms of spiritual, material, and historical deprivation. Loomis has been deprived of his song, his labor, and, most important for my purposes, his start. A start—a beginning—is a temporal marker, quite distinct, as Edward Said has made clear, from an origin,[1] an important distinction in understanding the work of August Wilson, whose opus is steeped in multifarious temporalities. As I have already noted, for Wilson, it's all about time.[2] It's about time, for example, that Memphis Lee reclaimed his land and that Boy Willie finally owned the land made fertile by the sweat of his ancestors. It's about time Troy Maxson finished his fence and Hambone got his ham and Risa found a man, and that Ma Rainey and Floyd Barton got to their respective Chicago recording studios; it's about time that Ma Rainey signed away her voice and that Levee got his chance to solo. And the difference between Levee's version of the blues and Ma Rainey's version is all about time. The play *Ma Rainey's Black Bottom*, moreover, is about the time when the value of music ceased to be its performance and became instead the record of its performance.

At any given time, since the beginning of recorded time, the record separates a "before" from an "after." Troy Maxson, therefore, is not in the record books as a home-run hitter because, his friend Bono explains, "You just come along too early," to which Troy responds, "There ought not never have been no time called too early."[3]

And this is something Wilson proves when he brings into the second half of his cycle the play *Jitney*, a play he wrote that came along too early. Thus, like Troy Maxson, Wilson with *Jitney* was reconfiguring the before/after relationship that informed his history by giving us the beginning of the cycle before it began. Because there are always two trains of thought running through his plays, however, Wilson also gives us, with *Jitney*, a culmination: the moment when the historical past represented in the cycle meets the present from which that history is recorded. From the moment of *Jitney*'s inclusion in the cycle, all of Wilson's plays will take place roughly in the present day—meaning roughly in a moment contemporaneous with their writing—with the exception of *Gem of the Ocean*, the play that provides the cycle's alternative beginning. Written after the end of the century that it, in Wilson's dramatic world, begins, *Gem of the Ocean*, like *Jitney*, is simultaneously a culmination and an initiation, for the dramatic world of which *Jitney* is the first instance will give birth to Aunt Ester, while the historical trajectory initiated by *Gem of the Ocean* will lead us to the crumbling inner-city neighborhoods of the post-1960s, the world where human dignity must continually reinvent itself in the face of decaying and confiscated property.

Jitney, set in the 1977 jitney taxicab station in the Hill section of Pittsburgh, thus reenacts the antebellum conflict between human rights and property rights. Space here does not allow even a cursory investigation of the multifarious and profound ways in which this conflict is intertwined, in the first half of the nineteenth century, with the Gordian knot of transcontinental nationalism. A few obvious points must, however, be stressed. First, the Union, in order to expand, needed not only to acquire territory but also to convert that territory into states—states that would participate as equal members in the complex system of legal reciprocity that allows the unimpeded flow of commerce and secures the universal sanctity of ownership. This process of reciprocity, which composes the legal concept of comity, becomes dysfunctional when specific states have laws, such as those surrounding slavery, that directly contradict one another. To resolve this contradiction by invoking the rationale of states' rights requires another contradiction: that the federal government has to enforce those states' rights; that is, that the innate rights of states are dependent on the supplementary power of the federal government. Under the instrumentalist philosophy of jurisprudence that dominated in the first half of the nineteenth century, a virtual mandate arose to protect the commercial and economic interests of the nation, which meant that, as the legal resistance to slavery rose in the non-slave states, so too did the federal impetus to protect nationally the states' rights of the slaveholding states. So strong, in fact, was this impetus that the decisions emanating from the strongly proslavery Supreme Court in the 1850s gave rise to fears in many—including Lincoln—that a pattern of decisions would lead to the de facto nationalizing of slavery.

As Thomas D. Morris succinctly points out, "As long as respect for the property interests of slave owners overshadowed the abhorrence of slavery, or concern for peaceful relations was greater than repugnance of the 'peculiar institution,' interstate comity, of course, could have provided a viable solution to the problems created after 1780 by the abolition of slavery in the North."[4] But as the "property rights" of slaveholders came under increasing threat from the personal liberty laws of non-slave states, and as the principle of comity became more and more impracticable, interstate commerce became more and more fragile. That fragility extended, needless to say, to territories that not only created new sites of contestation but also threatened to alter the legislative balance. Thus, national interests merged with slaveholding interests as long as those interests privileged property rights over personal liberty, and, even more important, as long as blacks—slave or free, South or North—remained silent and invisible in defining "national interests"; that is, in creating and delimiting the nation's public space.

In light of these legal disputes, the act of emancipation, by voiding the pending slavery-related cases, in effect precluded judicial affirmation of the primacy of human rights. In other words, emancipation was not a moment of liberation but a moment in which a formerly enslaved population was set loose in a world where human rights were usually contingent and property rights usually absolute. As the legal history of the last century-and-a-half has shown, property rights continued unabated to distribute and define liberties—so much so, in fact, that our laws now hold that a corporation can be treated as a person,[5] while people have fewer and fewer safeguards on the public regulation of their private lives.[6] Therefore, to cite one of numerous examples, the massive corruption of subprime lending, as a regrettable trait of the *private* sector, falls outside the purview of prosecutors, while the Patriot Act enables the Department of Justice to scrutinize the sex lives of public figures.

From one perspective, emancipation could be viewed as the action that prevented the nation from grappling with the implications of giving legal primacy to property, because it removed from the docket the most cogent test of property rights: the case of chattel slavery. This was in part what Ralph Ellison meant when he argued that, in the antebellum period, the Negro represented the moral burden placed on the democratic ideals that justified, in Lincoln's succinct phrase, "a new nation conceived in liberty and dedicated to the proposition that all men are created equal." With the end of Reconstruction—what Ellison has called the counterrevolution of 1876—the moral burden was not lifted; it merely went underground, became invisible.

That invisible world is Wilson's starting point, as it is manifest in every aspect of the jitney station, surrounded by vacant properties and empty lots that represent the lot of people who have descended from property—descended, that is, from a condition in which they constituted the capital that they were not allowed to acquire. Mark Twain summarized this dilemma concisely when Jim, referring to the $800 reward for his capture, says to Huck, "Yes—en I's rich now, come to look at it. I owns myself, en I's wurth eight hund'd dollars. I wisht I had de money, I wouldn' want no mo.'"[7]

The historical conditions of *Jitney* thus become the starting point for Wilson's dramatic cycle examining the conditions of history that produced that start. David Krasner marks *Jitney* as the source of the Wilson dramatic opus, the play that "evolved into the ten-play cycle."[8] As such, the play shares with all the historical dramas that will follow the recognition that history has been full of false starts—the first of which was the start of slavery in the New World, which itself was the false start of capitalism, invested as it was in the primacy of property, the supremacy of the marketplace, the heroicizing of trade.[9] That false start, moreover, was made possible by the Industrial Revolution, crucially dependent on the cheap price of cotton fiber, without which capitalism could not have amassed its capital.[10]

That start was concurrent with the birth of Aunt Ester, the matriarchal figure and spiritual leader whose presence informs the locale and sensibility of most of Wilson's plays written after 1992. Although her birth thus symbolizes the beginning of a specific Anglo-American economic practice, she was born in a very different place than that of the peculiar institution to which Wilson connects her birth. Her birthplace, we should remember, had to be Africa—not America—in that the practice of slavery was the necessary precondition for turning her from African into African American. Therefore, her African American identity was contingent upon a practice of slavery she did not initiate, but her initiation into slavery marked the beginnings of her African American identity. Once again, therefore, Wilson has doubled the beginnings. Aunt Ester marks the beginning of the peculiar institution that will culminate with the moment in which *Gem of the Ocean* will begin the chronology of plays that will dramatize the twentieth-century aftereffects of that institution.

If Aunt Ester marks the start of the slave trade, let me emphasize again that her origins, geographically and temporally, were elsewhere. She was a victim of the transatlantic traffic that subsumed her in an exchange system, subordinating her freedom and her identity to commercial interests that antedated her birth—commercial interests that mapped the New World as claimable property and the residents of the Old World as that property's managerial class. Thus began a set of special circumstances in which Africa became a way station in the flow of commercial traffic, never eligible, as America was, to assume its management. By the same token, as Krasner points out, Wilson's plays suggest that "to succeed, African Americans . . . establish specific locations in which they can flourish."[11] This leads me to two initial points: one being that, in this sense, the jitney station is Africa, and the second, that Aunt Ester's home at 1839 Wylie is the jitney station.

Let's start with Aunt Ester's home, as it reconfigures that way station that is Africa, at the start of the century that has rid itself of slavery's issues but not of its vestiges and implications. One in a line of lost souls—think of Sterling and Memphis in *Two Trains Running*—Citizen Barlow will thus visit Aunt Ester's house in order to get his start. But to go forward, Barlow will have to go back. Like Loomis and all of the Wilson characters who have had their song stolen, he will have to go back, because if he does not find his start in the past, he is likely to confuse it with his finish. For this reason, Barlow, using a boat made out of Aunt Ester's bill of sale, will travel again the Middle Passage, this time not as a superficial crossing of the sort registered in a shipping corporation's commercial log, but one that takes him under the surface to the sunken City of Bones in a manner that confronts the slave trade by invoking the combination of African and Christian traditions and rituals that characterized the postbellum African American church. "For Barlow," Harry Elam explains, "going to the City of Bones is a ritual act of cleansing in which the spiritual, the political and the historical all combine."[12]

It starts with capitalism

In this way, *Gem of the Ocean* is our initiation into the forces that produced the world from which Wilson initiated his historical cycle. But, notably, *Gem of the Ocean* is an initiation written in retrospect, and also a retrospective condensation of the properties of capitalism that produced the unresolved confusion of human rights and property rights, a confusion all too extensively— albeit not exclusively—operating in the interest of racial privilege. That condensation starts with the Middle Passage, the re-experiencing of which becomes essential to Barlow's initiation rites. In this construction, *Gem of the Ocean* is positioned not as the initial play of the cycle but as the culmination of a journey that must be compulsively reinitiated. Since Barlow's departure point is the New World, however, he does not so much repeat as retrace the Middle Passage. He takes it backward, in other words, so that he may *take it back* in both senses of the phrase: to retract it, and also to use it to find his path back to the present moment—the present place of departure for him, for the twentieth century, and for the Wilson cycle.

The scene of death by drowning, which the City of Bones memorializes, also returns us to the start of *Gem of the Ocean*, in that the play begins when Citizen Barlow attempts to see Aunt Ester so he can expiate his guilt over causing the death of Garret Brown. Brown had jumped into the river because he was falsely accused of stealing a bucket of nails actually stolen by Barlow. Rather than be punished for a crime he did not commit, Brown chose to stay in the water until he drowned. Brown did this, as Aunt Ester explains to Barlow, because, he had said, "I'd rather die in truth than to live a lie. That way he can say that his life is worth more than a bucket of nails" (*Gem*, 45). Aunt Ester thus sees Brown's decision as replicating the Middle Passage's disruption of the slave trade's economic logic. Brown was, in effect, refusing to allow his body to enter into an exchange system that could equate it with property.

This is the exchange system that Caesar advocates in the play, when, as constable, he justifies shooting a boy for stealing a loaf of bread: "He was a thief! He was stealing. That's about the worst thing you can do. To steal the fruits of somebody else's labor" (*Gem*, 36). A quintessential capitalist, Caesar describes at length the legal and semilegal ways he accumulated capital, clearly differentiating stealing from conning or swindling. Thus, the fact that he never stole anything in his life justifies his killing a man for stealing bread; at the same time, Caesar sees his own overcharging for bread as a public virtue:

> Yea, I sell magic bread. Got a big sign that say you only have to eat half as much to get twice as full. And I charge one and a half times as much for it. You don't understand I give the people hope when they ain't got nothing else. They take that loaf of bread and make it last twice as long. They wouldn't do that if they didn't pay one and a half times for it. *I'm helping the people.* (*Gem*, 35–36, emphasis added).

In making this distinction, Caesar seems to be refuting directly the Marxist doctrine that property is theft by turning Christ's miracle of the loaves into a capitalist parable, wherein not the bread but the profit from selling it is the magic multiplication Caesar's enterprise produces. This perverted miracle perpetrated against black people turns the miracle of capitalism into a black magic and Caesar into a form of antichrist, one who insists that the law is everything.

Figured this way, we can say that Caesar represents the state; that is, the law that makes Barlow free—that allows him to be a citizen. But as a constable, Caesar also rules the street, the public thoroughfare, the means and ways of traffic and transaction, the social and economic space where Citizen Barlow is citizen in name only. As Barlow explains, when he left Alabama only four weeks earlier, "They had all the roads closed to the colored people. I had to sneak out" (*Gem*, 42). These roads, closed at the beginning and at the end of the play, make the free black no longer the property of a specific master, but the universal property of the state.[13]

Instead of bestowing the freedom to travel, the public roads convert the stamp of blackness into currency in the same way that the official mark of the state has, since the inception of empire, converted first silver and then promissory notes—silver certificates—into money. On the coin of the realm, the face of Caesar is always and everywhere the inscription of the state on the entire state of economic affairs; the face of Caesar makes wealth real and reduces the material on which that face is imprinted to a substance used to bear the emperor's sign. The value of thirty pieces of silver is thirty pictures of Caesar. The face of Caesar is the foundation of capital in that it performs the miracle of converting not water into wine but matter into money; that is, Caesar's image makes the pieces a medium of standard exchange. In this way, Caesar is to money what blackness under slavery is to human beings: the sign of commodification. It is important to remember that unlike slavery in antiquity, slavery in America was a racialized condition valorized by genetics, even as the visible signs of the gene pool diminished. A fair-skinned "Negro," therefore, could circulate under slave law the way a well-circulated coin, from which Caesar's image had all but faded, could still pass as legal tender by allusion to the conditions under which it was minted. Thus, the features of a face, the tints of a complexion—even when diminished to hints—bear the signs not of race but of history, of the historically specific circumstances that commodified human subjugation in accordance with specific commercial practices and legal standards. Slavery, like money, functioned on the basis that specific markings certified the stamp of history as the apparatus of the state.

That is why the Caesar of *Gem of the Ocean* ironically misunderstands the nature of money when he says, "Money ain't got nobody's name on it."[14] In the system that has made Caesar wealthy and powerful, currency with nobody's name on it is worthless. In other words, all money has Caesar's name on it, in that it is tender of the realm. Money that has no name on it is shit, or, as Solly Two Kings calls the dog shit he collects to sell to tanners, "pure." Invoking a water metaphor, Caesar explains to Solly his belief about money: "It's floating out there go on and grab you some" (*Gem*, 33). Named after Old Testament kings David and Solomon, who were never subjects of the Roman Empire, Solly shuns the legal tender that, unlike his "pure," bears the brand of the state: the figurative image of Caesar.

Similarly, Solly will later reject that which is "floating out there" so he can attend instead to that which is sinking. Noting the failure of emancipation to deliver what it promised, he describes the current state of affairs:

They wave the law on one end and hit you with a billy club with the other. I told myself I can't just sit around and collect dog shit while the people drowning. The people drowning in sorrow and grief. That's a mighty big ocean. They got a law tied to one toe. Every time they try and swim, the law pull them under. (*Gem*, 60)

The law, in Solly's view, has thus replaced the Middle Passage in populating the City of Bones. The same rule of law that manufactures legal tender, that legally tendered in human cargo, and that legally emancipated the slaves, is thus connected to the force of law that drowned Garret Brown. And ultimately, the refusal to serve two kings, to render unto Caesar what Caesar claims as his, will cost Solly Two Kings his life.

Just as Solly must grapple with his names, whatever the consequences, Citizen Barlow must grapple with his. As Solly points out to him early in the play, "It's hard to be a citizen. You gonna have to fight to get that. And time you get it you be surprised how heavy it is" (*Gem*, 27). The site of citizenship, like the site of commerce, is the street, and *Gem of the Ocean*, set one year after W.E.B. Du Bois declared the informing problem of the twentieth century to be the color line, can be seen as initiating one aspect of what Sandra Adell has defined as the double bind of double consciousness,[15] in this case, manifest in the conflict between the state and the street.

This conflict thus connects Wilson's two beginnings, because the sites of both *Gem of the Ocean* and *Jitney*—havens sheltering families formed by mutual affiliation rather than bloodlines—feel the encroachment of the state, manifest in *Gem of the Ocean* as a set of arrest warrants and in *Jitney* as eminent domain. These two issues converge in the play that serves both as the cycle's end and as Wilson's last play, *Radio Golf*. At the same time, both *Gem of the Ocean* and *Jitney* are about taking one's business into the streets.

At the outset of *Gem of the Ocean*, Barlow is living on the streets just as Solly is making his living from what he picks up off the streets. The black workers, moreover, have taken *to* the streets. Because of Brown's drowning, "they was," Caesar states, "all over at the mill rioting" (*Gem*, 30). As Caesar sees it, this putting their business in the streets, which threatens to close the mill, will end up putting hundreds of black people on the streets—as loiterers, prostitutes, and disturbers of the peace. In that all of these activities are criminal, Caesar regards the streets for black people as pathways to jail.

But despite all of Caesar's attempts to enforce the law, the street and the state govern by different rules, and it is in that space of difference that the emancipated but not yet free black person must, in Wilson's world, negotiate the means for liberation. That is why Citizen Barlow must repeatedly take his business into the street. That is why his admission to the City of Bones must be the two shiny new pennies he finds on the street, not with the face of Caesar but of Lincoln, the newly minted shiny man; not the color of silver but of copper, a new coin with the datemark of the new century.[16] These new coins connect the Middle Passage to every place the street will lead: to the Great Migration, to Marcus Garvey, to the civil rights movement, and to the Black Power Movement.

In this initial moment of the twentieth century, Wilson thus uses the Middle Passage to juxtapose Aunt Ester's initiation into slavery with Barlow's into citizenship, that is, into the century that would equate freedom with free markets, into the entrepreneurial system that brought Aunt Ester to America as property and will bring Aunt Ester's property values to the present conditions of urban decay and urban renewal that inform *Jitney*, *King Hedley II*, and *Radio Golf*. Thus, urban renewal becomes one more restaging of the search for a new start effected by the conflict between property rights and human rights, between money and history: the conflict of serving two kings.

As this was the problem from the beginning of Christianity and from the beginning of slavery, it is also the problem we find at the beginning of Wilson's dramatic enterprise, where the jitney station is situated between the laws of the state—which license legitimate taxis, control property through eminent domain, and prosecute murders—and the rules of the street, which are always contingent and negotiable—the product of what Michel de Certeau has called the practices of everyday life. Thus, the jitney station is the unauthorized car service, controlled by Becker's rules, which dominate the station, the set, and, even in their violation, the tenuous world of the jitney drivers. This is a world where the law has little say, because in the 1970s the case is still that, as Wining Boy said in *The Piano Lesson*, the difference between a black man and a white man is that "the colored man can't fix nothing with the law" (*Piano*, 38).

The rule of law versus the law of rules and the role of the street

Instead, the black men in *Jitney* must fix things with one another through a series of negotiations, codes, and deals—none backed by the heft of legal sanction or the threat of police enforcement. Thus, if the set, with "Becker's Rules" written prominently on the wall, suggests a rigid world, the actions of the play make clear from the outset that we are in a world based not on rules but on deals. The play begins, in fact, with Youngblood and Turnbo arguing over the rules of checkers: "How you gonna jump him with the man sitting there!"[17] Youngblood says to Turnbo, "I got a man sitting there! Is you blind?" to which Turnbo responds, "Then put him where he belongs" (*Jitney*, 12). This is the first of Turnbo's many attempts in the play to put men where they belong, but the game disbands when Youngblood subsequently accuses Turnbo of cheating. Because rules, unlike laws, require mutual consent, and because the space of consent is also the space of negotiation, everyone in the station is trying to interpret the rules so as to cut some sort of deal for himself.

The "deal" thus not only defines the station's purpose—to facilitate an agreement struck between a driver and a caller—but delimits all activities that intersect there. Part of Turnbo's deal with a customer, for instance—another way he puts people in their place—is that, as he constantly stipulates, he won't wait; Youngblood, similarly, won't haul things he thinks will sully his car. The drivers make deals with one another over who will take the next call or under what circumstances they will accept the ride. Turnbo even argues with Youngblood about whether or not they had a deal about coffee. "If you're going next door," Turnbo says, "bring me back a cup of coffee," to which Youngblood responds, "I ain't your slave" (*Jitney*, 23). When Youngblood nevertheless returns with the coffee, Turnbo refuses to pay him for it, fomenting a vicious argument about whether Turnbo and Youngblood had, in effect, entered into a deal. The argument evokes Caesar's concern, in *Gem*, over the need for limiting black freedom—"It's Abraham Lincoln's fault," Caesar asserts, "He ain't had no idea what he was doing" (*Gem*, 34)—in that Youngblood and Turnbo are arguing about the conditions under which Youngblood is or is not a slave.

The alcoholic driver, Fielding, similarly, must negotiate the way he is or is not a slave to the bottle. Thus, he leaves the station to drink, and on his return argues with Becker about whether he has broken the "no drinking" rule and, further, if he has, whether that allows Becker to return his dues and break his agreement with the jitney station. Like so many in the Wilson canon, Fielding is not interested in getting his money back; he is interested in having his contract honored, because his status as equal party to a contract distinguishes him *from* property, making his humanity a fact of law. "This is a free country!" he shouts, "I'm a free man! You can't tell me what to do! This is the United States of America!" (*Jitney*, 50), asserting his right both to be a jitney driver and to drink. By evoking the name of the nation, Fielding is, like Citizen Barlow, making his business in the street an issue of the state—converting a rite of passage into the rights of citizenship. Similarly,

Shealy, the numbers runner, may take numbers at the jitney station and get messages there, but, by Becker's rules, may not use the station to operate his business. This situation puts him in constant negotiation with Becker, even while Becker is placing a bet with him. Shealy's entire enterprise exemplifies the tenuous world of contingent rules, in that his business is based on verbal exchanges and relationships of implicit trust for which there are no legal recourses. The irony of Shealy's double bind, therefore, is that while one of his rules is that "I don't be putting nobody's business in the street" (*Jitney*, 15), his own business, like those of the jitney drivers, is always in the street, because that is the place where they can—where they have to—make their living and deal with their lives.

Because putting business in the street turns private life into public property, however, it is also the process whereby the street acquires proprietary rights over individuals. This is why Turnbo puts others down for putting their business in the street, and, at the same time, it is why others accuse Turnbo of putting *their* business in the street. When Turnbo spreads the word that Youngblood is carrying on with his wife Rena's sister, Turnbo justifies his gossip on the grounds that Youngblood, by driving around in public with Rena's sister, had turned his life into public property. The conflict, restaging the earlier conflict between Youngblood and Turnbo over the coffee, pivots on the circumstances under which Youngblood's life is legitimately Turnbo's property. The business in the street, in other words, is the business of slavery.

Cigar Annie, the evicted woman standing in the middle of the street cussing out everybody from God to the gas man, although never actually seen in the play, serves to consolidate the confusion of property rights and human rights that business in the street produces. With "her furniture and everything sitting out on the sidewalk" (*Jitney*, 22), she is indistinguishable from her own property—a point she emphasizes by repeatedly raising up her dress, because, as Doub says, "that's all anybody ever wanted from her since she was twelve years old. She say if that's all you want . . . here it is" (*Jitney*, 22). By disowning the commercial rights to her own body—"here it is"—she replicates not only the landlord who is putting her personal property on the street but also the slave auction that, too, rendered a slave's body a property that she had no business controlling. But in her double bind, Annie's control of her body comes not from ownership but from using the street to stage its disowning, so as to restage the business in the street as a slave market. Annie has thus replaced the commercial laws of the slave trade with a personal deal that violates the conventional rules.

In light of Annie's double bind, Becker's "rules" can be viewed as an attempt to impose order where the law has failed. But if Becker runs the station—and his life—according to Becker's rules, those rules have not produced for him the deal he had hoped to get: "You look up one day and all you got is what you ain't spent. Every day cost you something and you don't all the time realize it" (*Jitney*, 36). A man who has for twenty years tried to manage rules for the business in the street not surprisingly figures his life in economic terms, a perspective affirmed, after his death, by his son: "He ain't got out of life what he put in it" (*Jitney*, 96).

The point I am making is that the street, in *Jitney*, comprises a private social and material economy authorized by the community, not the state. It is the composite of negotiation, rumor, and myth, where people construct the alternative history that Wilson will subsequently narrate back to the start of the twentieth century when he sends Citizen Barlow out into the street in defiance of Caesar's authority. That is why the *fear* of putting business in the street and the *necessity* of doing so are inextricably linked in *Jitney*. If the street is the antithesis of the private property and private lives that the characters crave, it is also the lifeline that allows them to pursue their dreams.

In pursuit of his dreams, Shealy, our quintessential agent of the street, has also made an elaborate deal with himself regarding women. After he was dropped by Rosie, a prior (albeit brief) love, he said to himself, "I was gonna find me another woman. But every time I get hold to one . . . time I lay down with them . . . I see Rosie's face. I told myself the first time I lay down with a woman and don't see her face, then that be the one I'm gonna marry."[18] Although this has never occurred—"with that little yellow gal works down at Pope's I seen Rosie's face . . . but it was blurry"[19]—and despite the fact that this has encouraged Shealy, the new "yellow gal" will not respond to Shealy's calls. Shealy's blurry face deal thus becomes a comic exaggeration of the ostensibly one-sided, unenforceable deal Becker had made with someone *he* loved. Becker had invested everything in Booster, his gifted, talented son, who broke the deal while in college years earlier, when, as Becker sees it, he threw his life away dating a rich white girl. As Turnbo tells it:

One day see her father was up here in the neighborhood, looking for one of them whores. He find one and she tell him to drive up the dead-end street there by the school, so she can turn the trick in the car. Don't you know they pulled right up in back of this gal's car where her and Booster done went to fool around! Her father recognizes the car and he goes over and looks inside and there's Booster just banging the hell out of his daughter! Well that cracker went crazy. (*Jitney*, 41)

All of the power relations that inform the business of the street in 1957 consolidate around what it means for the rich white father, as opposed to, for example, Cigar Annie, to "go crazy" in the street. Whereas the disempowered Cigar Annie, figuratively, and perhaps literally, the whore whose business twenty years earlier had brought the father to that alley, can only be regarded as mad—meaning insane—when she puts her business in the street by breaking the rules, the father's unruly behavior is *mad*—meaning manifesting the full force of appropriate anger—because, like Caesar, he can bring the law of the state down on the business in the street so that the police, accepting the girl's story that Booster had kidnapped and raped her, arrest Booster. On his first day out on bail Booster kills the girl, because, exactly like the drowned Garret Brown in *Gem of the Ocean*, Booster refuses to live a lie. And the lie—the big lie—rejected by the numerous warriors in Wilson's cycle is ultimately the lie that one can be conflated with property.

This is the lie that Citizen Barlow must dedicate his life to fighting if he is to earn his name. Thus, Wilson's penultimate play takes us back to the paradox with which we started, nearly twenty years earlier, in *Jitney*. Barlow's reenactment of the Middle Passage, which allows him to commune in the City of Bones with the spirits of his ancestors, enables him to proclaim himself the heir not only of those who survived the Middle Passage—and thereby made slave traffic profitable—but also of those whose lives were thrown away, those whose deaths denied the property rights of the slave traders and the profitability of their trade. This is one of the great ironies with which Wilson's history struggles: that the business in the street serves repeatedly, and often tragically, to remind us that it was the warrior—who fought on in the face of the impossible, who survived the Middle Passage and the ordeals of slavery—that made the slave system work, that made it profitable.[20] If everyone had died in transit, the slave traffic would have died with them, but some impossibly endured and, in ways small and large, even triumphed, ever confirming the high value of human property, the great value that slavery brought to American history, the enduring gift of capitalism.

CHAPTER 5
THE BOUNDARIES OF PROPERTY
AND THE PROPERTIES OF HUMANITY:
FENCES AND *JOE TURNER'S COME AND GONE*

Fences

Production history

Fences was workshopped at the O'Neill Conference in the summer of 1983 and opened at the Yale Repertory Theatre on April 30, 1985, where it was directed by Lloyd Richards and starred James Earl Jones as Troy, Mary Alice as Rose, and Courtney Vance as Cory. The same production had its Broadway premiere at the 46th Street Theatre on March 26, 1987. It ran for 525 performances.

Arrangement

As Wilson has repeatedly acknowledged, *Fences* is not a combo arrangement but rather, a powerful solo performance (the reason Wilson liked it least of his plays). Troy Maxson is the quintessential *warrior*, but one with a strong streak of *pragmatist* and perhaps an equally strong streak of *hustler*, and in the overtones of his duets with Death, perhaps a touch of shaman. Rose is one of Wilson's most powerful and striking blues singers, and Bono, like all Wilson *accommodators*, is the most consistent character. (If we consider the bassist, Slow Drag, paradigmatic, then we can see how each of Wilson's accommodators provides the steady bass line, against which the improvised harmonies unfold.) Cory, like Youngblood, combines the *earnest young man* with the *warrior*, and Lyons the (aging) *earnest young man* with the *hustler*. Gabriel adds to the combo the *man-not-right-in-the-head*, but, in a stunning finale, he combines this with the *shaman* capable of opening the gates of heaven.

Joe Turner's Come and Gone

Production history

After being workshopped at the O'Neill Conference in the summer of 1984, *Joe Turner's Come and Gone* opened at the Yale Repertory Theatre on April 29, 1986, directed by Lloyd Richards and starring Charles Dutton as Herald Loomis. The Broadway production featured the same cast, with the exception of Dutton, who was replaced by Delroy Lindo. It opened at the Ethel Barrymore Theatre on October 2, 1987, and ran for 105 performances.

Arrangement

This was Wilson's favorite play in the cycle. From the perspective of its arrangement, one can easily see why, in that it gives fullest orchestration to the panoply of instruments in his repertoire. Loomis combines the *man-not-right-in-the-head* with the *warrior* (a potentially dangerous combination, as illustrated by Hedley in *Seven Guitars*), but one with a level of force and menace that energizes all the other players, giving each a new vitality. Bynum, the *shaman* primarily and *historian* secondarily, is drawn from his marginal role as boarding house resident to a centrality emanating from the explanatory heft his part provides for Loomis's explosive improvisations. Holly, the other *historian*, is a *pragmatist-entrepreneur* with an *accommodator* wife, Bertha. Jeremy, very much like Lymon (*The Piano Lesson*) or Citizen Barlow (*Gem*), epitomizes the earnestness of young men newly come north, a blend of determination and wonder. (In many ways, they suggest younger versions of Floyd Barton [*Seven Guitars*].) Although none of the female singers—Molly, Mattie, or Martha—has a solo comparable to Rose's, Wilson provides each with a clear voice that sings a distinctive tune about female desire.

Property rights and property lines

The idea of a fence is inextricable from the idea of property. To construct a fence is to delimit, to divide up property, to separate the proper from the improper. The act of naming is fence-building; it is giving propriety to the named, marking it off as proper.

One could argue, furthermore, that this act of naming is the source of all rights. For if we apply a Western theological standard—by invoking some version of natural law—then we can trace these laws from the originary act of naming that separated order out of chaos, and that classified the order through God's agency and Adam's surrogacy, to the naming of a chosen people who would accept the restrictions and thus the inherent freedoms in God's law. If we reject theology in favor of a socially constructed understanding of rights, then naming is the act that creates the parties consenting to any social or personal contract. To put it simply, the unnamed have no properties and therefore cannot claim rights, for the claim to rights, regardless of how one constructs the source of those rights, is the claim that one belongs to the class—either general or particular—to which those rights accrue. The right to life, liberty, or the pursuit of happiness, for example, cannot be claimed for a car axle or a baseball bat; they do not have the necessary properties.

As this example suggests, one significant name that distinguishes a large body of rights is the name "human"; to be named human is to have claim to human rights. For the human race, as for the American Express card, membership has its privileges. (Even the term "human race" suggests the possibility of racial traits that are nonhuman.) In America, one of the privileges of being human is that one cannot be treated as property; another privilege is that one has property rights, that is, the right to treat that which is named nonhuman as property. Property has no rights; property rights, like human rights, are the property of humans. In one case, they are rights that protect the human, and in the other, they protect the human's ownership. Property can never be the damaged party or claim rights on its own behalf; the claims are made by the owner, and the damages accrue to him or her. The property itself is mute and neutral. A fence, then, is a sign of property rights. It thus implies an owner who is human and is manifesting his or her rightful claim. If a literal fence, by being part of a delimited property, represents *metonymically* the presence of property rights, the general concept of a fence or boundary *metaphorically* represents the necessary condition for the abstract accumulation of human rights. Just as the literal fence separates the owner's property from his or her non-property, the metaphoric fence separates human properties from nonhuman ones.

In antebellum America, race or skin color was just such a fence. It served to separate blacks from humans, denying blacks the properties of humans and giving humans property rights over blacks. About part of antebellum America, at least, we can say this with certainty. In the South, legal scripture and social precedent affirmed without flinching the distinction between blacks and humans, a distinction made fuzzy but not eliminated by the presence of Southern free blacks or even Southern black slaveholders.[1] In the North, on average, the boundaries were less clear, the fences less sturdy, although their power to separate was indeed bolstered by the Dred Scott decision and the Fugitive Slave Law.

The Dred Scott decision and the Fugitive Slave Law arbitrated between human rights and property rights by deciding that property rights were universal and human rights were local. The Fugitive Slave Law, passed as part of the Compromise of 1850, made it illegal, even in the North, to help runaway slaves or to refuse to assist in catching them. The Dred Scott decision, in 1857, went so far as to declare the Missouri Compromise, which created the Mason-Dixon line, unconstitutional because it violated the Fifth Amendment by depriving slaveholders of their property without due process of law. To put it another way, these laws and decisions mandated that the humanity of blacks be treated as a metaphor, while their nonhumanity—their condition as property—be treated as literal. The fact of their existence, implicitly, was that they had the properties of property, while the circumstances of their logistics might allow them to be treated *as if* they were human, as long as no one could claim that such treatment abrogated his or her property rights. In black American antebellum experience, to consider oneself human was to privilege a metaphoric representation of oneself over the literal "facts" of American culture. Within the codes of the dominant discourse, black humanity existed only as representation, only as its own simulacrum.

For black Americans, then, their humanity lay on the other side of the fence; it was not essential but contingent, a function not of experience but of imagination, situated not geographically but geopolitically. For black Americans, in other words, to consider oneself human was to hold that the truth was not literal but figurative. On some sites, holding to this figurative truth was prohibited by law; on others, it was not. The fence that divided these sites was the Mason-Dixon line. For the slave, that line represented the fence on the other side of which his or her humanity ceased to be figurative. As long as he or she believed that crossing it made one's humanity literal, the line itself was a literal division—a real fence across which lay the name of real humanity. If the Fugitive Slave Law and the Dred Scott decision mitigated that understanding, the failure of the Civil War and of Reconstruction, by eliminating the line but not the distinctions it represented, universalized it. The Mason-Dixon line, no longer literal, became the universal metaphoric fence that marked the properties of race as criteria for inhuman treatment.

The truth of the Mason-Dixon line, like the truth of black humanity, required privileging the figurative over the literal. With the failure of Reconstruction, the metaphoric truth of the Mason-Dixon line became endemic to black American experience; that is, it became a constant awareness that the construction of a site where black humanity became literal was always a personal feat, a function of knowing where the local Mason-Dixon fence lay and staying on the right side of it. This is a humanity constructed tactically and logistically against the larger strategic constructions working to create what de Certeau calls an "institution of the real."[2]

In this context, Wilson's drama investigates the implications of this condition by creating conflicts whose resolution requires inverting the traditional designations of "literal" and "figurative," and by situating those resolutions within the context of white American historical narrative in such a way as to reveal what Michel de Certeau and Hayden White have demonstrated is the figurative nature of all historical discourse. Both de Certeau and White, each influenced by Michel Foucault, explain how, in historiography, as in all institutionalized discourse, "facts" are the product of discourse, not its foundation.

In historiography, then, the figurative does not substitute for the literal; rather, it makes literal representation possible. From this perspective, the analysis of history becomes not the search for facts but the attempt to discover the privileged metaphors and the consequences of that privilege. Wilson's historicizing, I believe, impels such an examination of American history's representation of race. These traits, I think, typify all of Wilson's drama and, as well, his general attempt to construct a decade-by-decade chronicle of twentieth-century black American experience. *Ma Rainey's Black Bottom* brings into conflict the literal and the figurative value of Ma Rainey's music, as construed by black and white audiences or situated in black or white histories, and our understanding of the motivation for the brutal stabbing at the end depends on our privileging the figurative value of Levee's shoes. In *The Piano Lesson*, again, the figurative value of music, this time inextricably connected to the instrument on which it is produced, makes literal the ghosts who haunt the play. *Fences* and *Joe Turner's Come and Gone*, more than the others, however, emphasize the importance of the relationship between logistics and identity. Viewed in juxtaposition, moreover, they illustrate Wilson's interest in the historical context of this relationship.

The metaphoric Mason-Dixon line

In *Fences*, Wilson examines the effects of having to internalize that metaphoric Mason-Dixon line, as he describes Troy Maxson's struggle to build a fence around his property and thus create a site in which his properties can be considered human. A fifty-three-year-old garbage man who owns a small house in a run-down section of Pittsburgh, in 1957, Troy during the course of the play works at building a small fence around his meager back yard. At the same time, he works constantly to delineate his rights and responsibilities as husband, brother, worker, friend, and father. His name, Maxson, suggests a shortened "Mason-Dixon,"[3] a personalized version of the national division over the properties of blackness. His character similarly embodies the personal divisions that come from living in a world where the Mason-Dixon line exists as the ubiquitous circumscription of black American claims to human rights.

Troy lives in a house with Rose, his wife of eighteen years, and their seventeen-year-old son, Cory. The down payment for the house came from the $3,000 his brother Gabriel received in compensation for a Second World War head wound that left him a virtual half-wit, harboring the belief "with every fiber of his being that he is the Archangel Gabriel."[4] Troy takes pride at having housed and cared for Gabriel since the injury, and at the same time expresses shame at having had to rely on Gabriel's misfortune to provide the down payment he could never have acquired through years of honest labor. Having run away from a cruel and abusive father when he was a teenager, he found his way to the city, where he married and supported his family through theft until he was convicted of assault and armed robbery and sent to jail for fifteen years. There he learned to play baseball and gave up robbery. By the time he was released, his wife having left him, he met Rose, remarried, and after playing baseball in the Negro Leagues, became a garbage man.

The central conflicts in the play arise from his refusal to let his son play football or accept a football scholarship to college, and from his having fathered a daughter through an extramarital affair. But these are framed by conflicts with the father he fled, the major leagues that wouldn't let him play baseball, and Death himself, with whom Troy had once wrestled. Whatever else he loses, he vigilantly maintains his property and his property rights, demanding his authority within its confines, eventually building a fence around his yard and guarding the entrance with all of his human power against the force of Death, whose representation in human form is generally perceived to be metaphoric.

It is on these grounds—and on his home ground—that Troy chooses to be sized up. For in all other locales, he is a large man who has been underestimated. As a baseball player, and even as a garbage man, the world has not taken his measure. To "take the measure of a man" is to make a metaphor derived from a set of primary physical traits. "To measure up" means to fulfill a role in the same way one fills out a suit of clothes; "to take measure of oneself" means to assess one's ability to fill a specific role in the same way that one selects that suit of clothes. Implicit in all these metaphors is a set of objective physical standards—what Locke called primary characteristics—against which such intangibles as character, courage, loyalty, skill, or talent can be determined.

In the logistics of *Fences*, however, these standards form the variables measured against the standard of Troy Maxson's largeness. From the outset of the play, his size is a given: "Troy is fifty-three years old, a large man with thick, heavy hands; it is this largeness that he strives to fill out and make an accommodation with. Together with his blackness, his largeness informs his sensibilities and the choices he has made in life" (*Fences*, 1). And after his death, as Rose explains to Cory, "When I first met your daddy, . . . I thought here is a man you can open yourself up to and be filled to bursting. Here is a man that can fill all them empty spaces you been tipping around the edges of. . . . When your daddy walked through the house, he filled it up" (*Fences*, 93). Cory perceived Troy as "a shadow that followed you everywhere. It weighed on you and sunk in your flesh. It would wrap around you and lay there until you couldn't tell which one was you any more" (*Fences*, 93), but Rose argues that Cory is just like his father:

> That shadow wasn't nothing but you growing into yourself. You either got to grow into it or cut it down to fit you. But that's all you got to make life with. That's all you got to measure yourself against that world out there. Your daddy wanted you to be everything he wasn't . . . and at the same time he tried to make you into everything he was. (*Fences*, 93)

In addition to establishing Troy's size as the standard, both negative and positive, Rose is setting that standard against the standards asserted by the dominant white culture. Cory, in other words, is being urged not to measure himself against Troy, but to use Troy's size as a defense against the other, implicitly figurative, norms of "that world out there."

In so doing, Rose is asking him, in fact, to continue his father's quest. For the problem of the play can be seen as Troy's attempt to take measure of himself in a world that has denied him the external referents. His struggle is to act in the literal world in such a way as to become not just the literal but the figurative father, brother, husband, man he desires to be. The role of father is the most complex, because he is the father of three children from three different women. The children, precisely seventeen years apart, represent Troy's paternal responsibilities to three successive generations of black children. As each of these children makes demands on him, he must measure up to his responsibilities, and for each generation he measures up differently.

When his older son, Lyons, a struggling musician, regularly borrows money from him, Troy puts Lyons through a ritual of humiliation constructed out of the process of differentiating Lyons from himself: "I done learned my mistake and learned to do what's right by it. You still trying to get something for nothing. Life don't owe you nothing. You owe it yourself" (*Fences*, 18). At issue here is not only Troy's sense of himself as role model but also his sense of himself as negative example. He is both the father to emulate and the father not to emulate: Lyons should be like Troy by not making Troy's mistake. This lesson has a double edge, though, because the earlier, error-ridden life that Troy has learned to reject included not only his criminal acts but also his marriage to Lyons's mother and his fathering of Lyons. At that point in his life, we later learn, he felt he was not ready to be a father or to accept the responsibilities of fatherhood. For Lyons to recognize Troy's mistakes, then, is for him to acknowledge the inappropriateness of his own existence.

Troy deals with his younger son, Cory, in the same way. Like Troy, Cory is a talented athlete. Although a superstar in the Negro baseball leagues, Troy was never given a chance to play in the white leagues. Believing that white America would never allow a black to be successful in professional sports, he refuses to allow his son to go to college on a football scholarship. Once again, he becomes what he sees as a positive example for his son by virtue of his ability to reject himself. In a completely self-contained economy, he becomes both the model of error and the model of correction.

In regard to sports, particularly, he does this by constructing a division between personal history and American history. An extraordinary baseball player, whose talents are compared with those of Babe Ruth and Josh Gibson, Troy unfortunately was over forty when professional baseball was first integrated. When his friend Bono says that he "came along too early" (*Fences*, 9), Troy rejects his statement with a triple negative: "There ought not never have been no time called too early" (*Fences*, 9). In his critique of Bono's historical analysis, Troy is exposing its figurative nature and, by implication, what Hayden White has identified as the tropic nature of all history. Whereas Bono privileges the events of American professional sports integration as the given fact, Troy privileges the athletic requirements of the sport, not the political requirements surrounding it, as the context that determines meaning. To suggest that there was a right time to meet the requirements of a sport is to reveal that the requirements are figurative, just as suggesting that one can meet those requirements too early is to reveal that the time frame is figurative. At stake again is the dominant discourse—the one echoed by Bono—that takes the time frame of segregation as a fact in light of which a black player's physical ability can be seen as metaphoric.

For Troy to assert that his physical ability can be valorized only within a time frame that is racially determined is to impose the Mason-Dixon line onto his body. And if, as I have suggested, the name "Maxson" suggests this imposition from outside, the name "Troy" suggests the creation of a defensive wall, the internal resistance against alien assaults, with each assault being the precursor of Death. After the death in childbirth of his girlfriend, therefore, Troy issues his challenge to Death in terms of the wall he is constructing between himself and it:

> I'm gonna build me a fence around what belongs to me. And I want you to stay on the other side. See? You stay over there until you're ready for me. Then you come on. Bring your army. Bring your sickle. Bring your wrestling clothes. I ain't gonna fall down on my vigilance this time. You ain't gonna sneak up on me no more. When you ready for me, . . . that's when you come around here. . . . Then we gonna find out what manner of man you are. . . . You stay on the other side of that fence until you ready for me. (*Fences*, 77)

This is the metaphoric fence constructed to complement the literal fence Rose had been requesting from the outset. When Death accepts Troy's challenge, he confirms Troy's mastery over the literal, his power to turn his property into the visible recognition of his human properties, such that his responsibilities to his family, his athletic prowess, and his physical presence confirm his ability to confront Death—and hence to construct his life—on his own terms. In his terms, as he stated earlier in the play, "Death ain't nothing but a fastball on the outside corner" (*Fences*, 10). Rose's description of Troy's death confirms that terminology: "He was out there swinging that bat and then he just fell over. Seem like he swung it and stood there with this grin on his face . . . and then he just fell over" (*Fences*, 91). The inference is not only that he had protected his family by striking a final blow at Death but, more significantly, that he was able to do so because Troy made Death come to him on Troy's terms. Although Troy's challenge may be seen as figurative, Death's accepting it makes it literal, and thus the man-to-man battle between Troy and Death becomes a literal fight and simultaneously affirms Troy's power to create a site, however small, in which the figurative becomes literal. The conversion not only reduces Death to a man but also affirms Troy's status as one.

Within the context of the play, moreover, Wilson affirms the literal status of that conversion by having Gabriel perform a similar feat. Released from the mental hospital in order to attend Troy's funeral, Gabriel arrives carrying his trumpet. Although it has no mouthpiece, he uses it to "tell St. Peter to open the gates" (*Fences*, 99). After three attempts, with no sound coming from the trumpet, "he begins to dance. A slow, strange dance, eerie and life-giving. A dance of atavistic signature and ritual. He begins to howl at what is an attempt at song, or perhaps a song turning back into itself in an attempt at speech. He finishes his song and the gates of heaven stand open as wide as God's closet" (*Fences*, 100).

Gabriel's ability to invert the literal and the figurative thus confirms our understanding of Troy's death at the same time as it revises our understanding of Gabriel's marginality or "madness." For we can read his wound as a function of attributing literal power to such figurative institutions as nation and warfare. As a soldier in the Second World War, he invested his primary literal claim to human rights—his human life—in support of a figurative structure—the United States—that on the very site of his investment, the segregated armed forces, denied the status of that life as human. One can only assume that the part of his brain blown away in the war contained the beliefs and conceptions that allowed him to accept the figurative status of his own humanity. Lacking that part of his brain, he is not functional within the dominant white culture, as is evidenced by his numerous arrests as well as his institutionalizations.

The Mason-Dixon line, marking off the site where he may consider himself literally human, has become for Gabriel the walls of the mental institution. By the end of the play—providing a virtual survey of the institutionalized power critiqued by Michel Foucault—all the Maxsons are disciplined within figurative Mason-Dixon lines.[5] With Gabriel in the mental hospital, Cory in the armed services, Lyons in prison (we could conceivably even add Rose's recent involvement with the church), they find only this moment of relief within the boundary of the fence that Troy built. In the play's final pronouncement, with Gabriel speaking now as prophet and miracle worker rather than as marginalized madman, he asserts and demonstrates that the order of things—the relationship of figurative to literal—should be reversed: "And that's the way that go!" (*Fences*, 100).

This is a tactical victory, a method of subverting and resisting the strategic power of the dominant culture. For that culture has urged the black American man to flight with the implication that his humanity was the function of logistics; confined by sites that denied literal confirmation of that humanity, the culture has offered the promise of an elsewhere, a site where the literal and figurative reconfigure. To pursue that promise, to seek that site, often meant sacrificing familial responsibilities. Instead of pursuing that site at the expense of his family, Troy created it in order to protect them. As Rose, referring to the fence, noted to Cory, "Oh, that's been up there ever since Raynell wasn't but a wee little bitty old thing. Your daddy finally got around to putting that up to keep her in the yard" (*Fences*, 91).

In this way, Troy fought not only Death but also history. For the normative discourse of white American history, in 1957, was one of progress and assimilation. Textbooks promoted the idea of the melting pot and of upward mobility; historical films and dramas reinscribed the myth of the nuclear family; and despite the continued presence of Jim Crow laws, segregated schools and facilities, rampant denial of voter rights, and extensive discrimination in housing and employment, American history and, more important, its popularizations represented the United States as a land of equal opportunity, with liberty and justice for all. Those whose personal narratives failed to confirm this hegemonic discourse became invisible; as Ralph Ellison so dramatically illustrated in *Invisible Man*, they fell outside of history. Despairing of the possibility of altering dominant historical discourse, Troy devotes himself to reconfiguring the paternal patterns that compose his personal history.

The walking blues

In thus making himself the positive and negative model for his sons, he also makes his father a positive and negative model. For unlike many men of his generation—Bono's father, for example—Troy's father refused to leave the family, however much he detested it. As Troy points out, "He felt a responsibility towards us. Maybe he ain't treated us the way I felt he should have, but without that responsibility he could have walked off and left us, made his own way" (*Fences*, 51). In contrast, Bono points out:

Back in those days what you talking about, niggers used to travel all over. They get up one day and see where the day ain't sitting right with

them and they walk out their front door and just take on down one
road or another and keep on walking. . . . Just walk on till you come to
something else. Ain't you never heard of nobody having the walking
blues? (*Fences*, 50–51)

The "back in those days" to which Bono refers is the period in which
Joe Turner's Come and Gone is set. And the play, we could say, is very
much about exactly those "walking blues" that Troy's father rejected.
Set in a Pittsburgh boarding house, perhaps not far from the site that
would eventually become the Maxson home, it becomes the intersection
at which we meet numerous characters like Bono's father, each with
his or her own form of walking blues. The characters, in other words,
have literalized the idea signified by the Mason-Dixon line—that a site
exists where they become human. For each of the characters, that quest
for humanity is for a form of completeness that their circumstances,
and history, have denied them. It may be economic security or fair
employment practices, or a mate, or a family. The haunting specter of
this quest comes in the form of Herald Loomis, a man traveling with his
eleven-year-old daughter, searching for his estranged wife, from whom
he had become separated during his seven years of forced labor on a
Southern chain gang.

In numerous ways, this experience is all too typical. For Southern
blacks, it indicates the ways in which the Emancipation effected by the
Civil War was only figurative. Loomis, first of all, was forced into a slave-
labor situation of the same sort that most of the men in *The Piano Lesson*
were. Nearly half a century after Emancipation, he still could be denied his
human rights and treated as property. After seven years, when he is freed
from the chain gang, he experiences the situation of a newly freed slave.
Rent of his roots, without family, home, or job, he is in an environment
that still fails to recognize his human rights. Although he is looking to start
anew, everywhere around him his circumstances replicate the past. Under
such conditions, many came to assume that the future lay elsewhere. They
looked for their human rights—that is, the legal and social confirmation of
their status as human—in a place, just as their antebellum ancestors had,
rather than in time, as their parents had. In this sense, especially in light of
the exacerbated violence against blacks in the turn-of-the-century South,
the characters with the walking blues in *Joe Turner* can be seen as walking
on a historical treadmill, arriving at neither a time nor a place at which
their humanity was construed as literal. Instead, they replicate infinitely the

quest for freedom; for the site, in other words, where they are construed as having the properties of humans.

The play thus equates these walkers to newly freed slaves. In the preface, for example, Wilson writes:

> From the deep and the near South the sons and daughters of newly freed African slaves wander into the city. Isolated, cut off from memory, having forgotten the names of the gods and only guessing at their face, they arrive dazed and stunned, their heart kicking in their chest with a song worth singing. They arrive carrying Bibles and guitars, the pockets lined with dust and fresh hope, marked men and women seeking to scrape from the narrow, crooked cobbles and the fiery blasts of the coke furnace a way of bludgeoning and shaping the malleable parts of themselves into a new identity as free men of definite and sincere worth.[6]

Only the words "sons and daughters" differentiate those described here from the newly freed. Because the generational shift, in other words, has produced no concomitant shift in status or identity, these migrants imply that a shift in locale will do so.

Seth Holly, the Northern-born black owner of the boarding house, questions their goals, but he does not dispute their status as newly freed slaves:

> Ever since slavery got over, there ain't been nothing but foolish-acting niggers. Word get out that they need men to work in the mill and put in these roads . . . and niggers drop everything and head North looking for freedom. They don't know the white fellows looking too. White fellows coming from all over the world. White fellow come over and in six month got more than what I got. But these niggers keep on coming. Walking . . . riding . . . carrying their Bibles . . . Niggers coming up here from the back-woods . . . looking for freedom. They got a rude awakening. (*Joe Turner*, 6)

Like Troy Maxson, Holly underscores the difference between the narrative history of white America—one that incorporates personal narratives of effort, achievement, and reward into a coherent national narrative of progress—and the narrative history of black Americans, who, again like Ellison's invisible man, continue to run like an escaping slave toward an ever-receding horizon. Within the dominant discourse, Holly sees the black emigrants as still—vainly—trying to escape slavery.

To put it another way, he is recognizing the figurative power of the Fugitive Slave Law, the power to deny blacks their human properties, regardless of their locale. That power, Wilson makes clear, is economic and applies as much to Holly himself as it does to the tenants who pass through his house. For Holly, too, is a man whose labor is being exploited. As he himself acknowledges, even a property owner like himself was quickly surpassed economically by white emigrants. But Holly is also a tradesman, making pots with the raw materials furnished by a white peddler named Rutherford Selig. Although Holly ought to be able to capitalize on his skills, because he is dependent upon Selig for both materials and distribution, he cannot amass enough capital to set up a shop of his own and hire other workers in the community. Instead of returning to the community, the surplus value of his labor becomes the profit of the white community. Nor will that community finance Holly's attempts to capitalize his labor with a loan unless he puts his property up as collateral. Holly had inherited his property from his father, who was a free man; for Holly, therefore, as for Troy, the property signifies the site on which he has human properties, the site on which he is the *subject with* property rights, not the *object of* property rights. Refusing, therefore, to jeopardize his property, he nevertheless becomes the virtual property of Selig, with the fruits of his labor circumscribed completely by Selig's allowance and demand. The connection between this relationship and slavery is underscored in several ways. First, Selig enters immediately after Holly announces that the blacks looking for freedom have "a rude awakening." More significantly, Selig is also known as the People Finder, a name he gets because his door-to-door and town-to-town travels enable him to locate people for a fee, in much the same way as a slave catcher did. This connection is later made by Selig, himself, who identifies his current practices as deriving from his family's historical connection with the slave trade:

My great-granddaddy used to bring Nigras across the ocean on ships . . . it set him well in pay and he settled in this new land and found him a wife of good Christian charity and with a mind for kids and the like and well . . . here I am, Rutherford Selig. . . . Me and my daddy have found plent Nigras. My daddy, rest his soul, used to find runaway slaves for the plantation bosses. He was the best there was at it. . . . After Abraham Lincoln give all you Nigras your freedom papers and with you all looking all over for each other ... we started finding Nigras for Nigras. Of course, it don't pay as much. But the People Finding business ain't so bad. (*Joe Turner*, 41).

This speech is significant for several reasons. The first is its anachronistic quality, which suggests that Selig worked with his father as a slave catcher, and that he started tracking blacks for blacks immediately after the Civil War. Since Selig is in his early fifties, however, he was under ten years old in 1865. This conflating of time does not seem to me so much an error as a recognition of continuum, a recognition of the ways in which Selig's role is no more a significant break with that of his slave-selling and slave-catching ancestors than Loomis's is with that of slaves.

The speech also validates Holly's (and Maxson's) sense of dual histories. As Selig acknowledges, slavery enabled the slave merchants to establish coherent families with histories, traditions, extended lineage, while it left the slaves "all looking all over for each other." White America, the speech indicates, historically rewarded the practice of the slave trade—with both money and respect—while it historically punished the victims of that practice. This is "historical" discrimination in that it created a continuum— an institutionalized repetition of practices that, despite some differences (e.g., level of profit, abolition of some laws in some areas), compose a coherent pattern of discipline and exploitation transcending the alleged historical rupture of the Civil War. While the principles fought for in and established by that war—most notably, that the United States would not be a slaveholding nation—cannot, I think, be underestimated, the failure of the nation to address adequately the implications of Emancipation and to institutionalize the human rights of black Americans gives the Civil War a different position and significance in black American history than in the dominant historical narratives of white America.

The failure of those historical narratives to acknowledge black American history, then, becomes another form of historical discrimination. It is not just the history of denying blacks their human rights but also the practice of denying the story of that denial—or at least the significance of that story—in the dominant discourse named "American" history.

In this context, even attempts to bind the rifts created by the practice of slavery become another source of profit for the former slave catchers. If the black's body is no longer the property of the slave catcher, his or her name, identity, location are. His profit comes from controlling the economy in which these properties are exchanged for money, in just the same way as he controls the economy in which Holly's labor is traded. Selig's control over this human exchange, however, is even more extensive, in that he represents the institutions and practices that have initially reduced blacks to the property whose properties he trades upon. As Holly's wife, Bertha, points out,

> You can call him a People Finder if you want to. I know Rutherford Selig carries people away too. He done carried a whole bunch of them away from here. Folks plan on leaving by Selig's timing. They wait till he get ready to go, then they hitch a ride on his wagon. Then he charge folks a dollar to tell them where he took them. Now that's the truth of Rutherford Selig. This People Finding business is for the birds. He ain't never found nobody he ain't took away. (*Joe Turner*, 42)

This characterization draws direct parallels between Selig and the mythic Joe Turner. Joe Turner is the name, immortalized by a blues song, of the man who caught blacks to work on his chain gang. In catching Loomis, he broke up Loomis's family. Unable to work the land herself, his wife, Martha, was thrown off her tenant farm, and after five years of waiting for Loomis to return, she presumed him dead and went North, leaving their daughter in the care of her mother. When Loomis was released by Joe Turner, he set out for the North in search of his wife. At the same time, however, explains Martha, who had returned for her daughter, "I wasn't but two months behind you when you went to my mama's and got Zonia. I been looking for you ever since" (*Joe Turner*, 89).

Reclaiming their songs

Just like the newly freed slaves that Selig described, in other words, Loomis and Martha were "all looking all over for each other." When Loomis gives Selig the dollar to find Martha, he is paying Selig to find somebody whom Joe Turner took away. This creates a parallel between Loomis and Holly, both black Americans living in the aftermath of captivity and delimited by the economy created by that aftermath. That economy is constructed out of a dual historical perspective that marginalized the victims of slavery while it valorized the practitioners; it is an economy in which black labor becomes the property that allows white society to deny blacks their human rights. In transcending time, this economy denies blacks their participation in the American historical narrative, and this motivates Wilson's call for an alternative historical project, suggesting that in the performing arts—those inscribed in what de Certeau has called the practices of everyday life—can be found the site of black American history: the traces of its African origins, the scars of bondage, the economy of otherness, the encoded language of ghettoization, the arts and customs forged by the conditions of a double diaspora. As much criticism has noted, black American literature needs to be read through an awareness of such practices as storytelling (and the folkloric), the blues, black vernacular, folk art, and the "dozens."

Wilson thus privileges music as the source of a reality that transcends logistics, making it in all of his plays the link between humanity and history. As Bynum points out to Loomis, Joe Turner's ability to exercise his property rights over Loomis's body was an attempt to steal not merely Loomis's labor but also his claim to human rights. In describing his captivity by Joe Turner, he implicitly raises this issue:

> I asked one of them fellows one time why he catch niggers. Asked him what I got he want? . . . He told me I'm worthless. Worthless is something you throw away. Something you don't bother with. I ain't seen him throw me away. . . . I ain't tried to catch him when he goin down the road. So I must got something he want. What I got? (*Joe Turner*, 73)

At stake here is the contradiction implicit in enslavement. To treat a person as property is to deny his or her human worth, while to steal and guard that person is to ascribe some inherent value to him or her. Holly's explanation—"He just want you to work for him. That's all"—Loomis finds inadequate: "I can look at him and see where he big and strong enough to do his own work. So it can't be that. He must want something he ain't got" (*Joe Turner*, 73). To Holly's literal explanation, in other words, Loomis gives a literal response, thus pointing out that a person's desire to have someone do his or her work and the formulation of that desire into a master-slave relationship cannot be attributed simply to the need to get work done. To accept this literal formulation, Loomis must allow that his only properties are *qua* property, that he does not have human rights, which are being stolen along with his labor. So Loomis returns to that which he has or is, beyond the tangible property of producing labor or of being a machine. Since acknowledging his worth simply as machine legitimizes Joe Turner's use of him, he instead points out that such a need is an inadequate explanation. This turns him to the figurative construction of his worth, but he makes the turn in the form of a question, the answer to which Bynum supplies:

> That ain't hard to figure out. What he wanted was your song. He wanted to have that song to be his. He thought by catching you he could learn that song. Every nigger he catch he's looking for the one he can learn that song from. Now he's got you bound up to where you can't sing your own song. Couldn't sing it them seven years 'cause you was afraid he would snatch it from under you. But you still got it. You just forgot how to sing it. (*Joe Turner*, 73)

In this response, Bynum not only answers Loomis's question but also explains why Loomis himself doesn't know the answer. Since the song, as Wilson represents it, is one of the sites of black American history, it is the authority upon which rests Loomis's claim to human rights. To steal that song is thus to deprive Loomis of the claim and thereby to legitimize the treatment of him as property. At the same time, Loomis's attempt to protect his song, in the way he was unable to protect his body, has forced him to suppress that song in the same way that Berniece in *The Piano Lesson* forced herself not to play the piano. In denying Joe Turner access to the source of his claim to human rights, he has also had to deprive himself of that access. In consequence, now that Joe Turner has come and gone, Herald Loomis doesn't know whether he is coming or going. The figurative source of his claim to human rights, his song, has turned into a literal search for logistics, the walkin' blues. Hence, he searches for his lost wife not to recapture her—which would replicate Joe Turner's enslavement—but rather, to recapture the history he lost when he suppressed his song. As he points out, he wants to find Martha so that he can start again:

> That's the only thing I know to do. I just want to see her face so I can get me a starting place in the world. The world got to start somewhere. That's what I been looking for. I been wandering a long time in somebody else's world. When I find my wife that be the making of my own. (*Joe Turner*, 72)

The temporal and the geographic are inextricably connected in Loomis's speech. He is looking for a starting *place*, a site from which to initiate his entrance into *time*, into history. That entrance into history, in turn, is figured as the creation of a place, a world of his own. He is estranged from that place, however, not by distance but by time: "wandering for a long time in somebody else's world." In thus refiguring Moses's experience of being a stranger in a strange land, Wilson exposes the ways that black Americans have lived outside of the governing metanarratives of white Western culture. Though he is the slave who has wandered for years and arrived at the destination north of the Mason-Dixon line, it provides no promised land, that is, no property on which his claims to human rights are literal; and although he seeks to return to his origins, unlike Odysseus, he has no homeland to claim, that is, no property on which his claims to human rights once were literal. Loomis, in other words, seeks a figurative place with literal power, and Wilson provides it by imbuing it, like Troy Maxson's fence and Gabriel's identity, with superiority over its literal representation.

The song becomes a truer form of history than white historical discourse, and being bound to his song allows Loomis a historical identity as a human being that no geographical site allows. Troy Maxson is similarly bound to a song about his dog Blue. And his son, like Loomis, finds a starting place when he sings Blue's song and thus binds himself to his father's blues. The song is an elegy for a hunting dog. "Blue laid down and died like a man," the song tells us. "Now he's treeing possums in the Promised Land" (*Fences*, 98). In Blue's song, as in the blues, the dog crosses the true Mason-Dixon line to the Promised Land, the land, in other words, that promises conversion from beast to man, servitude to freedom—the figurative land on which one acquires human properties instead of being the property of humans. This is indeed Troy Maxson's song, and when his son and daughter sing it together, Gabriel can arrive to prove that the song's claim, which has become theirs, is real.

If reality is authorized for black Americans by performance and for white America by text, Wilson's plays, as both text and performance, mediate between the site of dominant discourse and the practices of black American life. In this regard, we can view his project to create a decade-by-decade cycle of plays as an attempt to make history, that is, an attempt both to construct an event and to construct the story in which it figures. This is figurative history, but as we have seen, in the context of American history, to privilege the figurative, to invert its relationship to the literal, has been a means to construct a claim for the human rights of black Americans.

CHAPTER 6
THE PROPERTIES OF THE PIANO
AND THE LEGACY OF HUMAN
PROPERTY: *THE PIANO LESSON*

Production history

After being workshopped at the O'Neill Conference in the summer of 1987, it opened on November 26 of that year at Yale Repertory, under the direction of Lloyd Richards, with Samuel L. Jackson as Boy Willie, Starletta DuPois as Berniece, Carl Gordon as Doaker, Rocky Carroll as Lymon, Tommy Hollis as Avery, and Lou Myers as Wining Boy. With the same cast, other than Jackson, who had been replaced by Charles Dutton, the play had a Boston production in January 1988. The same production, with S. Epatha Merkerson replacing DuPois, opened on Broadway on April 16, 1990, at the Walter Kerr Theatre, where it ran for 328 performances.

Arrangement

The Piano Lesson provides almost the full spectrum of Wilson's instrumentation, with each part clear and distinct. Doaker epitomizes the Wilson *historian* and *accommodator*, as does Boy Willie the Wilson *warrior* and *pragmatist-entrepreneur*. Lymon typifies his *earnest young man*, and Wining Boy combines in perfect harmony the *hustler* and the *shaman*. In prolonged mourning for her husband and for her parents, Berniece is one of Wilson's most soulful blues singers, albeit without the show-stopping solo that he gives to Alice (*Fences*) or Tonya (*King Hedley II*). The *man-not-right-in-the-head* is Avery, if viewed through the eyes of Boy Willie, but it's Boy Willie as seen by Berniece or, at times, by Lymon, Doaker, or Wining Boy. At the end of the play, Wining Boy in his drunken state overwhelms the other contenders for the part, such that the crescendo that ends the play pits a collaboration of madness against the reality of ghosts.

In the middle of *The Piano Lesson*, Wilson's play set in 1936 Pittsburgh, Wining Boy, a semi-retired piano player and singer in his fifties, explains why he is no longer working as an entertainer:

> That piano got so big and I'm carrying it around on my back. . . . You wake up one day and you hate the whisky, and you hate the women, and you hate the piano. But that's all you got. You can't do nothing else. All you know how to do is play that piano. Now, who am I? Am I me? Or am I the piano player?[1]

Wining Boy, a gambler, rambler, and con-man, here is singing a blues refrain, wherein the piano stands in for the medium of the blues and the life of a blues man. Wining Boy has paid a surprise visit to his brother, Doaker, a railroad man who shares a house with their niece, Berniece, and her ten-year-old daughter, Maretha. The house's living room is also a repository of a rare, elaborately carved piano, which Berniece's father, Boy Charles (the brother of Doaker and Wining Boy) stole from the descendants of Robert Sutter, the slaveholder who paid for the piano with two of his slaves, Berniece's grandfather and great-grandmother.[2]

Unlike the highly visible and uniquely ornate piano in Doaker's living room, the "piano" to which Wining Boy refers is the figurative implement that connects his lifestyle to the blues tradition he has inherited and to the community that, in that tradition, he enchanted. In the orchestration that Wilson created for *The Piano Lesson*, Wining Boy harmoniously combines the shaman and the con-man. Wining Boy's figurative piano, therefore, is magical, while Berniece's carved piano is literally haunted, and although the piano to which Wining Boy refers is not the one specific to the play's action, the question he raises, about whether one owns a piano or is owned by it, is at the heart of the play. For, like *Fences*, *The Piano Lesson* engages the distinction between owning property and being property. And, as in *Fences* and *Joe Turner*, the concept of property, of what may be owned or stolen and who may own or steal, is inextricably linked to the definition of and limitations upon black humanity.

The play has a relatively simple plot: Berniece's brother, Boy Willie, and his friend, Lymon, have driven a truckload of watermelons from Mississippi to Pittsburgh, where they intend to sell them and divide the profits, so that Lymon can stay in the North and Boy Willie can return to Alabama to purchase the land on which his ancestors had worked as slaves. He expects to get the remainder of the money for the land purchase by selling the carved piano he co-owns with Berniece. Because she refuses to part with the piano, even though she also refuses to play it, she and her brother are in direct conflict that builds to a near-fatal crisis and finally resolves when, to assist the Boy Willie in his battle with the ghost of Sutter (the man from whom the piano had been stolen and the grandson of the slaveholder who had owned Boy Willie and Berniece's family), Berniece uses the piano to summon ancestral power, after which Boy Willie abandons his demand to sell the piano as long as Berniece continues to play it.

The piano's properties

At the same time, because of the piano's multifarious properties, the plot of *The Piano Lesson* could be seen as Wilson's most complex plot. When the audience looks at the piano, Wilson explained, it begins "to find out more, and more, and more. Every time you look at it, you see something different. You learn it was stolen. You learn this happened, and that happened. And every new piece of information you find out about the piano, the piano changes" (*Conversations*, 55–56). Thus, the piano interweaves numerous narratives and conflicts, each emanating from a different set of its properties. As Doaker explains to Lymon, "To understand about that piano, you gotta go back to slavery time" (*Piano*, 42). In antebellum America, the piano had belonged to a Georgian named Nolander, who sold it to Robert Sutter in exchange for Berniece's grandfather—at the time nine years old—and her great-grandmother. Sutter purchased the piano as an anniversary gift for his wife, Miss Ophelia, who loved the gift but also longed for the slaves for whom it had been exchanged.

At that time, Doaker explains to Lymon, Robert Sutter had used "one and a half niggers" (*Piano*, 42) to buy the piano. But as "time go along" (*Piano*, 43), Miss Ophelia missed the slaves (in the way one might miss pets), so much so that she became sick. In order to cure Miss Ophelia, Robert Sutter instructed Berniece's great-grandfather, Willie Boy, an accomplished wood sculptor, to carve the images of his wife and son—Miss Ophelia's "pet" slaves—into the piano's surface. "When Miss Ophelia seen it . . . she got excited. Now she had her piano and her niggers too. She took back to playing it and played on it till the day she died" (*Piano*, 44). Willie Boy, however, also decorated the piano with many additional engravings: members of Berniece's family tree and crucial scenes from the family's history. These engravings turned the piano from a musical instrument or a piece of furniture into a unique work of art, a unique historical document, and a unique historical artifact.

Each of these properties reflects an array of narratives lodged in dramatic conflict. The first source of conflict is between Robert Sutter's purposes and Willie Boy's usurpation of them. Put simply, Robert Sutter wanted to please his wife, who could enjoy the music she could produce on the piano and satisfy the nostalgia for her lost (pet) slaves through the images its surface produced. But through Willie Boy's artistry, the piano produced a surfeit of images. "When Mr. Sutter saw the piano with all them carvings on it, he got mad. He didn't ask for all that. But see . . . there wasn't nothing he could do about it" (*Piano*, 44).

This situation indirectly echoes a personal experience Wilson had in a Boston bar where he quickly became aware, from the composition and demeanor of the crowd and the difficulty he had in ordering a drink, that it was a de facto white establishment. Initially, he intended to finish his drink and expeditiously depart, but when he heard rhythm and blues coming from the jukebox, he instead started savoring his drink and making room for himself at the crowded bar. "You can't say," he told me, "that you want my music here but you don't want me."

In the same way that there was nothing anyone could do about Wilson's making room for himself at the bar, there was nothing that Robert Sutter could do about Willie Boy's using his artistry to make room for himself, his family, and its traditions on the piano. Just as the white record company profited from Ma Rainey's voice—her musical labor—Robert Sutter got a nice price for Willie Boy's labor. "See, everything my granddaddy made Sutter owned cause he owned him" (*Piano*, 43). Similarly, Robert Sutter owned the piano as musical equipment in the same way that Sturdyvant and Irvin owned Ma Rainey's recordings, that is, owned the apparatus that made her art available. But no matter how grafted to the structures, technologies, and privileges of white commerce, Willie Boy's art was his own, the immutable product of the community whence it came, exemplified and particularized by his family's role in the history of that community. In this way, Willie Boy functions visually as Ma Rainey did audibly when she explains that she did not invent the blues: "They say I started it . . . but I didn't. I just helped it out. Filled up that empty space a little bit" (*Ma Rainey*, 83).

In the same sense, no one could stop Wilson from making room for himself at the Boston bar, because the room was already there, made not by him but by the history that produced the music and that produced him. The jukebox did more than supply a set of recorded sounds; it extended into that white bar a black space or, more precisely, a space of invisible black history. For the same reason, the piano's worth is always overdetermined;

it provides more than one asks for: not just the sentimental memories of animate property but also the unsentimental history that rendered people as property and that animated their artful resistance as the indelible trace of the human rights fixed to the surface of property rights. But in a nation with asymmetrical laws, those human rights can be subordinated or compartmentalized. As Wining Boy points out at another point in the play, "the difference between the colored man and the white man [is that] the colored man can't fix nothing with the law" (*Piano*, 38).[3]

The piano's complexity, therefore, emanates from Robert Sutter's legally trading for it and Willie Boy's subversively engraving it, both of which acts took place in what Doaker called "slavery time" (*Piano*, 42) but have a profound postbellum legacy for the family. Berniece and Boy Willie's mother, Mama Ola (b. 1876), and father, Boy Charles (b. 1879), were both born at the moment of Reconstruction's failure, and were both haunted by the legacy of slavery. Boy Charles, Doaker explains, was obsessed by the piano, because "It was the story of our whole family and as long as Sutter [the grandson of Robert Sutter] had it . . . he still had us. Say we was still in slavery" (*Piano*, 45). For Boy Charles, in other words, "slavery time" is not a historical era, but a state of mind and an organization of power that had not abated with Emancipation.

This theme pervades the play, which is replete with anecdotes of exploitation and forced labor. Lymon has no intention of returning to Mississippi, for example, because, as he explains, "The sheriff looking for me. All because they gonna try and make me work for somebody when I don't want to. They gonna try to make me work for Stovall when he don't pay nothing" (*Piano*, 77). Both Lymon and Boy Willie have spent time on Parchman Farm, an example of what Douglas Blackmon has called "slavery by another name." In his Pulitzer Prize–winning book, Blackmon documents in extensive and painful detail the practice, between the end of the Civil War and the Second World War, of legally condoned, de facto black slavery.[4] "By 1900," he points out, "the South's judicial system had been wholly reconfigured to make one of its primary purposes the coercion of African Americans to comply with the social customs and labor demands of whites"[5] (Blackmon, 7).

> The records demonstrate the capture and imprisonment of thousands of random indigent citizens, almost always under the thinnest chimera of probable cause or judicial process. . . . The original records of county jails indicated thousands of arrests for inconsequential charges or for violations of laws specifically written to intimidate

blacks. . . . Repeatedly, the timing and scale of surges in arrests appeared more attuned to rises and dips in the need for cheap labor than any demonstrable acts of crime. Hundreds of forced labor camps came to exist, scattered throughout the South—operated by state and county governments, large corporations, small-time entrepreneurs, and provincial farmers. These bulging slave centers became a primary weapon of suppression of black aspirations.[6]

Parchman Farm, a massive prison constructed on the site of a Mississippi plantation and specifically identified as a place where Boy Willie, Lymon, and Wining Boy have done time, was described by historian David Oshinsky as "the quintessential penal farm, the closest thing to slavery that survived the Civil War."[7] Wining Boy calls it "my old stomping grounds" (*Piano*, 37). Even Lymon's father was incarcerated and would have gone to Parchman Farm had Lymon's mother not bribed the sheriff with two hundred dollars, the last fifty of which she got from Wining Boy. "Now I figured it . . ." he explains, "without that fifty dollars the sheriff was gonna turn him over to Parchman. The sheriff turn him over to Parchman, it be three years before anybody see him again" (*Piano*, 63).

Boy Willie's and Lymon's stay at Parchman was the result of their having taken a job hauling lumber, for which, no doubt, they were underpaid. In compensation, they dropped off the truck a small amount of lumber from each load, planning to pick it up after the job was complete. This kind of situation exists in a tacit relation to economies that allow people to pay slave wages in exchange for looking the other way when goods are skimmed. The unspoken arrangement, however, requires two conditions, the first being that the value of the amount skimmed must never equal the amount saved by underpaying for the work. More important, this supplementary contract must remain tacit. The crucial difference between paying Boy Willie and Lymon a low hauling fee *plus* 5 percent of the profits instead of allowing them to skim 5 percent of the wood is that it maintains a silent asymmetry, wherein their labor is always haunted by gratuitous dependency, such that Boy Willie and Lymon can only approach fair value for their labor as long as they renounce the right to claim it. By tacit agreement, their supplementary compensation must be marked as theft, even though, as Boy Willie knew, it was not:

BOY WILLIE   We ain't stole no wood. Me and Lymon was hauling wood for Jim Miller and keeping us a little bit on the side. We dumped our little bit down there by the creek until we had enough to make a load. Some fellows seen us and we figured we better get it before they did. (*Piano*, 53)

The fellows who saw them drop the wood were white men, we know, because Boy Willie and Lymon "saw the sheriff with them" (*Piano*, 53). They had brought him along so that the law could fix (meaning "rig") the skimming agreement to reflect white privilege by rewriting the tacit agreement so that the "stolen" wood would not belong to the black men who hauled the lumber but to white men who had done no work at all. This event exemplifies the hypothetical story Wining Boy originally used to explain the difference between the white man and the colored man:

> You say I'm gonna go out and get me a whole pot of these berries and cook them up to make a pie or whatever. But you ain't looked to see them berries is sitting in the white fellow's yard. Ain't got no fence around them. . . . Now the white man come along and say that's my land. Therefore everything that grow on it belong to me. He tell the sheriff, "I want you to put this nigger in jail as a warning to all the other niggers. Otherwise the first thing you know these niggers have everything that belong to us."
>
> . . .
>
> Now Mr. So and So, he sell the land to you. And he come to you and say, "John, you own the land. It's all yours now. But them is my berries. [. . .] You got the land . . . but them berries, I'm gonna keep them. They mine." And he go fix it with the law that them is his berries. (*Piano*, 38)

It is important to note how subtly the story of hauling the wood connects to the question of property that informs the play: Because lumber is secretly interchangeable with labor, the distinction between wood and work blur, making Boy Willie's and Lymon's effort indistinguishable from someone else's property. Let me make clear that I am not saying all exchanges of labor for material goods are displacements of slavery. Rather, I am saying that when social conditions allow the exchange to be visible only as theft, the "stolen" portion of the labor becomes no different from other owned property, in the same way that Willie Boy's labor—like Willie Boy and his wife and child—were the property of Robert Sutter.

The ghost of property rights inhabiting the purview of the law presides as well over Boy Charles's claiming of the piano. When Boy Charles took it, he did so, as Wining Boy explains, "because he figure he had more right to it than Sutter did. . . . If Sutter can't understand that, then that's just the way that go" (*Piano*, 57–58). Lacking the ability to fix things with the law, Boy Charles regarded Sutter's property rights as contingent (in the same way that Sutter relegated contingent status to Boy Charles's human rights). In contradistinction to Sutter's personal bill of goods, Boy Charles asserted his personal Bill of Rights by stealing the piano on July 4 to declare his independence from the laws with which the white man could fix things. Even though Boy Charles felt the piano was rightfully his, however, he knew he must acquire it under the rubric of theft, as though legitimate ownership could actually accrue to someone who obtained a piano in exchange for human beings. The piano legally belonged to Sutter because the colored man could not use the law to fix (meaning "redress") the confusion of humans with property, whereas the white man could use the law to fix (meaning "stabilize permanently") that confusion of humans and property as a legitimate equivalency.

In both instances, the attempt to resist this asymmetric construction of legitimacy, and, by implication, the confusion of people and property that it legitimizes, is fixed (meaning "corrected") by the law, as it oversees the execution of the resisters. After Boy Charles took the piano, the sheriff trapped him in a railroad car, which the white posse, whose actions the sheriff authorized, burned to the ground. Similarly, when Crawley, Boy Willie, and Lymon tried to collect the skimmed lumber, and they found the sheriff waiting for them, Boy Willie and Lymon ran, while Crawley made the fatal decision to use his gun to assert his "right" to the wood. By running, Boy Willie and Lymon were acknowledging that in the eyes of the law, a portion of their labor was someone else's property. Crawley, on the other hand, refusing to accept a law he could not fix, was fixed by the law.

Crawley's death took place only three years before the start of the play's action, and Boy Willie's and Lymon's forced servitude is even more recent. In this context, "slavery time" extends into the present day of the play, which explains why the Great Depression is never mentioned, even though the play is set in the depth of it. *The Piano Lesson*, in other words, takes place along an alternative historical trajectory that makes the Great Depression irrelevant. What *is* relevant is the historical trajectory that haunts the family. Berniece has the piano because her father took it from the heir of the slaveholder who traded away his father and grandmother. If the piano resulted in her father's immediate execution, Berniece believes it also caused the slow death of her mother, Mama Ola. "You always talking about your daddy," Berniece shouts at Boy Willie, "but you ain't never stopped to look at what his foolishness cost your mama. Seventeen years' worth of cold nights and an empty bed" (*Piano*, 52).

Even though Boy Willie recognizes that the piano is suffused with the family's grief—in fact, *because* he does—he wants to turn that grief into capital. He wants, in other words, to redeem the value of the labor Robert Sutter usurped. "The only thing that make that piano worth something," he argues "is them carvings Papa Willie Boy put on there" (*Piano*, 51). But is the value of the carvings in their uniqueness, that is, in the record of their sui generis relationship to history, or is the value simply in their beauty, in the artistry that transcends time? Thus, the question is not whether Willie Boy made the piano valuable but rather, what constitutes the nature of that value.

This is why different characters value the piano for different reasons and also why clearly identifying each reason is far from simple. The antique dealer values the piano a-historically: the carvings for him are tantamount to fictive, in that they mark no legal transactions or any historical record of specific people. Rather, for the dealer, the piano contains arbitrary faces and generic narratives. Only for those who already know the stories inscribed on the piano does it relate a version of history. For Berniece, the carvings trace a painful history, drowned in her family's blood: the blood relatives she never knew, the blood shed by her father to acquire the piano, the blood shed by her mother's hands in polishing the piano, the bloodshed endemic to slave trade and the violence inherent in making humans property. The quality of the bloodshed is so intense that, for Berniece, the piano is too toxic to touch.

Boy Willie occupies a position between Berniece and the dealer, in that he recognizes that the aesthetic value of the piano is an effect of historical circumstances. By investing that history with a teleology, he feels that the value that his grandfather added to the piano and, thus, the value that the family gained when his father died to acquire it was something to be used: "Now, I'm supposed to build on what they left me" (*Piano*, 51). Both Berniece and Boy Willie understand that the piano represents resistance to the history that made it everything it is. But for Berniece, it consolidates the toxic past of slavery as generic violence, inscribed as the specifically violent disruption of her family tree, while for Boy Willie, the piano provides the means to triumph over those violent disruptions.

In this regard, one of the properties of the piano is its capacity to own and to be owned at the same time, because it is not just the product of labor but the producer of music, of a specific kind of music that, similarly, is owned by African Americans and also owns them. The reason that Wilson made room for himself at the Boston bar was because, if the music was his, he was entitled to the royalties. They were his royalties not because he wrote the music or the lyrics, but because, as an African American, he paid for them with his history. In this sense, the piano literalizes African American history as the site whence the music comes.

The piano, however, is only recognizable as that historical site because of Willie Boy's labor. Willie Boy used his talents to expose a truth that was always already there, a truth that Robert Sutter and his progeny tried to make invisible, even when it was audible. It is no coincidence that Wining Boy's meditation on his relationship with the piano comes immediately after a discussion about coerced labor, in the midst of which the group of men are unified by singing a work song, "O Lord Berta, Berta." In this sense, in other words, four men who have had their labor coerced invoke that experience through the music that the experience produced as a way of expressing intolerable conditions and, simultaneously, of making those conditions tolerable. As Harry Elam explains:

> The scene symbolizes the personal hardship and collective social memory of unfulfilled dreams and compensatory separations that blacks suffered under enforced enslavement. Yet, even as the song expresses the pain of these men, it also proclaims their will to survive. (*Piano*, 27)

But Willie Boy's carvings were the product of forced labor. He was commanded by Robert Sutter to apply his craft to the piano's surface, but in so doing he converted forced labor into art and history. As Elam points out, "as evidenced by the carved piano, . . . a European instrument that the African American Charles family adopts and appropriates and makes its own, . . . African American culture has always involved adaptation, appropriation and hybridity" (*Past*, 31). Willie Boy thus turned Robert Sutter's command that the piano represent Miss Ophelia's lost slaves into the means by which Willie Boy made his history and art a permanent aspect of Sutter's instrument and of Miss Ophelia's consciousness. Willie Boy thus made his family's presence visible, their labor palpable, and their history legible in the same way that Wilson made his presence visible at the bar.

The piano as possessed

To put it another way, the engravings on the piano haunt the artistry and conscience of white America in the same way that African American music does.[8] This perspective has extreme resonance in *The Piano Lesson* because the play is a ghost story or, actually, a compendium of stories about the ways a piano is possessed. Most explicitly, the ghost of Sutter—Robert Sutter's grandson—has come to Berniece's house. After Sutter died from falling down a well, Berniece saw his ghost in her home. So did Doaker. Since the land Boy Willie wants to buy is up for sale because of Sutter's death, Berniece believes Boy Willie has killed Sutter and thinks that Sutter's ghost has followed Boy Willie to Pittsburgh. Doaker, however, notes that Sutter arrived just after his death—about three weeks before Boy Willie—and he believes "Sutter here cause of that piano. I heard him playing on it one time" (*Piano*, 57).

If Sutter's death initiates the action of the play, then the arrivals in Pittsburgh of Sutter and Boy Willie provide alternative versions of the play's objective and trajectory, such that one of the play's conflicts is over who owns its plot. Is it the story of a man posthumously reclaiming his stolen property or of a man finally wrenching it away from a ghost that is illegitimately possessing it?

Because Boy Charles equated Sutter's ownership of the piano with Sutter's ownership of the family, the possession of the piano by Berniece and Boy Willie represents resistance to slavery (a resistance made all the more cogent in light of the fact that, as the play's stories of forced labor have made clear, slavery had not been abolished). As long as Boy Willie and Berniece possess the piano, Sutter does not possess them. That is why the crisis, finally, is less about whether Berniece will allow Boy Willie to sell the piano than about how either of them can stop the piano from being possessed by Sutter. The literal and the figurative in African American history, as I have noted, are not discrete qualities but properties bound interdependently in the laws and practices surrounding the status of black humanity. Thus, the piano's being possessed—that is, haunted—by Sutter cannot be separated from Boy Willie's family and their piano's being possessed—that is, enslaved—by him. These forms of ownership can be disarticulated only if the colored man has the capacity to fix things with the law, a circumstance that would make black humanity a foundational concept rather than a contingent privilege.

From this perspective, Boy Willie is opposed diametrically not to his sister but to Sutter, who wants to maintain the fixity of the old order, which the piano threatens in two ways. It evidences subversion of that order, and it also represents the means to acquire the power of that order's capital. Because Sutter's claim on the piano is not a claim on property but on power, Sutter's ghost, by playing on the piano, is attempting to repurpose it into an obstacle to Boy Willie's teleological narrative. Sutter, in other words, is converting the piano from a source of black capital to a sign of the white man's ability to fix things with the law. Sutter wants to assert posthumously his legal control over the piano in order to fix (meaning "stabilize") the history of white supremacy, instrumentalized as the primacy of property rights over human rights. Implicitly recognizing that this is the way the law fixes things for white people, Boy Willie rejects the law: "I don't go by what the law say. The law's liable to say anything. I go by if it's right or not. It don't matter to me what the law say" (*Piano*, 38–39). For Boy Willie, what is right is that the piano be viewed not only as the product of forced labor but as the medium of exchange that will make that labor productive for the people coerced into performing it.

But Sutter is far from the only ghost involved; the piano's talismanic heft derives from the plethora of ghosts that inhabit it, including Berniece's parents and ancestors. Berniece, Elam points out, "is unwilling to accept the import of the past for the present. And yet she, more than any other character, on some conscious level recognizes the presence, the coexistence, of the ancestors" (*Past*, 201), even though "[My Mama] say when I played it she could hear my daddy talking to her. I used to think them pictures came alive and walked through the house. Sometime late at night I could hear my mama talking to them. [. . .] I don't play that piano because I don't want to wake them spirits" (*Piano*, 70).

Mama Ola, Berniece angrily reminds her brother, "polished this piano with her tears for seventeen years. For seventeen years she rubbed on it till her hands bled. The she rubbed the blood in . . . mixed it up with the rest of the blood on it. Every day that God breathed life into her body she rubbed and cleaned and polished and prayed over it" (*Piano*, 52). In this context, Mama Ola functioned as sacred vessel, transforming God's breath into her blood and tears, in a sanctifying ritual codified by her prayer. Mama Ola's daily rites thus allowed the piano to make music by combing secular and spiritual labor: "'Play something for me, Berniece. Play something for me, Berniece.' Every day. 'I cleaned it up for you. Play something for me, Berniece'" (*Piano*, 52). This daily cleansing, followed by the repeated incantation, makes clear the conditions under which Berniece could use the piano, and, since Mama Ola's supplication must be granted, the conditions under which Berniece *must* play the piano. But after Mama Ola's death, Berniece could not sanctify the piano in the way her mother had: "I shut the top on that piano and I ain't never opened it since. I was only playing it for her" (*Piano*, 70).

The ghosts of the four hobos who were burned to death in the boxcar along with Boy Charles also inhabit the piano's troubled legacy. Because the train to which that boxcar belonged was called the Yellow Dog, Boy Charles and these hobos became known as "The Ghosts of the Yellow Dog." And in the seventeen-year span since Boy Charles's death, the Ghosts of the Yellow Dog had been blamed for the deaths of twelve white men connected with their incineration, all of whom fell down wells. According to Elam, the Ghosts of the Yellow Dog were participating "in a policy of racial redemption. They have not only avenged their deaths but the deaths of other black men who were wrongly killed by white vigilantes" (*Piano*, 198–99).

Although Elam is no doubt correct, it is important to note that the race of the four hobos is never stated, so that, regardless of their race, they come to represent all random victims of the violence several times displaced: from the violent conversions of African people to African American properties; from the conversion of property to legal tender, in which a white man could acquire legal rights to an instrument purchased first with the labor stolen from people, and then with the stolen people themselves. The hobos thus consolidate the violence of the cumulative thefts originating in the relentless attempts to steal humanity and commodify the remains. Even if the hobos were black, by being identified solely as "hobos," they are defined by their liminal state, their anonymous homelessness, their state of transience, which made them the pure receptacles of the violence inherent in pitting human rights against property rights. The inability to connect them to the piano's history or ownership, furthermore, reduces them to its pure retributory violence, making them the pure instruments of retribution. Whether or not they operate according to divine law, they unquestionably operate outside of white law, and therefore they cannot be fixed, or at least not by the same legal authority that empowered slavery by another name.

Although Berniece discounts the idea of the Ghosts of the Yellow Dog, she is certain she has seen Sutter's ghost, and she is also haunted by the ghost of her husband, Crawley. Avery, another transplant from Mississippi, who is working as a Pittsburgh elevator operator at the same time as he is trying to start his own church, is Berniece's frustrated suitor. At the heart of his frustration is his rivalry with a ghost. "You can't go through life," he tells Berniece, "carrying Crawley's ghost with you" (*Piano*, 67). In exchange for Crawley's ghost, Avery is offering Berniece the Holy Ghost. In a dream, Avery was led by three hobos to a room with a flock of people having the heads of sheep and a second room where he meets Jesus, who offers to join him in leading this flock through a valley filled with wolves: "If you go, I'll go with you," Jesus tells Avery (*Piano*, 25), to which Avery responded, "Come on. Let's go" (*Piano*, 25), at which point Avery woke up believing he "had been filled with the Holy Ghost" (*Piano*, 25). While Berniece is supportive of Avery's vision, she regards skeptically his endorsement of the Ghosts of the Yellow Dog: "God is the Great Causer. He can do anything. He parted the Red Sea. He say I will smite my enemies. Reverend Thompson used to preach on the Ghost of the Yellow Dog as the hand of God" (*Piano*, 69).

Exorcising the confusion

If, as Elam claims, the Ghosts of the Yellow Dog represent a form of African ancestral worship (198–201), and Avery seems to be conflating or confusing Christian and African beliefs,[9] this is one of many confusions that haunt the play. Shortly after Boy Willie arrives at Doaker and Berniece's home, Berniece encounters Sutter's ghost at the top of the stairs. According to her, the ghost was calling Boy Willie's name, leading Berniece to conclude that Boy Willie, not the Ghosts of the Yellow Dog, had pushed Sutter down the well. Boy Willie's denial makes perfect sense:

> You telling me I'm gonna go out there and hide in the weeds with all them dogs and things he got around there . . . I'm gonna hide and wait till I catch him looking down his well just right . . . then I'm gonna run over and push him in. A great big old three-hundred-forty-pound man? (*Piano*, 14)

But Berniece rejects Boy Willie's defense and, particularly, his blaming the Ghosts of the Yellow Dog: "You can talk all you want about that Ghosts of the Yellow Dog stuff if you want. I know better" (*Piano*, 15). Berniece is clearly confused by ghosts. While she does not believe in the Ghosts of the Yellow Dog, she believes in Sutter, because Sutter's ghost, she believes, has followed Boy Willie to her house.

Berniece also believes that Boy Willie has killed Sutter and, in addition, was responsible for Crawley's death:

> Boy Willie, I want you and Lymon to go ahead and leave my house. Just go somewhere. You don't do nothing but bring trouble with you everywhere you go. If it wasn't for you Crawley would still be alive. (*Piano*, 15)

Berniece follows up her conflation of the deaths of Sutter and Crawley (and by implication, we later learn, of Boy Charles and Mama Ola), which haunt her consciousness, taint the piano, and consolidate around the presence of Boy Willie, with a general statement about what Boy Willie represents to her: "I want you and Lymon to go on and take all this confusion out of my house!" (*Piano*, 16).

This desire to rid the house of confusion is central to Berniece's motivation. Ghosts comprise fundamental confusions between life and death because they act like living people even though they are dead, and they represent an Other-world while inhabiting this one. The dual status of ghostliness, *The Piano Lesson* makes clear, emulates the dual status of African Americans, that is, a status that confuses the owner and the owned, the biological and the historical, legacy and history. The dead, after all, relinquish their property rights, and, like their literal and figurative estates, their bodies become the property of the living. Similarly, to be an African American circumscribed by the laws and the realities of Jim Crow America is to have one's body represent the ghost of the African enslaved and the ghostliness of the body that has the properties of enslavement; the black American, as the ghost of enslavement, can inhabit the living world of Jim Crow America marked as Other, having different properties and therefore different property rights.

For this reason, Berniece's confusion entails tracing the ghosts back to the violence that ended their lives. But the piano can only serve as the medium for unraveling the lineage of personal and institutional violence when it is maintained by the necessary rites, whether they be Mama Ola's purification ritual or Wining Boy's shamanistic blues (more about this below). Instead of viewing the piano as a musical instrument or viewing the music as the culmination of daily ritual, Berniece can only see the piano as the artifact of a secular history infused with pride, retribution, and pointless deaths:

> For what? For a piano? For a piece of wood? To get even with somebody? I look at you and you're all the same. You, Papa Boy Charles, Wining Boy, Doaker, Crawley . . . you're all alike. (*Piano*, 52)

By making the piano "a piece of wood," Berniece can add Crawley to the piano's other victims. Although he had nothing to do with the piano's theft, he did die over lumber—pieces of wood—in much the same way as Papa Boy Charles died over the piano, that is, at the hands of the sheriff. So long as Berniece sees the piano as a "piece of wood," her husband and her father both resisted the law for the same thing. But what enables Berniece to reduce the piano to a piece of wood is the absence of Mama Ola's ritual, the ritual that Berniece can neither perform nor forget. The piano functions, as Michael Morales points out, both as "a mnemonic device for the transmission of oral history [and as] a sacred ancestral altar, bridging the world of the living to that of the dead" (*Piano*, 106). In rejecting both of these roles, Berniece has deprived the piano of its instrumentality. At the same time, she extends its history to include Crawley's death, making Boy Willie and Lymon accessories to that death in the same way as Doaker and Wining Boy were to Boy Charles's. In both cases, three men of the same generation went to claim their "piece of wood," and in both cases one was killed by the sheriff.

Just as the piano merges several generations of the family's history, so too does Berniece's understanding. Both Doaker and Boy Willie try to convince her that she is wrong about Boy Willie's causing Crawley's death. "It ain't his fault" (54), Doaker tells her. Boy Willie tells her the same thing: "I told you I ain't responsible for Crawley" (54). To each of them she responds, "He ain't here" (*Piano*, 54). But of course, the piano's lesson is that they all are *here*, not as people or as images carved on its surface, but as parts of a history that those images convey, a history wherein labor was stolen as if it were property, wherein the attempts to claim what should have been the legal fruits of that labor resulted in irreparable damage because it could not be fixed with the law.

This confrontation between Berniece and Boy Willie over the cause of Crawley's death is interrupted by Maretha's scream, coming from upstairs, where she has seen Sutter's ghost. Thus, the pattern of call-and-response, Berniece's evocations of Crawley: "He ain't here, is he? Is he?" "He ain't here" (*Piano*, 54) are answered by the scream, in effect responding to the list of men who are not "here" by announcing that Sutter *is* here.

This moment, which ends the first act, frames Berniece's confusion with the panoply of ghosts she is trying to avoid, both those in whom she believes and those whom she denies. She believes in Sutter's ghost, but not in the Ghosts of the Yellow Dog; she accepts Avery's Holy Ghost, but remains haunted by Crawley's ghost, and is afraid to engage with her father's ghost, her mother's ghost, or the ghosts of her grandparents and great-grandparents. She is confronting, in other words, the fundamental dilemma of historiographers and, as I have pointed out, the problem of the historical record, in that if she doesn't write the record, it gets written for her; and if she can't right the record, she gets wronged by it. Thus, the lesson she needs to learn from the piano is that her task is not to avoid ghosts but to choose correctly among them; if she doesn't play the piano, Sutter does.[10] According to Elam, Berniece's "neglect of the piano, her unwillingness to confront the ghosts of her past [is what] allows the ghost of Sutter to return and contest them for ownership of the piano" (*Past*, 123). "While it is easy to sympathize with Berniece's desire to forget her painful memories," according to Yoruba belief, Morales underscores,

> if we draw a parallel between the piano and African ritual practice, the spiritual and physical consequences of forgetting her past and not using the piano are very serious. . . . Ritual neglect of the ancestors not only results in the loss of ancestral protection from forces destructive to living members of the lineage, but it also threatens the very existence of the ancestors who require the food of sacrifice to maintain their existence in the realm of the dead. (109)

Preparing for the response

Maretha's scream thus sets up the binary structure of the play, which works not to rid the piano of its ghosts, but to invoke those ghosts who will enable the piano to perform in a way worthy of the labor that gave it value rather than of the practices that turned that stolen labor into capital. Just as, at the end of the first act, Maretha calls on her mother to fend off Sutter's ghost, at the end of Act II, Berniece will call on her own mother to do the same. The second act is structured, in other words, to allow Berniece's response to answer her daughter's call at the end of the first.

In order to facilitate Berniece's climactic response, many conditions must be met. The first is that Berniece has to be released from the spell that is stultifying her. Her sexual unavailability to Avery and her emotional unavailability to her brother are both symptoms of her alienation from all the piano represents. If Crawley, as a violent man, an oppressed man, and a dead man, obstructs her access to the piano, it is because Berniece has internalized that obstruction.

We see that obstacle dissolve, however, when Boy Willie and Lymon come back to the house after a night on the town. First, Boy Willie brings back Grace, a woman he has met at the bar. In a comic fiasco, Boy Willie, who has not told Grace that he does not have his own bedroom, attempts to have sex with her on the couch in the middle of the living room, which results in their overturning a lamp, waking up Berniece. Appalled by

Boy Willie's disregard for the propriety of her home, Berniece asks Boy Willie and Grace to leave, indicating several times: "Boy Willie, I don't allow that in my house" (*Piano*, 74), "You know I don't allow that in my house" (*Piano*, 74), "I can't allow that around here" (*Piano*, 74), and "I'm sorry miss. But he know I don't allow that here" (*Piano*, 74). Although she is explicitly obstructing Boy Willie's sexual desires, Berniece is also reflecting her prohibitions on her own libido, something already noted by Avery: "Who you got to love you? Can't nobody get close enough to you. Doaker can't half say nothing to you. You jump all over Boy Willie. Who you got to love you, Berniece?" (*Piano*, 67). When Avery says: "How long you gonna carry Crawley with you, Berniece? [. . .] Life got all kinds of twists and turns. It don't mean you stop living. That don't mean you cut yourself off from life" (*Piano*, 67), Berniece responds "I just ain't ready to get married right now" (*Piano*, 67); in other words, she doesn't allow *that* in her house.

Immediately after Berniece throws Boy Willie and Grace out, Lymon returns. He has been less successful than Boy Willie, even though he is wearing a "magic" green suit that Wining Boy sold to him for the purpose of meeting women. Unfortunately, Lymon's problem is that he cannot meet the kind of woman to whom he is attracted. As he puts it, Wining Boy "told me if I wear this suit I'll find me a woman. He was almost right" (*Piano*, 77). Lymon then enters into a long discussion with Berniece about his regrets regarding women: "I just dream about women. Can't never seem to find the right one" (*Piano*, 78). The fact that Berniece reassures him ("She out there somewhere. You just got to get yourself ready to meet her" [*Piano*, 78]) is less important than that her reassurance reveals a sympathetic side of her personality, heretofore hidden from the audience, from the other characters, and, at least since Crawley's death, from herself. Her compassion for Lymon also seems to facilitate an opening up of her own desires, as reflected by her confession, "That's what I'm trying to do" (*Piano*, 78).

This confession slowly leads to a more intimate conversation, wherein Lymon compliments Berniece on her appearance and makes Berniece a gift of a bottle of perfume, a drop of which he tenderly puts behind her ear. He then gives her a kiss, a kiss that she returns before going up the stairs. Complete with its magic elixir, this scene provides the enchanted moment when Berniece, like Sleeping Beauty, wakes from her spell, a point confirmed by the stage direction that ends the scene: "LYMON *picks up his suit coat and strokes it lovingly with the full knowledge that it is indeed a magic suit*" (*Piano*, 80).

Released—at least potentially—from her mourning, Berniece puts in place the next element necessary for her to respond to Maretha's scream in the face of Sutter's ghost: She asks Avery to perform a ritual to rid the house of Sutter's ghost, a ritual that most critics see the play as discrediting. Elam, for example, calls it an "aborted Christian exorcism" (*Past*, 201), and Morales says that Avery's Christian exorcism "only seems to feed Sutter's power, rather than diminish it."[11] About Boy Willie's denigration of Avery, his Christian beliefs, and his exorcism ritual (Boy Willie throws water from a kitchen pot to mimic Avery's ritual of sprinkling water), Wilson has pointed out that the scenes are not indictments of Christianity. "The Christian church is one of the reasons that we're still here. It's one of the institutions that has in fact enabled our survival . . . Spiritually, the Christian church has been important for us" (*Conversations*, 177). It might be more accurate, therefore, to read Avery's ritual as a vital part of the play's resolution. If Avery's actions had no power, his exorcism would not have evoked the confrontation with Sutter's ghost so that Boy Willie, Berniece, their ancestors, and the Ghosts of the Yellow Dog could join forces against Sutter. In addition, it is important to remember, as I have noted, that Avery's Christianity, reflecting one strain of interpretation of the African American church, incorporates the Ghosts of the Yellow Dog, which reflect African avenging spirits. As Wilson has pointed out, although there is no question that the church is probably the most important institution in the black community, "it's an overlay of African religions onto the Christian religion. The original African religions we stripped away from them. They weren't allowed to practice these religions" (*Conversations*, 77). Incarnated as hobos, moreover, the Ghosts of the Yellow Dog share a kinship with the three hobos in Avery's dream who led him to Jesus.

Thus, earlier in the play, when Avery seems to be conflating Christianity and what could be called superstition, his perspective is preparing us for the final scene, wherein what he calls "the Great Causer" is not one entity but rather, the community of competing interests, beliefs, authorities, powers, and spirits transformed into a combo around the piano. Even Sutter, as the impetus for expulsion, is essential to the final product, in the same way as without the practice of slavery, we would not have the blues as we know it; in the same way as without the theft of the piano from Sutter, we would not have the Ghosts of the Yellow Dog. Those ghosts are indeed the avatars of the ancestors upon whom Berniece calls. It takes these ancestors, their avatars, her brother, and her faith to free the piano from Sutter's possession. Such is the powerful legacy of white supremacy that all the community of natural and supernatural forces can do—at best!—is stave Sutter off, not defeat him.

This full community, in other words, operates in the way the blues does. As Ma Rainey explained, "The blues help you get up in the morning. You get up and know you ain't alone. There's something else in the world. Something's been added by that song. This be an empty world without the blues" (*Ma Rainey*, 83).

In this context, Wining Boy serves as a blues shaman. As the stage directions that introduce him note: "He is a man who looking back over his life continues to live it with an odd mixture of zest and sorrow" (*Piano*, 28). This mixture of zest and sorrow, characteristic of the blues, resonates with his description of his now-deceased wife, Cleotha, which echoes Ma Rainey's language:

> Many a night I sat up and looked over my life. Said, well, I had Cleotha. When it didn't look like there was nothing else for me, I said, thank God, at least I had that. If ever I go anywhere in this life, I done known a good woman. And that used to hold me till the next morning. (*Piano*, 32)

Wining Boy's shamanistic role is also suggested by the fact that he explicitly links his identity as gambler to that of priest when he says, regarding Avery, "You got the preacher on the one hand the gambler on the other. Sometimes there ain't too much difference between them" (*Piano*, 30). Wining Boy has also been inspired by the Ghosts of the Yellow Dog:

> I said everything can't go wrong all the time . . . let me go down there and call on the Ghosts of the Yellow Dog, see if they can help me. I went down there and right there where them two railroads cross each other . . . I stood right there on that spot and called out their names. They talk back to you, too. (*Piano*, 34–35)

This meeting at the crossroads, of course, emulates (or in the timeline of the play, anticipates) Delta blues pioneer Robert Johnson's legendary meeting with the Devil, wherein he exchanges his soul for the mastery of the blues.[12] In this way, Winning Boy simultaneously locates himself in the blues and the occult traditions. We might, in fact, argue that this is exactly the enchanted place occupied by all of Wilson's shamans.

In addition, as I noted, Wining Boy's magic suit allowed Lymon to release Berniece from her spell. Just prior to the exorcism, moreover, Wining Boy crucially intervenes to disrupt the cycle of violence that has so scarred and burdened the family. When Boy Willie is trying to remove the piano from the house, Berniece threatens to shoot him with Crawley's gun. Each sibling seems so adamant that another death over the piano looks immanent. As Lymon says to Boy Willie, "The way I figure it . . . I might be wrong . . . but I figure she gonna shoot you first" (*Piano*, 99). At that moment, a very drunk Wining Boy enters the house and insists on playing the piano while singing a song he wrote for Cleotha, making it impossible for Berniece to shoot or for Boy Willie to move the piano. Then, Wining Boy throws his drunken body on the piano and says repeatedly that "he ain't taking the piano" (*Piano*, 102) and "He got to take me with it!" (*Piano*, 102).

Wining Boy's song to Cleotha averts the violence that has haunted the family and the piano, and it helps us see how Cleotha, whom Wining Boy regarded as the spirit of the blues, is less a ghost than an angel and muse. With a name that seems to combine the Muses of History, Clio, and of Comedy, Thalia, she serves as a guardian angel who evokes the site where, for Wilson, history and comedy intersect as the blues. This is why Wilson, as he has pointed out, configures the historical moment for his plays not by reading history books but by playing the blues records of the period. And this is why Wining Boy's and Cleotha's transformative qualities are signaled by Wining Boy's describing Cleotha simultaneously as object of a blues lyric, as muse, and as guardian angel:

> Much as I loved Cleotha, I loved to ramble. . . . We got married and we used to fight about it all the time. Then one day she asked me to leave. Told me she loved me before I left. Told me, Wining Boy, you got a home long as I got mine. And I believe in my heart that she always kept me safe. (*Piano*, 31–32)

If Wining Boy is the play's embodiment of the blues, Cleotha is its guiding spirit, the spirit of the blues that brings Wining Boy to Berniece at the exact moment when she must be released from the piano's spell in order to save the piano and to save her family, whose history and blood it bears.

Each character's reasons for valuing the piano help make it clear that value is not essential but contested and therefore is a function of continuous struggle. This theme informs all of Wilson's work. As we have seen with regard to *Jitney*, and will continue to see as we delineate the tenets of Wilson's world, when one can fix nothing with the law, one is subject to the law of negotiation, to rules established through informal contract, on the street. What is valorized at the end of *The Piano Lesson*, therefore, is neither Berniece's nor Boy Willie's standards for value but rather that, when one can fix nothing with the law, one must struggle relentlessly for the right to ascribe value rather than be the subject of valuation. That fight, moreover, requires a coalition whose individuals have discrete goals and purposes.[13]

Whether, or on what terms, the exorcism succeeds, and in what way it eliminates confusion, may be open to debate, but what is clear is that it gives the piano an important new property as the instrument of (incomplete) exorcism, aptly complementing its role as the center of the play's myriad blues confusions, which follow from the way that confusion over the properties of humanity has been historically instrumentalized.

The lesson of *The Piano Lesson*, therefore, is not to attempt to eliminate the confusion of the blues—that is, all the historical, economic, and racial confusions that the blues embody—but to play them continuously. Neither Boy Willie nor Berniece defeats Sutter's ghost; they merely render him temporarily powerless. To do so requires the cooperative strength not just of Berniece and Boy Willie but also of their ancestors. The battle with Sutter's ghost, therefore, "transforms the conflict that threatened fratricide and the destruction of the kinship group into the conflict against a mutual enemy that only the combined action of the kinship group can resist."[14] Their struggle, moreover, must be relentless. Because they cannot fix anything with the law, the minute they relent, they will lose control of their property and of their human properties.

CHAPTER 7
URBAN RENEWAL BY ANY MEANS NECESSARY: *TWO TRAINS RUNNING*

Production history

Under the direction of Lloyd Richards, *Two Trains Running* opened at the Yale Repertory, starring Lawrence Fishburne as Sterling, Samuel E. Wright as Holloway, and Al White as Memphis, with Samuel L. Jackson as Wolf and Ella Joyce as Risa. The same production had its Broadway premiere at the Walter Kerr Theatre on April 13, 1992, with several changes in the cast: Anthony Chisolm replaced Jackson, Roscoe Lee Brown replaced Wright, and Cynthia Martells replaced Joyce. It ran for 160 performances.

Arrangement

A fitting arrangement for a blues score intended to reflect the tone of 1969, *Two Trains* has a surfeit of *warriors*. In addition to those seen on stage—Memphis, Sterling, Hambone, and Holloway—the background is saturated with warfare, as personified by Malcolm X and Martin Luther King, whose enmity toward one another (for the bulk of Malcolm's life) was matched by their shared antagonism toward white supremacy, an antagonism that resonated in the world of *Two Trains* in the form of rallies, protest, assassinations, police brutality, and urban riots. Even in their disagreements, however, Memphis, Sterling, Hambone, and Holloway find common chords and shared thematic strains. A discordant, potentially violent, harmony emerges from the sundry other elements Wilson attaches to their warrior themes: Memphis is very much the *pragmatist-entrepreneur*, Sterling the *hustler* with hints of the *man-not-right-in-the-head*, Holloway the *historian* with links to the *shaman*, and Hambone the *man-not-right-in-the-head*, with traces of a (destroyed) *earnest young man*. Resembling Coltrane's late work in *A Love Supreme* and thereafter, the conflicting warrior strains build to a volatility consonant with the incendiary historical moment. Even the *accommodator*, Risa, is scored with a warrior level of passive aggressiveness. The other *accommodator*, Wolf, is also a *hustler*, and the other *entrepreneur*, West, as a funeral home-owner, is in the enterprise of death. The shaman, Aunt Ester, plays from offstage, while Risa sings her sullen blues throughout.

Two trains of religious thought

Like *The Piano Lesson*, *Two Trains Running*, the play Wilson wrote immediately after it, is engaged in exploring and possibly reconciling conflicts between the spiritual beliefs that inform the African American community. This is one indication of how Wilson does not view history as teleological or orchestrated by driving themes or metanarratives. While the persistence of historical practices—what Elam calls the past as present— saturate all the aspects of African American life portrayed in his plays, those practices exist for Wilson in the specific permutation of the performative moment. Hence, in Wilson's world, African American religion, or any form of belief system, is not a body of doctrine or practice, but rather, the improvisational deployment of myriad cosmologies, consolidated in the moment of action.

In this regard, in *The Piano Lesson*, Wilson is accurately reflecting the debates over the nature of African American Christianity. While some scholars have argued that it is an adaptation of African traditions, practiced under the cover of worship permitted by the slaveholder, others have claimed that the numerous violent, eclectic disruptions of the slave trade effectively severed Africans from their traditions and forced them to construct a version of Christianity reflective of their current circumstances. While the African American church became a strong force in the Abolitionist Movement and, subsequently, in the civil rights movement, in the twentieth century other claims on African American faith emerged in relation to sub-Saharan African beliefs and rituals and, perhaps most significantly, in relation to the Muslim religion, the most prominent representation of which was the Nation of Islam, a black separatist group that rose to prominence in post– Second World War America under the leadership of Elijah Mohammed and his most distinguished disciple, Malcolm X. Thus, the civil rights movement, primarily southern, Christian-based, and integrationist, whose most prominent figure was MLK, vied for black followers with the separatist black Muslims.

As James Cone explains,

> Martin King's dream and Malcolm's nightmare were primarily defined by two distinct religious traditions in the African-American community. One was Christian, imported from Europe but redefined in the light of black people's struggle for dignity in American society. The other was Muslim, originally Asian and African but reshaped to express the hostility of American blacks to white oppressors.[1]

Malcolm's political and social views, therefore, his commitment to black separatism, and his criticisms of the civil rights movement were firmly based on his religious convictions, as much as was the activism of MLK. "Malcolm was a deeply religious person who identified his life's work as a mission from God, mediated through the Messenger. His highest aspiration was to be one of God's ministers" (Cone, 152). Cone explains:

> The reason that sympathetic interpreters often miss the central role of religion in Malcolm's thinking is that religion is commonly separated from struggles for justice. That is why Martin had such a difficult time getting the white church involved in the civil rights movement, and why liberation theologians in the Third World are so controversial today. Many people think religion has everything to do with an individual's personal relationship with God and nothing to do with society and one's fight for justice in it. When Malcolm X identified the fight for justice as *the central religious act*, his message was usually misunderstood. His friends often avoided the subject of religion and ignored the strict moral code he faithfully obeyed. Malcolm's enemies accused him of using religion as a façade for fomenting hate and violence. (Cone, 164)

Despite their both having deep religious convictions grounded in the Bible, these two leaders, for the bulk of their public careers, were in direct conflict over the goals and interests of African Americans, owing to their fundamental disagreement about the value of Christianity. "In Malcolm's view," Cone points out, "Christianity was proven both false and wicked by its age-old association with white people" (Cone, 166). Malcolm felt that "Christianity is the white man's religion. The Holy Bible in the white man's hands and in his interpretations of it have been the greatest single ideological weapon for enslaving millions of non-white human beings" (quoted in Cone,

166). Only in the last year of Malcolm's life, after he had traveled to Africa and broken with the Nation of Islam, did he find some common ground with and degree of respect for MLK, who, at around the same time, was starting to acknowledge the broader social and economic implications of his agenda, implications that intersected most extensively—although never completely—with Malcolm's in the last year of MLK's life.

By 1969, the year in which *Two Trains Running* is set, the ideals of both men were impacting African American communities, especially in northern urban areas, where two decades of inner-city decay (correlated with the commensurate flourishing of white middle-class suburbia) and a half-decade of urban riots had created much turmoil for black Americans about the possibilities for and nature of change. The assassination of MLK, in 1968, brought a dramatic end to the era of nonviolent protest, the tenets of which had been in decline since 1963. At the same time, the efficacy of black separatism remained dubious for the majority of African Americans: if it appeared that Malcolm more accurately diagnosed the problematic racial dynamics of the nation, many deemed him less astute regarding successful pragmatic solutions. To the extent that his motto, "by any means necessary," could be associated with the looting and rioting that was destroying many inner-city communities, the slogan struck many as less productive than self-destructive.

Needless to say, many black Americans, especially in the 1960s, did not find themselves identifying with either Malcolm or MLK, some because they were drawn in a more militant direction by the Black Power Movement, and some because they placed their faith in more traditional, conservative religious leaders. Others looked to nontraditional spiritual leaders, and some just prayed that their number would come in.

Two Trains Running takes place in the epicenter of such a divided community, the Hill section of Pittsburgh, where urban renewal programs were boarding up buildings, one by one, and condemning long-standing establishments.[2] If *The Piano Lesson* is haunted by the ghosts of "slavery time," Memphis's restaurant, where the play is set, is located in a Pittsburgh ghost town, a glut of buildings vacated in the name of "eminent domain." Memphis, one of the last holdouts on his block, is engaged in a legal battle over the amount the city owes him for the deed to his restaurant. The first offer, which he is appealing in court, was $15,000; he wants $25,000 (in 2018 the equivalent of approximately $185,000). With the neighborhood's deterioration, business has shriveled, and the restaurant's entire staff is reduced to Memphis and the sullen (or perhaps passive aggressive) waitress,

Risa, who is also the cook. The regulars in the restaurant include Wolf, a numbers runner who uses the restaurant as one of his bases of business; Holloway, a retired house painter; West, the affluent owner of the funeral parlor across the street; and Hambone, who "is in his late forties. He is self-contained and in a world of his own. His mental condition has deteriorated to such a point that he can only say two phrases, and he repeats them idiotically over and over."[3] The cause of Hambone's mental deterioration is an agreement he made to paint the fence surrounding Lutz's Meat Market, across the street from the restaurant. "Lutz told him," Memphis explains to Sterling, "if he painted the fence he'd give him a chicken. Told him if he did a good job he'd give him a ham. He think he did a good job and Lutz didn't" (*Two Trains*, 23). In consequence, Hambone has spent every morning for nearly a decade confronting Lutz when Lutz opens the market, to demand his ham. Hambone even waits in front of the store on Sunday, in case Lutz shows up. Over this period, however, Hambone's fixation has resulted in his being able to say only "I want my ham" and "He gonna give me my ham."

Time, death, faith, and (urban) renewal

The play is framed by the death of the Prophet Samuel, a charismatic religious leader renowned for the wealth he had accumulated, who is lying in state at West's funeral parlor. So vast and loyal is his following that, before West stopped them, people had started charging mourners a dollar each to view the Prophet Samuel's corpse. Prior to the beginning of the play's action, Memphis's wife of twenty-two years has left him. "She up at her sister's house," Memphis tells Wolf. "She been up there two months since she left" (*Two Trains*, 4). Although her reasons for leaving remain a mystery to Memphis, his description of her departure provides some clues:

> I ain't asked her nothing but to get up and make me some bread. And she got up and walked out the door. I know she don't expect me to make it myself. I went down there and saw her. Asked her what the matter was. She told me she was tired. Now how you gonna get more tired than I am? (*Two Trains*, 5)

The arrival at the restaurant of Sterling, a thirty-year-old man who has just been released from prison, initiates the play's action, such as it is, in that Sterling is the only agent of change we see on stage. He aggressively courts

Risa, irritates Memphis, and annoys Holloway; he buys a gun from Wolf, and attempts to help Hambone. Little else by way of plot occurs, although in the end Sterling's number does come in and he does win Risa's affection. During the span of the play's action, however, several events occur offstage: Memphis gets $35,000 from the city, the Prophet Samuel is buried, and Hambone dies in his bed. Sterling confronts the mobsters who halved the payout for his winning number, and both Memphis and Sterling visit Aunt Ester, a shamanistic figure alleged to be 322 years old (although when Sterling asks her directly, she says 349).

Larger offstage events also infuse the world surrounding the restaurant. A rally commemorating Malcolm X's birthday takes place, at which the police take photographs of the protesters. A drugstore burns down; the arson is blamed by some on Black Power activists but presumed by many others to have been committed by the owner to collect the insurance. Regardless of motive, the incident raises the possibility of Memphis's restaurant also being burned. "There is violence in the air, it seems," Stephen Bottoms accurately points out, "simply as a result of the helplessness felt by the local residents."[4]

Structurally, therefore, *Two Trains Running* does not depend on actions, revelations, and reversals in the Aristotelean sense of those terms. "Audiences who expect the wealth of stories that are told in Memphis's café to wind up as parts of a neatly arranged plot soon discover that this is not to be."[5] Rather, it is an extended contemplation on faith and death in a precarious time. In other words, the deaths of the Christian Prophet Samuel and the Black Muslim minister, Malcolm X, form the backdrop for the play. These deaths suggest alternative ways that the precarious Hill community, or more generally African Americans, can invest faith or construct hopes.

To these unseen spiritual leaders, the play adds Aunt Ester, who will become a major figure in the Wilson cycle. Drawing directly on African faith—based on her age, she was either born in Africa or among the first slaves born in America—Aunt Ester represents black powers that are neither Christian nor Muslim. This implicit suggestion of African influence on black Christianity—also important in *The Piano Lesson*—is underscored by the fact that the Prophet Samuel had launched his career by visiting Aunt Ester. At first, Bottoms notes, Aunt Ester sounds like another Prophet Samuel, but "she differs significantly from Samuel in that her ministry centres not on the acquisition of money, but on its unimportance" (Bottoms, 153). "By significantly shaping African American cultural identity," Shannon points out, she makes sense out of the absurdity of the situations of the people in the black community, "and shows them how to realize their own agency."[6]

Like *Ma Rainey*, this play is all about time. Fifteen years after *Brown v. Board of Ed.*, fourteen years after the Montgomery bus boycott, six years after the 1963 March on Washington, five years after the assassination of Malcolm, and one year after the assassination of MLK, black America was running out of patience, and the nation was running out of time. *Brown II*, dealing with implementation of *Brown v. Board of Ed.*, ordered states to implement desegregation with "deliberate speed," a phrase steeped in oxymoronic temporality. At the same time, both Malcolm and MLK pointed out that the speed of change was being played in the tempo of delay. As MLK said in his 1963 "Letter from a Birmingham Jail," addressed to eight white "liberal" clergymen who requested that he moderate his tactics, "I guess it is easy for those who have never felt the stinging darts of segregation to wait" (154). MLK follows with a list of eleven detailed vignettes of injustice, each starting with the temporal marker "when" (e.g., "when you have seen hate-filled policemen curse, kick, brutalize and even kill your black brothers and sisters with impunity" [155]). This paragraph of the letter concludes:

> There comes a time when the cup of endurance runs over, and men are no longer willing to be plunged into the abyss of injustice where they experience the bleakness of corroding despair. I hope, sirs, you can understand our legitimate and unavoidable impatience. (157)

Malcolm found this mode of appeal unacceptable. He thought, Cone explains, that

> King was guilty of using the moral standards of criminals—that is, whites—to evaluate the behavior of their victims. Why should the victims of crime, Malcolm would ask him, try to make themselves worthy of the respect of criminals? (Cone, 72)

So, it is about time that white America recognized its responsibilities to black Americans, or it is about time that black Americans stopped asking America and started taking. It is the time for action or for taking the right actions in time, because in 1969 black urban communities seemed to be running out of time, as did, possibly, the entire powder keg of America. Specifically, just as Memphis's wife ran out of patience serving Memphis, he is running out of time to sell his restaurant. Soon the city may condemn the property and pay what it wishes; in addition, because it is mid-May (a rally in the play celebrating Malcolm X's May 19 birthday), the community is braced for the possibility of the kind of riots that plagued many American cities throughout the second half of the 1960s. That celebration, as Shannon explains, is not a "pro-Malcolm demonstration but [an] exposé of what has come of his legacy."[7]

The two preceding summers had been particularly brutal. In a few weeks in July 1967, large-scale riots in Newark, New Jersey, lasted six days and resulted in more than 700 injuries and over twenty deaths. A week later, the National Guard and the federal troops, assisted by tanks, engaged in firefights in the streets of Detroit. Over 1,000 people were injured or killed, and over 2,000 stores were looted or burned. This escalating state-supported violence gave increasing cogency to Malcolm's call for black people to arm themselves. And MLK's assassination in April 1968 ignited numerous riots, most notably those in Chicago, Washington, and Baltimore.[8]

Given, furthermore, that the restaurant is not insured, it seems urgent that Memphis settle with the city, lest his worth go up in flames. West, who is trying to buy the property from Memphis before the city does, also feels the urgency to press for a deal. Sterling is looking for a job, but not necessarily at the frenetic pace with which he pursues Risa. And Memphis is also running out of patience with Sterling (which he indicates in terms of how much time he thinks Sterling has left before he returns to jail):

I give that boy three weeks. . . . And he gonna be laying over there across the street or back down there in the penitentiary. You watch. Three weeks. (*Two Trains*, 68)

I changed that, Holloway. I give him two weeks. (*Two Trains*, 79)

In contradistinction to these rapid tempos, a number of the characters march to a slow, steady beat. Just as she passively shuns Sterling's upbeat courtship, Risa moves with a purposeful slowness that actively defies Memphis's barrage of rapid orders. Similarly, Wolf continues his steady practice of using Memphis's phone to take numbers, despite Memphis's demands that he desist, demands slightly less constant but also more emphatic than those Memphis snaps at Risa. The slowest but also the steadiest tempo comes from Hambone, who, for nine years, has been demanding his ham from Lutz.

In this regard, Hambone resembles MLK, a point elaborated by Bottoms:

Set in the context of the 1960s, his simply *asking* for justice, instead of demanding or even taking what he believes is his, reads in part as an assimilationist acceptance of white authority—an authority which is never going to grant him his due. . . . Wilson is perhaps implying a link to the civil rights movement's insistence on nonviolent protest, which indeed many blacks were "tired of hearing" by the later 1960s. (Bottoms, 150)

Hambone's big mistake, as Memphis explains, was letting someone else decide what his labor was worth. Hambone, in other words, had placed himself in the same position as did Boy Willie and Lymon when they were hauling lumber. The difference between what their labor was worth and what they were getting paid for it could only be made up by practices that the law would call theft. Thus, it was left to others to decide whether they could obtain full value for their work, just as it was left to Lutz to determine whether Hambone deserved a ham or a chicken for his work. Because Lutz's persistent denial of Hambone's decade-long demand for fairness has, from its inception, taken the form of offering Hambone a chicken, the impending urban unrest that makes Lutz's butcher shop vulnerable to looting and immolation threatens, at any moment, to become an example of Malcolm's chickens coming home to roost.

Logics

The tension of this blues rendition comes from the same source as the tensions—focused by MLK and Malcolm—in the world outside Memphis's restaurant: the competing ontologies of two warriors with radically different visions of black rights, lodged in different systems of logic. When Memphis first enters, the stage directions tell us that his greatest asset is "his impeccable logic" (*Two Trains*, 1). Punctuating the logic of eminent domain, for example, Memphis emphatically asserts: "These white folks crazy. Tell me they can give me anything they want for my building. Say it got a clause. I told them I don't care nothing about no clause. What kind of sense that make if they can give me what they want?" (*Two Trains*, 57). Although Memphis, like Boy Willie or Hambone, lacks the ability to fix things with the law, he refuses to acknowledge the legality of the law. Like Boy Willie, he asserts what is "right" over what is "legal."

Sterling, on the other hand, is characterized by "the combination of his unorthodox logic and straightforward manner" (*Two Trains*, 16). It is no surprise, therefore, that Memphis is annoyed by Sterling. After their first encounter, Memphis says, "The boy ain't got good sense" (*Two Trains*, 27), a point he reiterates late in the play, "Something's wrong with that boy. That boy ain't right," when he warns Risa to "stay away from him. He ain't gonna do nothing but end up right back down there in the penitentiary" (*Two Trains*, 85). And yet Sterling's critiques of injustice share with Memphis an inherent critique of the concept of "justice." As Memphis argues at one point: "Ain't no justice. That's why they got the statue of her and got her blindfolded. Common sense would tell you if anybody need to see she do" (*Two Trains*, 42). This is the same criticism Sterling has of the rigged economy when he explains why he robbed a bank:

> I figured a man supposed to have money sometime. Everybody else seem like they got it. Seemed like I'm the only one ain't got no money. I figured I'd get my money where Mellon got his from. (*Two Trains*, 45–46)

As Bertolt Brecht said, "What is the robbing of a bank compared to the founding of a bank?" In the same spirit, Sterling made a gift to Risa of flowers taken from the accumulation in front of West's funeral parlor, placed there by the numerous followers of the Prophet Samuel. When she says that she doesn't want flowers "you stole from a dead man" (*Two Trains*, 62), Sterling says, "He don't mind. The man got so many flowers West don't know where to put them." In both cases, Sterling is pointing not to uneven social distribution, but to the logical inequities upon which it is based. Or, to put it another way, he is questioning the ways in which posthumous ownership functions as a cornerstone of injustice. Despite the differences in their approaches and sensibilities, Memphis shares Sterling's distrust of the posthumous ownership when he refuses to celebrate Malcolm's birthday on the grounds that "Dead men don't have birthdays" (*Two Trains*, 40).

What I want to call a "confluence of disagreement" between Sterling and Memphis is perhaps most sharply focused by the play's crucial debate about life and death, which examines the complex relationship between the life of bodies and the life of ideas, concepts, agendas. Hence, Sterling and Memphis, most explicitly, but also Holloway and Hambone, in fact arrive via different logical paths at similar conclusions, attesting to the vitality of concepts that transcend the lives of their strongest proponents. This is particularly apparent in the discussion that Memphis and Sterling have about Malcolm, in which Holloway is a significant participant. Holloway is a man who, after years of frustration, has decided to exempt himself from the fray of the natural world. As the stage directions explain, he is

> *a man who all his life has voiced his outrage at injustice with little effect. His belief in the supernatural has enabled him to accept his inability to effect change and continue to pursue life with vigor.* (*Two Trains*, 5)

When Sterling says to Memphis that he would have followed Malcolm because he was "the only one who told the truth. That's why they killed him" (*Two Trains*, 41), Memphis replies: "Niggers killed Malcolm. When you want to talk about Malcolm, remember that first" (*Two Trains*, 41). At this point, Holloway, instead of addressing the racial politics of Malcolm's death, underscores its inevitability: "They killed all the saints. Saint Peter. Saint Paul. They killed them all. When you get to be a saint, there ain't nothing else you can do but die. The people wouldn't have it any other way" (*Two Trains*, 41). From Holloway's perspective, martyrdom is a social phenomenon rather than a religious one. Hence, Holloway can group Malcolm with white Christian saints despite Malcolm's abhorrence of Christianity and of whites, a grouping whose oddity is underscored when Holloway ironically compares Malcolm to Jesus: "I remember when Malcolm didn't have but twelve followers" (*Two Trains*, 40).

For Holloway, martyrdom is about the conditions of possibility under capitalism. Implicitly foregrounding the historical relationship between the rise of capitalism and the institution of slavery, Holloway had explained:

> If you ain't got nothing . . . you can go out here and get you a nigger. Then you got something, see. You got one nigger. If that one nigger go out there and plant something . . . get something out of the ground . . . even if it ain't nothing but a bushel of potatoes . . . then you take that bushel of potatoes and go get you another nigger. Then you got two niggers. Put them to work and you got two niggers and two bushels of potatoes. See, now you can go buy two more niggers. That's how you stack a nigger on top of a nigger. White folks got stacking . . . and I'm talking about they stacked up some niggers! Stacked close to fifty million niggers. . . . They couldn't find you enough work back then. Now that they got to pay you they can't find you none. If this was a different time, wouldn't be nobody out there on the street. They'd all be in the cotton fields. (*Two Trains*, 35)

Holloway's allusion to cotton fields anticipates extensive twenty-first-century historical scholarship that shows how profoundly the rise and success of capitalism depended on the Industrial Revolution, fueled by a textile industry that could only flourish if the cost of cotton was kept artificially low by slave labor. Because both the Industrial Revolution and the slave trade proliferated ancillary commerce, especially in the shipping trades and the sundry commercial enterprises to which shipping was foundational, slavery enabled the amassing of capital that turned banking and investment into the huge and hugely profitable pillar of capitalism.[9] Holloway is also anticipating the common ground that Malcolm and MLK would find, late in both of their lives, wherein each would recognize that the enemy wasn't so much whiteness or segregation as the economic system that made racial antipathy advantageous.

In this context, Memphis's adding MLK to Holloway's list of saints seems particularly apt: "You right about that. They killed MLK. If they did that to him, you can imagine what they do to me or you. If they kill the sheep, you know what they do to the wolf" (*Two Trains*, 41). When Sterling argues that they are having the rally "for black power. Stop them from killing the sheep" (*Two Trains*, 41), Memphis attacks "these black power niggers" (*Two Trains*, 41): "These niggers talking about freedom, justice, and equality and don't know what it mean [. . .] There ain't no justice. Jesus Christ didn't get justice. What makes you think you gonna get it?" (*Two Trains*, 42). At the same time, however, as Memphis seems to be dismissing Malcolm's ideas and the Black Power Movement that took inspiration from them, Memphis also reflects directly one of Malcolm's core beliefs: "You can't do nothing without a gun. Not in this day and time. That's the only kind of power the white man understand" (*Two Trains*, 42).

At a later point in the play, Holloway would explain the way in which the white man understands a black man with a gun:

A nigger with a gun is bad news. You can't even use the word "nigger" and "gun" in the same sentence. You say the word "gun" in the same sentence as the word "nigger" and you in trouble. The white man panic. Unless you say, "The policeman shot the nigger with his gun" . . . then that be alright. Other than that he panic. He ain't had nothing but guns for the last five hundred years . . . got the atomic bomb and everything. But you say the word "nigger" and "gun" in the same sentence and they'll try and arrest you. Accuse you of sabotage, disturbing the peace, inciting a riot, plotting to overthrow the government and anything else they can think of. You think I'm lying? You go down there and stand in front of the number two police station and say, "The niggers is tired of this mistreatment—they gonna get some guns," and see if they don't arrest you. (*Two Trains*, 86)

This speech, particularly specific to 1969, indicates a more precarious aspect of the world surrounding Memphis's restaurant. Specifically, it marks exactly the moment when Holloway's supposition was being tested. As the Black Panther Party for Self-Defense was promoting the arming of African Americans as a response to police violence, violent police actions were mounted against militant blacks. One of the most notable was the police-orchestrated assassination of Chicago Panther leader Fred Hampton, just seven months after the time when *Two Trains* takes place. Hampton, who was drugged by an undercover agent who also supplied police with the layout of Hampton's apartment, was the victim of a 4:00 a.m. police attack, in which he was first wounded, then dragged from his bed, semiconscious, and shot in the head.

Thus, Memphis, like Malcolm, seems to be defying an (unwritten) law of law enforcement.

Immediately after Memphis's diatribe against black power, Hambone enters, declaring, "He gonna give me my ham. He gonna give me my ham" (*Two Trains*, 43), which causes Memphis's ire to peak. First he orders Risa not to serve Hambone, and when she does anyway, he throws out Hambone's cup of coffee, and then throws Hambone out of the restaurant.

Memphis   Come in here running off at the mouth. I'm tired of hearing that.
Risa   He don't bother nobody.
Memphis   He bother me. Let him go on over there and get his ham. It ain't like Lutz hiding from him. That man crazy. He let Lutz drive him crazy. Well, go on over there with Lutz and tell *him*. Don't tell me. Man been around here ten years talking the same thing. I'm tired of hearing it.
(*Memphis slams the restaurant door closed.*) (*Two Trains*, 42)

If we recognize that Hambone's tactics evoke those of MLK, Memphis's antipathy at this juncture becomes one more way in which he is tacitly endorsing Malcolm's philosophy, despite his rejection of the man. Like

Malcolm, he rejects asking the white man for anything and he has no time for nonviolent protest, seeing, as Malcolm did, that it had never produced adequate results: "The white man is our first and main enemy. Our second enemy are the Uncle Toms, such as Martin Luther King and his turn the other cheek method" (quoted in Cone, 99).

If Hambone's monomaniacal logic is inimical to Memphis, it is frustrating to Sterling, who at one point attempts to reeducate Hambone by getting him to say "united we stand" and "divided we fall," but Hambone immediately reverts to "I want my ham!" and instead of correcting him, Sterling at first joins in, also shouting "I want my ham!" And then each time Hambone shouts "I want my ham!" Sterling shouts "Malcolm lives!" until Memphis enters and stops them. Hambone thus ends up educating Sterling, or at least converting Sterling to his cause, a conversion that allows Sterling to connect the tactics of MLK with the goals of Malcolm. This connection can also be found in Holloway's analysis of Hambone's behavior:

> He might be more in his right mind than you are. He might have more sense than any of us. . . . He trying to shame Lutz into giving him his ham. And if Lutz ever break down and give it to him . . . he gonna have a big thing. . . . That's why I say he might have more sense than me or you. Cause he ain't willing to accept whatever the white man throw at him. It be easier. But he say he don't mind getting out of bed in the morning to go at what's right. I don't believe you and me got that much sense. (*Two Trains*, 29–30)

Although he uses tactics of asking for that which he should take, Hambone also refuses to take "whatever the white man throw at him." This too is Memphis's philosophy, rejecting what Memphis calls "'old backward southern mentality': When I come up here they had to teach these niggers they didn't have to tip their hat to the white man" (*Two Trains*, 30). Memphis refuses to let the city determine what his property is worth, as governed by their assessors. As he points out, "They forcing me to move out . . . close up my business . . . well, I figure they ought to pay me something for that. I don't care what the building is worth or how much I bought it for" (*Two Trains*, 38). Echoing exactly Hambone's position, Memphis asserts his right to determine the worth of his property. "They ain't the only one that got a clause. My clause say they got to pay me what I want for it" (*Two Trains*, 58).

The warrior faith

However nuanced the discussion of tactics, values, and world views in the debates over Malcolm and over Hambone, to the extent that Hambone evokes MLK, we need to remember that these perspectives are grounded in faith. Because, as Cone puts it,

> As different as Martin's and Malcolm's religious communities were, Martin's faith, nonetheless, was much closer to Malcolm's than it was to that of white Christians, and Malcolm's faith was much closer to Martin's than it was to that of Muslims in the Middle East, Africa, or Asia; this was true because both of their faith commitments were derived from the *same* black experience of suffering and struggle in the United States. Their theologies, therefore, should be interpreted as different religious and intellectual responses of African-Americans to their environment as they searched for meaning in a nation that they did not make. (Cone, 122)

In *Two Trains Running*, this confluence of attitudes toward work, race, and rights circumscribes a place of faith, lodged neither in dogma nor in charisma, but in the kind of truth created by a community and made apparent indirectly. It is in this context, I think, that we should understand the apparent immortality of Aunt Ester, as it stands in stark contrast to all the play's dead religious leaders—Malcolm X, the Prophet Samuel, and by surrogacy through Hambone, Martin Luther King. Aunt Ester thus represents the unseen living power of Africa as a function of African American faith, a faith that, through her, empowers both Memphis and Sterling. Her telling each of them to put twenty dollars on a rock and cast it into the river is one of many ways that, as Barbara Lewis points out, she bears "kinship to the female water divinities of Africa" (149). But, if we consider that "bread" is also slang for money, it is also Aunt Ester's version of casting one's bread upon the water, as advised in Ecclesiastes 11:1.[10] Both Memphis and Sterling do so and reap returns, which in turn allows Memphis to return to Mississippi in order to pick up the ball, as Aunt Ester put it, and reclaim his land by whatever means necessary, as Malcolm put it, which is also how Sterling claims Hambone's ham.

The connection of Hambone's death with MLK grows even stronger if we take into consideration that some of the events in *Two Trains*, including the rally commemorating Malcolm's birthday, are drawn from experiences Wilson himself had in 1968, shortly after MLK's death.[11] Hambone's death, however, evokes MLK heroically as well as critically. Only after Hambone's death do we learn that "(WEST:) Man had so many scars on his body . . . I ain't never seen nothing like that. All on his back, his chest . . . his legs" (*Two Trains*, 91). These scars identify Hambone, despite his derided "passive resistance," as having been one of Wilson's privileged warriors, arguably, based on the number of scars, the most courageous and battle-worn of them all, such that Hambone may unify all the warriors, living and dead, who populate Memphis's restaurant and, by extension, black America in 1969. Hambone, Elam points out, "represents the corporate black body, the black nation as a whole, the surrogate for all those black souls who have passed on without receiving their just due" (*Two Trains*, 192–93). As "surrogate," Hambone represents the population metonymically; he is one of many, including Malcolm and MLK. But in his scarification, he also represents symbolically these leaders as well as the people who followed them. He stands for them, as a symbol of their pain and sacrifice. Finally, he represents them in that he speaks on their behalf, the way that a spokesperson represents other figures and transmits their ideas. "Hambone's absent dead body speaks," Elam emphatically tells us. "Rather than an embodied presence on display, his spirit is present and the power of the spirit conveyed in the absence of the material body" (*Two Trains*, 193).

Because of the triply powerful representative status Hambone achieves at the end of the play, his core assertions deserve closer attention. "I want my ham" expresses a very specific desire, not for what Hambone should be given but for what is already his: he does not want *the* ham, but *his* ham. Thus, the ham is not something that he wants Lutz to give him, but something he wants Lutz to return. When Hambone did a good job of painting the fence, the ham became his, in the same way that the rights to full citizenship became the property of African Americans the minute their labor, as well as their freedom, was taken from them. In this way, Hambone is summarizing the point of Holloway's discourse on "stacking niggers." He is also articulating the position Memphis has come to, regarding the deed to his land in Mississippi. Because he will demand what is already his, he is going to tell Stovall, "I want my land."

Similarly, Memphis has finally accepted Hambone's second assertion, in effect proclaiming, "he gonna give me my land." But Memphis is *not* addressing Stovall any more than Hambone's second assertion addresses Lutz. As an act of faith, it is directed at Hambone himself—a reminder and encouragement to keep going—and, as a way of keeping his eyes on the prize, it is an expression of assurance to everyone willing to join the cause.

Consider how, as such, "he gonna give me my ham" echoes the great civil rights lyrics: "we shall overcome"; "like a tree that stands by the water, we shall not be moved"; "before I'll be a slave, I'll be buried in my grave, and go home to my Lord and be free."

The scars on Hambone's legs—set off in the script from the mention of the other scars—indicate, moreover, a special bond between Hambone and Risa that extends beyond the singular compassion that she shows for him throughout the play. It indicates their common cause, their shared dedication to the cause of human rights, extended by Risa to the area of women's rights. At exactly the moment when the most militant factions of the Black Power Movement were manifesting profound sexism, Risa joins Hambone's form of silent warfare.[12] The spirit of Hambone's silent warfare, moreover, as Shannon points out, "turns the floundering Sterling into a man of action."[13] Wilson, Elam explains,

> suffuses the mourning for the death of Hambone at the end of [the play] with a call to action and a cacophony of sound. As the other characters listen to Memphis plan for his future, the crash of breaking glass and a whirl of a burglar alarm are heard. Then the young rebel Sterling enters bleeding but carrying a ham stolen from Lutz's window, a blood sacrifice for Hambone's casket. Rather than asking Lutz for reparation, Sterling claims for Hambone that which was long due. His act and Hambone's death unite the community in celebratory revolution. (*Past*, 72)

The play ends with Sterling, a bit bloodied, carrying a large ham: "Say, Mr. West . . . that's for Hambone's casket" (*Two Trains*, 110).

CHAPTER 8
"SAD STORIES OF THE DEATH OF KINGS": *SEVEN GUITARS* AND *KING HEDLEY II*[1]

Seven Guitars

Production history

Seven Guitars opened in Chicago at the Goodman Theatre in January 1995 under the direction of Walter Dallas, and then was performed in Boston in September 1995 under the direction of Lloyd Richards. That production opened on Broadway at the Walter Kerr Theatre on March 28, 1996. With the exception of the role of Hedley—first played by Albert Hall, then by Zakes Mokae, and finally by Roger Robinson—the cast remained intact: Michelle Shay as Louise, Ruben Santiago-Hudson as Canewell, Tommy Hollis as Red Carter, Viola Davis as Vera, Keith David as Floyd, and Roslyn Coleman as Ruby. It ran for 188 performances.

Arrangement

The complexity of the arrangement in *Seven Guitars* comes from the confrontation of two doomed *warriors*, Floyd (who still shows traces of having been an *earnest young man* and strong desires to be an *entrepreneur*) and Hedley (who still shows traces of having been an *entrepreneur* but has become very clearly the *man-not-right-in-the-head*). Canewell, the *accommodator*, and Red Carter, *the hustler*, play backup to this titanic confrontation between men denied their destiny. This quartet has a lead singer, Vera, and two talented backups, each singing a different version of the blues.

King Hedley II

Production history

Under the direction of Marion McClinton, *King Hedley II* was first performed at the Pittsburgh Public Theater in December 1999. It was then performed in Seattle, Chicago, and Washington, before its Broadway premiere at the Virginia Theatre on May 1, 2001. Over the year-and-a-half of regional previews, the cast underwent numerous changes. The Broadway production featured Brian Stokes Mitchell as King, Viola Davis as Tonya, Leslie Uggams as Ruby, Stephen McKinley Henderson as Stool Pigeon, Monte Russell as Mister, and Charles Brown as Elmore. It ran for seventy-two performances.

Arrangement

King Hedley II is very much a blues song about the death of kings. Ruby, now retired, the only one of the blues singers to survive from the trio in *Seven Guitars*, clings to an older version of the blues, popular in the 1940s, the 1950s, and even the 1960s, while, in counterpoint, Tonya's blues manifests the hard, rock-inflected blues of the 1980s. Canewell, having witnessed the violence that destroyed Floyd and subsequently many other black warriors, can no longer be the *accommodator*. (To the extent that the 1980s provide anything worth accommodating, Ruby must attempt to do so with her older version of the blues.) Canewell has abandoned the accommodator part to become Stool Pigeon, someone who must simultaneously play the parts of *historian*, *man-not-right-in-the-head*, and *shaman*. King and Elmore are both *warriors* and, like most pretenders to the throne, they are also both *hustlers*, as is Mister.

The legacy of a king

In many ways, *Seven Guitars*, set in the 1940s, picks up where *The Piano Lesson*, set in the 1930s, leaves off by consolidating the goals articulated in the plays of the two preceding decades—cutting a record in Chicago, as in *Ma Rainey*, and acquiring the land that rightfully belongs to the family, as in *The Piano Lesson*. In *Seven Guitars*, each goal is embodied by a principal warrior. Floyd Barton, newly out of the workhouse, has been gaining notoriety from a hit blues recording. His agent has arranged for another recording session in Chicago, which, Floyd believes, will launch a successful performing career. Floyd's primary goal, therefore, is to get his pawned guitar out of hock, but he also wants to convince his estranged girlfriend, Vera, to accompany him to Chicago. As he explains to her: "A man that believe in himself still need a woman that believe in him."[2] Vera, however, remains very reluctant, because Floyd had previously walked out on her for another woman, with whom he went to Chicago for his first recording session. King Hedley, the play's other warrior, believes he will receive a legacy from his deceased father for the purpose of buying a plantation and thereby becoming a "big man."

The play's action takes place in the backyard of the small house in the Hill section of Pittsburgh, on the first floor of which Vera lives.[3] The second floor is divided into two apartments. Louise, a woman twenty years older than the 27-year-old Vera, occupies one of those apartments. Hedley, who lives in the other apartment, is a man in his sixties who suffers both from mental and from physical problems. Although he has contracted tuberculosis, he refuses to go to a sanitarium because of his intense fear of being taken away by white government officials. This fear, which becomes increasingly—perhaps clinically—paranoid, derives from his earlier life in Haiti, where his father died from medical neglect. The burden that Hedley bears throughout his life is that his father died before he could forgive Hedley for asking his father why he was not like Toussaint L'Overture, in response to which his father kicked him in the face: " 'I forgive you that you kick me,' Hedley said to his father, 'and I hope as God is with us now but a short time more that you forgive me my tongue' " (*Seven Guitars*, 87). Unfortunately, as Hedley soon discovered, when he offered this apology, his father had already died. The forgiveness that Hedley sought, therefore, only came years later, when his father in a dream promised that he had given the legendary (alcoholic and mad) blues musician, Buddy Bolden, money that Bolden would bring Hedley to buy a plantation.

Both Floyd and Hedley, in other words, are seeking to claim a rightful estate linked implicitly to a royal lineage, made explicit by Hedley, who noted with pride that he killed a man because "He would not call me King. He laughed to think a black man could be King. I did not want to lose my name, so I told him to call me the name my father gave me, and he laugh. He would not call me King, and I beat him with a stick" (*Seven Guitars*, 67).

The common aspirations that bond Floyd and Hedley are underscored by their shared chant, in which Floyd encourages Hedley's claim to his inheritance:

Floyd (*begins to sing*) "I thought I heard Buddy Bolden say . . ."
Hedley What he say?
Floyd He said, "Wake up and give me the money."
Hedley Naw. Naw. He say "Come here. Here go the money."
Floyd Well . . . what he give you?
Hedley He give me ashes.
Floyd Tell him to give you the money. (*Seven Guitars*, 23–24)

Floyd repeats versions of this exchange with Hedley two more times in the play, in this way echoing Sterling and Hambone in *Two Trains*, the play Wilson wrote immediately before *Seven Guitars*. In the case of Sterling and Hambone, however, the bond is based, as I have noted, on the values shared by Martin Luther King and Malcolm X. By echoing in *Seven Guitars* the Hambone-Sterling relationship, Wilson further underscores the common ground shared by the two African American activists, because, in this case, Hedley, who resembles Hambone (the avatar of MLK), holds Malcolm's black nationalist position, explicitly inspired in *Seven Guitars* by Marcus Garvey and Garvey's belief in an Ethiopian dynasty. Hedley's discovery of Garvey had enabled him to forgive his father and reclaim the name "King." "Yes," Hedley says, "The Bible say Ethiopia shall rise up and be made a great kingdom. Marcus Garvey say the black man is a king" (*Seven Guitars*, 40).

In *Seven Guitars*, however, the common ground between Floyd and Hedley attaches to the men's expectations of restoration of their rightful place, based on lineage and nobility. Floyd talks constantly about the success he will have after he records his next record, and Hedley predicts continuously not only that he will get his father's money from Buddy Bolden but that he will be a big man, something he associates, following Garvey, with the triumph of the Abyssinian rule: "Ethiopia," he shouts, "shall stretch forth her wings and every abomination shall be brought low" (*Seven Guitars*, 19).

This notion of triumph, however, takes place in the face of the systemic obstruction of Floyd's and Hedley's rights and options, a problem that plagues Floyd's entire combo. Floyd had been given ninety days in the workhouse for vagrancy—or as Floyd calls it, "worthlessness"—and, previously, Canewell, had been arrested in Chicago when he played his harmonica on the street:

> I said "If I'm gonna stand here and play I might as well throw my hat down . . . somebody might put something in it." The police said I was disturbing the peace. Soliciting without a license. Loitering. Resisting arrest and disrespecting the law. They rolled all that together and charged me with laziness and give me thirty days. (*Seven Guitars*, 22)

Red Carter, Floyd's drummer, had been once arrested for having too much money. "I had more money than the law allowed. Must have . . . because the police arrested me, put me in jail. Told me that if I had that much money I must have stole it somewhere" (*Seven Guitars*, 42).

Like most of Wilson's characters, Floyd and his combo have been thwarted repeatedly by their inability to fix things with the law. As Floyd accurately summarizes his fix, "They got you coming and going. Put me in jail for not having enough money and put you in jail for having too much money" (*Seven Guitars*, 42). Floyd's fix, moreover, applies not only to criminal law but also to civil law. After he was released from the workhouse, he tried to collect the thirty cents per day to which he was entitled, but he was told he didn't have the proper paper. (Being illiterate, he had made no distinction between the letter certifying the state's debt to him and the envelope in which it came.) Next, he was unable to redeem his guitar from the pawn shop because the ticket had expired (while he had been incarcerated), so instead of paying back the ten-dollar loan, he would have to purchase the guitar from the pawnbroker for fifty dollars. At this point, he has his final exchange with Hedley about getting money from Buddy Bolden:

> **Hedley** (*singing*) "I thought I heard Buddy Bolden say, "Here go the money. King take it away."
> **Floyd** Broke as I am, I need to have Buddy Bolden bring me some money. I'd take it away. I'd tell him, "Wake up and give me the money."
> **Hedley** No. No. He say, "Come here, here go the money."
> **Floyd** That's what I'm talking about. I need to have somebody say that to me. Bad as I need some money, I wouldn't care who it was. Buddy Bolden or anybody else. High John the Conquerer. Yellow Jack. Brer Rabbit. Uncle Ben. It could be anybody.
> **Hedley** It's my father's money. (*Seven Guitars*, 70)

The Theatre of August Wilson

As in all of Wilson's work, the ground for black legacy in white America—the basis for the place Wilson claimed at the Boston bar—is the blues. King Hedley was named King by his father after King Buddy Bolden, and it is to the name of King Buddy Bolden that Floyd is ultimately appealing for the money to get his guitar and to go to Chicago. Because Floyd here is claiming the right to his legacy from the same King who gave Hedley his title and who holds the promise of his father's inheritance, theoretically the two warriors are in conflict for the same estate ("my father's money"), something Hedley implicitly acknowledges when he then tells Floyd:

> You are like a king! They look at you and they say, "This one . . . this one is the pick of the litter. This one we have to watch. We gonna put a mark on this one. This one we have to crush down like the elephant crush the lion!" You watch your back! The white man got a big plan against you. Don't help him with his plan. (71)

The tragedy of a king

Hedley's warning foregrounds one of the most crucial connections between the two men—that they are both doomed. Hedley is dying of tuberculosis, and the play commenced with Floyd's funeral. In *Oedipus Rex*, Aristotle's exemplary tragedy, when Oedipus undertakes his charge to rid Thebes of the plague by discovering who killed the previous king, the first person he calls upon is the blind seer, Tiresias, who immediately tells him the truth—that he, Oedipus, is the killer. Although the fact that the who-done-it is solved in the first fifteen minutes of the play might temper some claims that *Oedipus* initiated the mystery genre, structurally it is crucial that Tiresias be interrogated first, for the same reason that Floyd's funeral has to precede the rest of the action in *Seven Guitars*: tragedy requires that fate be inescapable.

When he was starting to write *Seven Guitars*, Wilson told me that he wasn't sure of the plot—he always worked from characters, not plots—but he was sure that, from the outset of the play, he wanted the audience to know that the main character was dead, so that, as the play unfolded, the audience would think constantly that it was too bad that Floyd had died. At one stage in the writing, moreover, the play was supposed to be a mystery, and, like *Oedipus*, it still retains elements of the genre. In both cases, while we know that the king has been killed, the mystery of how and why remains.

For this reason, Hedley's warning to Floyd about the money is portentous, as Hedley, in a drunk and delusional state, confusing the money Floyd stole (in a jewelry store robbery) with Buddy Bolden's money, will kill Floyd with his machete. In consequence, this dispute over their claims to legitimacy will destroy both of them, as well as the next generation, whose fate is set by this moment, in the same way that Antigone's was set when her father slew his father.

We see that fate fulfilled in *King Hedley II*. In the middle of the *Seven Guitars*, Ruby, Louise's 25-year-old niece, arrives from the South to stay with her. She needed to get away because her former boyfriend, Elmore, had killed her current boyfriend, Leroy. In addition, Ruby is pregnant, although unsure whether Leroy or Elmore is the father. Attractive and (perhaps naively) flirtatious, she garners attention from all of the men, including Floyd, despite his attempts to win back Vera; Red Carter, despite the fact that his wife had just given birth to his son; and Hedley, despite the fact that he is nearly forty years older than Ruby.

Late in the play, Hedley, deranged with fear and anger, expressing a lifetime—in fact, several generations—of racial oppression, brandishes a newly acquired machete, rails at the gods, proclaims repeatedly "the black man is not a dog" (*Seven Guitars*, 88), and asserts the unqualified defiance of the white men who want to take him away. Ruby attempts to quiet and comfort him, which evokes from him violent assertions of his manhood: "I offer you to be the Lily of the Valley. To be Queen of Sheba. Queen of the black man's kingdom. You think I am a clown. I am the Lion of Judah!" (*Seven Guitars*, 89). This becomes an appeal to which Ruby succumbs:

(*Ruby goes over and takes the machete from Hedley. She lays it down on the bench. Hedley grabs her and kisses her violently. Hedley is feverish with lust. He tries to find an opening to touch flesh.*)
Ruby   Slow down baby. It's all right. Ruby help you. Here. Ruby help you. (*She lifts her dress and gives herself to him out of recognition of his great need.*) (*Seven Guitars*, 89–90)

King Hedley II takes place in the same backyard, thirty-seven years later. The neighborhood has deteriorated badly; the backyard is barren and the house next door has been torn down. Ruby, now sixty-one, has returned to Pittsburgh after spending a career on the road as a professional singer, leaving her son, whom she named King after his presumptive father, King Hedley, to be raised by Louise. Louise has recently died, and Ruby has come back to sell the house.

The violence involving King's presumptive father, Hedley, and actual father, Leroy, has infested the world of the play, such that prolific violence has become normal life. King has spent seven years in jail for killing a man named Pernell, who refused to call him by his proper name and who subsequently scarred his face with a razor blade. He shot Pernell repeatedly at point blank range, in the same way that Elmore, thirty-seven years earlier, had shot Leroy. In killing Pernell, King believed he was honoring his father, Hedley, who had also killed a man for refusing to call him King. Now that King is out of jail, Pernell's cousin is seeking to avenge him. Nor is the neighborhood infused with the unofficial royalty that solidified the African American community in earlier decades. *Seven Guitars* is informed by the unseen presence of Joe Lewis, who, as heard in a radio broadcast during the play, retains his boxing title, or by Marcus Garvey and Toussaint L'Overture, the nobility who occupied Hedley's consciousness. Absent too are the contemporary figures of MLK and Malcolm, whose presences preside over the world of *Two Trains Running*. Aunt Ester, the shamanistic consolidation of African American survival, who represented in that play the matriarchal alternative to (or perspective on) the politics of Malcolm and MLK, is ailing at the outset of *King Hedley II*, and in the first scene Stool Pigeon (formerly Canewell) announces her death.

King, furthermore, is not consciously connected to the blues tradition, the last vestige of which is represented by his mother, Ruby, whom, in light of her abandonment of him, King explicitly rejects, telling her, "My mama dead. Louise my mama. That's the only mama I know" (*King Hedley II*, 12). Estranged from her, from the blues tradition, and from the political traditions that have made black lives matter, he lives exclusively in a world of death, violence, and revenge. Unlike his predecessors in the Wilson canon, he was imprisoned for serious crimes rather than police caprice or the furtherance of "slavery by another name." He is currently involved in selling hot refrigerators, so that, for him and his companions, illegal activity and immanent violence have become a way of life.

How can you call me King?

To put this in the context of the Shakespearean histories, the world in *King Hedley II* is one of civil war effected by the death of the king and the absence of an uncontested heir. As Harry Elam explains, when Stool Pigeon gives King the machete with which Hedley killed Floyd, King doesn't know what to do with it:

> The violent history inscribed on the machete places demands on King that he does not yet comprehend. King wants to understand what his birthright is and how he lives up to his name. Where is his kingdom? Like Shakespeare's Hamlet or Prince Hal, Wilson's King desperately wants to know how, in a world rocked by chaos, can he follow his father's legacy and yet remain true to himself.[4]

Prince Hal, like Hamlet, has a tenuous relationship to the throne. In Hamlet's case, his uncle has usurped his ascendancy, by murder and by marriage; in Hal's case, ascendancy is less in doubt than is the legitimacy of his father's, Henry IV's, crown, a legitimacy tested in civil war. Regardless of their titles, moreover, Hal and Hamlet both appear manifestly unsuited to the role of king. Hamlet, a scholar ripped from the throes of actively not writing his soon-to-be-unfinished dissertation, has a head full of high ideas, lofty ideals, and intellectual doubt, all inimical to the decisive demands of sovereignty. Hal, on the other hand, seems to lack noble ideals as well as the intellectual rigor worthy of the crown.

If King, like them, lacks an understanding of how to fill his role, he also lacks the knowledge that his lineage is false, that he is not the heir to King Hedley's title. In other words, central to both *Seven Guitars* and *King Hedley II* is the issue evoked repeatedly in both plays: what does it mean to call someone King, or to refuse to? This is a question of great concern to Shakespeare, not only in most of his tragedies (*King Lear*, *Hamlet*, *Macbeth*) and all his histories but also in romances, such as *A Winter's Tale*, or in *A Midsummer Night's Dream*, in which Oberon must teach Titania, and in so doing teach himself, the authority entailed in being King of the fairies. At the heart of *Julius Caesar* reside the implications involved for Rome, and for Caesar himself, in distinguishing Caesar, the man, from Caesar, the emperor.

These issues are foregrounded in *Richard II*, where we see a huge disparity between King Richard's right to be king and his ability to do so. Like Hamlet, Richard II seems able to play every role but the one that history demands of him, and in the end his inability to fill the role to which he is the rightful heir costs him his crown and his life. When this fate starts to become apparent, he recognizes the dubious legacy of being a king:

> For God's sake let us sit upon the ground
> And tell sad stories of the death of kings:
> How some have been depos'd, some slain in war,
> Some haunted by the ghosts they have deposed,
> Some poisoned by their wives, some sleeping kill'd,
> All murdered—for within the hollow crown
> That rounds the mortal temples of a king
> Keeps Death his court, and there the antic sits,
> Scoffing his state and grinning at his pomp,
> Allowing him a breath, a little scene,
> To monarchize, be fear'd, and kill with looks;
> Infusing him with self and vain conceit,
> As if this flesh which walls about our life
> Were brass impregnable; and, humour'd thus,
> Comes at the last, and with a little pin
> Bores through his castle wall, and farewell king!
> Cover your heads, and mock not flesh and blood
> With solemn reverence; throw away respect,
> Tradition, form, and ceremonious duty;
> For you have but mistook me all this while.
> I live with bread like you, feel want,
> Taste grief, need friends—subjected thus,
> How can you say to me, I am a king? (*Richard II*, 3.2.155–77)

For *King Hedley II*, the frustrations articulated by Richard II consolidate around the ability to propagate. In a time of danger and uncertainty, King subordinates his life to his lineage. The "barren ground" of which Richard speaks is the site on which *King Hedley II* takes place, and that ground focuses the first and the last actions of the play. At the outset, King attempts to plant his seed in that ground, and throughout he tries to protect his small circle of dry earth in the hope that it will reach fruition. Profoundly shrunken in size from the small plot, three decades earlier, that Troy Maxson eventually fenced in, this barren land—upon which he may sit and tell sad stories of the death of kings—is literally the site where four decades earlier Floyd had buried the money that was going to take him to Chicago, the money that King Hedley believed to be the seed money for the plantation his father had bequeathed him, the money that caused Hedley to kill him on the ground now reduced to King's barren realm. By the end of the play, that small plot of land is cordoned by barbed wire and circumscribed by a ritual game in which King will attempt to use Hedley's machete to exact revenge from Elmore for killing King's actual father, Leroy ("the [alternate] King"). This piece of barren earth, indeed, becomes the hollow crown that rounds the mortal temple of King, the place where King will die, and, if we interpret the meow at the end of the play as the implied resurrection of Aunt Ester's cat, the kingdom that his blood will sanctify.

CHAPTER 9
THE CENTURY THAT CAN'T FIX
NOTHING WITH THE LAW:
RADIO GOLF

Production history

Radio Golf had its Broadway premiere at the Cort Theatre on April 20, 2007, a year-and-a-half after Wilson's death, but its out-of-town premiere was two years earlier, in April 2005 at the Yale Repertory, under the direction of Timothy Douglas. In the two years that followed, it was performed in Los Angeles, Seattle, Baltimore, Boston, Chicago, and Princeton; all of these productions, like the Broadway production, were directed by Kenny Leon. Three members of the cast—James A. Williams as Roosevelt, John Earl Jelks as Sterling, and Anthony Chisolm as Old Joe—remained consistent (with the exception of Jelks for the Boston production) from Yale to Broadway. Harmond and Mame, however, were played by several actors; on Broadway, Harry Lennix played Harmond and Tonya Pinkins played Mame. It had sixty-four performances on Broadway.

Arrangement

In some ways, the arrangement of *Radio Golf* is deceptively simple. Instead of being the lead singer, Mame is the *accommodator*, but her limited role suggests how little room there is for that theme. The play, in fact, is about the failure of accommodation, as indicated by Roosevelt, for whom the role is a guise beneath which we find the strong strains of the *hustler* and the *pragmatist-entrepreneur*. The play is arranged so that Harmond, who starts out as a *pragmatist-entrepreneur* and *accommodator* (i.e., a politician), confronts two generations of *warriors*, Old Joe, who is also both historian and *man-not-right-in-the-head*, and Sterling, who is either a perverted *pragmatist-entrepreneur* or a *man-not-right-in-the-head*. In attempting to accommodate them and harmonize with Roosevelt, Harmond is forced to play a spectrum of parts sampled from the cycle and the century. Opting for discord over harmony, Harmond, in almost symphonic style, emerges as a *warrior* in a world where the song of a shaman must inspire through memory rather than active power.

Conclusion and renewal

Although *Radio Golf*, the last play August Wilson wrote as well as the play set in the last decade of his ten-play cycle, may be his most complex in the way it interweaves elements of the nine plays that precede it, its plot is relatively simple. At the outset, Harmond Wilks, a successful, wealthy Pittsburgh real estate developer, who is the leading candidate to become the next mayor—and first black mayor—of Pittsburgh, is opening a campaign office in the run-down neighborhood of Bedford Hill (or the Hill, as it is commonly called). With his longtime friend, Roosevelt, he is also co-partner of the Bedford Hills Redevelopment Corporation, a massive urban renewal project in the Hill, the financial viability of which depends on the federal assistance that accrues to the neighborhood's officially being declared a blighted area. The plans for the renewal project, which will encompass several square blocks, entail leveling the building at 1839 Wylie formerly owned by Aunt Ester, the matriarchal and shamanistic figure who died in the 1980s at the age of 338, her birth coinciding with the introduction of slavery in America. The house was acquired at auction by Harmond's company, Wilks Realty. While he is setting up his office, Harmond is visited by Sterling, the supporter of Malcolm X who, returned from jail in 1969, initiated the action of *Two Trains Running*, and by Old Joe Barlow, the son of Black Mary and Citizen Barlow, who met at the beginning of *Gem of the Ocean* in 1903. As these characters put Harmond in touch with his ethnic *past*, his partner Roosevelt and Harmond's wife, Mame, point him toward what they perceive as a post-racial *future*. Roosevelt, recently promoted to vice president at Mellon Bank, has, with the help of a wealthy white benefactor, Bernie Smith, become a minority (in both senses of the word) partner in a radio station. As it does with his connection to the Bedford Hills Redevelopment Inc., his ethnicity puts his white backers in line for major profits because of government programs aimed at assisting minorities, no matter how little control Roosevelt actually exercises.

That *Radio Golf*, a play about affluent, prestigious African Americans, is frequently referred to as August Wilson's only play about middle-class African Americans (or about African Americans with middle-class aspirations) tells us less about the play than about the conceptual relationship in American discursive practice between race (especially the African American "race") and class. Contemporary American culture certainly provides copious references to *rich* African Americans—Michael Jordan, Oprah Winfrey, Herman Cain—but rarely, if ever, to *upper-class* African Americans. In his television series, widely heralded as being about "middle-class" African Americans, Bill Cosby played a doctor, Cliff Huxtable, married to a lawyer. Clearly, their income level would have put them in, or at least very close to, the top 2 percent of all American households (especially in the 1980s, before the Clinton administration, when banking regulations were radically changed, making possible a new class of Wall Street–based super rich). But if the Huxtables were middle class, what does a black person have to do to enter the *upper* class? Harmond Wilks has a real estate empire and is the mayoral race front-runner; his partner, Roosevelt, is a bank vice president and part owner of a radio station. In what sense are these people middle class?

The answer to that question, in fact to many of the questions in *Radio Golf*, lies in the other nine plays of "The Wilson Century," because with the cycle chronologically complete, Wilson did not only know that *Radio Golf* would function as an epilogue; he also knew intimately the corpus of work that *Radio Golf* would conclude, and thus the quest that it would renew.

For Wilson, we must remember, conclusion and renewal were always intertwined: endings did not resolve but initiate, such that he adamantly refused to finish any work until he knew the first lines of the next one. His craft, like history itself, especially in the way he employed history, was a springboard for the imagination, a platform for what would come next, as certain in its eventuality as it was unpredictable in its trajectory. These factors in Wilson's approach to writing become particularly cogent in that, in the final stages of revising *Radio Golf*, Wilson also knew it would be his last play. In other words, fate had impelled that this epilogue be his most emphatic renewal.

In this context, the theme of "urban renewal," which becomes an informing metaphor for both the most perverse and the most idealistic forces in the play, requires careful scrutiny. In its most common usage, "urban renewal" has functioned as a generic term for government-supported projects in the 1950s, 1960s, and 1970s, which led to the destruction of traditional ethnic neighborhoods, either through acts of "slum clearance," which removed minority populations from urban areas to clear ground for commercial or cultural projects such as New York's Lincoln Center, or for massive housing projects generally viewed as degenerating rather than improving the quality of life of their lower-income residents.[1] In contradistinction to these forms of urban renewal, the play posits a revitalization based on the kind of historical renewal foundational to a cohesive community and on the spiritual renewal that emanates from faith in the value and power of that cohesion.

To understand how Wilson converts a conclusion into a renewal, we need to identify the structures and themes that tie *Gem of the Ocean* to its bookend, *Radio Golf*.[2] Because Wilson wrote these two plays in chronological order, after he had completed the other eight plays, they constitute a de facto prologue and epilogue of the cycle, in that when he wrote *Gem* he was fully aware of the century it would introduce and the cycle of plays that would reflect his interpretations of or riffs upon that century, the century that several historians have dubbed "The American Century."[3]

As bookends for the century, the two plays invite, in fact impel, us to engage with Wilson's sense of progress. How have things changed for African Americans between 1903 and 1997? *Radio Golf*, after all, is a literal sequel to *Gem of the Ocean*, featuring the descendants of the characters in *Gem* and making the site of *Gem*, Aunt Ester's house, central to *Radio Golf*'s conflict. In both a genealogical and a logistical sense, therefore, *Radio Golf* is about the fate of *Gem of the Ocean*, its characters, and their home.

As a symbol of the proverbial "American Dream," the privately owned home signifies the kind of middle-class life that flourished in America's post–Second World War era, with the rise of extensive housing developments and the suburban communities they created. The affordable, new suburban home, equipped with modern appliances and delimited by a fenced-in backyard, contrasts sharply with the contemporaneous inner-city house in *Fences*, where Troy Maxson lives, devoid of a fence and of a television set.[4] Often unarticulated in discussing the rise of suburbia and the middle-class lifestyle it provided is how it emerged at the expense of African American urban communities and how it initiated forms of de facto segregation not possible in multifarious urban areas. The interstate highway system that connected the suburbs to the cities in effect destroyed old black communities, thus eliminating the home equity that would have facilitated trading up to suburban homes, if suburban developers had been willing to sell to African Americans, which, for the most part, they were not.[5] In the 1950s, such discrimination was not yet illegal, and in practice it carried on into the 1960s and 1970s, while in the 1980s the process of "white flight" accelerated. Thus, Aunt Ester's house, like Troy Maxson's house or the houses in *Seven Guitars* and *King Hedley II*, unavoidably connotes a class divide, one that made middle-class life an accessible reality for much of white America while it remained only an "aspiration" for much of black America.

But that class divide occurs over an undefined and problematically amorphous conceptual space, a mental topography upon which class lines are drawn. For several reasons, class has been a complicated concept in America, one not resembling, especially for African Americans, the traditional European model of class upon which Marx formulated his analysis. In one sense, the United States was supposed to be a classless society, in which all members had equal say and shared equal opportunities. Jeffersonian democracy anchored itself to the small farmer, whose model of self-sufficiency insulated him from large vested interests and thus made him more amenable to public welfare and the common good. While this model of democracy was in its conceptual incipience, however, others believed, as the Federalist Papers attest, that the security of the nation rested in the hands of an elite class, deemed by virtue of their wealth and education to be better suited to govern. While both positions agreed that privilege was not a simple birthright, they were less clear about the limits of equality. None would extend it to women, and it was agreed that only those who owned property could vote. Large landowners—the plantation class in Virginia, for example—enjoyed such levels of respect and influence in the social hierarchy that they have been referred to as the Tidewater "aristocracy." They nevertheless earned more of their wealth from production, the growing of cash crops, than from investments or from the rents and taxes paid by their tenants. The point is that if one attended to *how* they earned, rather than to *how much* they earned, this upper class was bourgeois, not aristocratic. Thus, in the sense, at least theoretically, that anyone could work his way up to the highest rung in the social and economic order, America was classless.

This model of classlessness, nevertheless, coexisted with a permanent underclass of slave labor, an underclass legally linked to race. While bloodlines could not promise a seat at the top, they could guarantee a position at the bottom, so that America was a classless society that entailed, by law, a racial underclass. Space would not permit even a cursory overview of the social and legal permutations of this class-race relationship over the nation's first century, which included Supreme Court decisions and armed insurrections as well as agitation, legislation, and migration, not to mention a civil war. At the beginning of the twentieth century, as America transitioned from the Gilded Age to the Progressive Era, the nation had validated the claims made by its strongest proponents and by its strongest opponents. It had created virtually limitless economic opportunity, with aspects of that opportunity furthering inequity rather than equality.

Because, at the dawn of the twentieth century, the cost at which labor could be sold was low, the working class had good reason to organize around common material interests. They constituted something like the traditional Marxist proletariat. At the same time, the nation's entrenched racial hierarchy often created a bigger class divide between black and white working people than any solidarity fostered by their common interests. Labor unions often barred African Americans, and, left outside the labor movement, they all too frequently became strikebreakers. Moving north into what we now call the Rust Belt, African Americans frequently provided labor at low wages that shackled them as well as inhibited union organizing.

Given that the 1903 world of *Gem of the Ocean* exists at the cusp of these trends endemic to the Progressive Era, it is not surprising that the play is framed by labor issues, by the treatment and rights of workers. Incorrectly accused of stealing a bucket of nails, Garret Brown chose to drown rather than acknowledge that he was guilty of a crime he did not commit. As Aunt Ester explains to Citizen Barlow (who actually stole the nails), Brown needed to prove that his life was worth more than a bucket of nails. What remains unsaid is that the *only* way available to him to prove this was to stay in the river until he drowned. In so doing, Brown joined the millions of Africans in the City of Bones, that place beneath the Ocean that houses the souls lost in the Middle Passage, those people who died instead of living as slaves, who, like Brown, rejected the conditions of their labor at the cost of their life. Like the Africans crossing in the hulls of slave ships, Brown faced a choice delimited by unequal power and underwritten by racial hierarchy. There was no union to protect his rights, nor any grievance process, just as there was no process to protect Citizen Barlow from having to give kickbacks to keep his job. These two inequities serve metonymically to reflect the working conditions in the mill that eventually foment a riot. Because the riot causes the city to clamp down on African Americans, it is much more clearly a race riot than a labor protest. Although the union movement was under way at that point in American history, *Gem of the Ocean* at no point suggests that the workers are protesting for the right to organize. They are simply rebelling against racial oppression.

Race and/as class

Thus, being black means belonging to a *class* defined by curtailed rights and restricted opportunities, a class essential in its own immobility to the upward mobility of white America. Caesar's speeches in *Gem* reflect the clash between the alleged freedom provided by the marketplace and the actual class restriction accruing to race. When he first meets Barlow, Caesar suggests that Barlow go to Philadelphia: "It's too crowded here. Too many niggers breed trouble" (*Gem*, 31). He then offers Barlow a quarter.

> I'm gonna see what you do with that. These niggers take and throw their money away. I give one fellow a quarter and he turn around and give it to the candy man. . . . He can't see it's all set up for him to do anything he want. See he could have bought him a can of shoe polish and a rag. If he could see that far he'd look up and find twenty-five dollars in his pocket. Twenty-five dollars buys you an opportunity. You don't need but five dollars to get in the crap game. That's five opportunities he done threw away. (*Gem*, 32)

Caesar has thus parlayed his illegal activity such that it has allowed him to epitomize the law, which entails his benefiting from a process that helps maintain a racial caste system.

But if Caesar is extreme, he is not anomalous in Wilson's plays, where we can repeatedly trace the inextricable relationship between race and the law. We first meet Ma Rainey, for example, when a policeman with whom she has had an encounter escorts her into the recording studio. For Ma, the altercation entails her identity: "Tell the man who I am" (*Ma Rainey*, 48), she repeatedly demands of her white manager, Irvin. As a star, she is an important source of profits, while simultaneously, as a black troublemaker, she is a social disruption that threatens the growing urban centers and the flow of capital that they facilitate. Ma Rainey is outraged that her status as Mother of the Blues is not apparent to the officer, just as the officer is outraged that a black troublemaker should assume an aristocratic attitude. In the end, the charges and countercharges, the facts of the event, the events of history, become irrelevant, because the matter is resolved not by distinguishing truth from fabrication, innocence from culpability, but by Irvin's bribing the officer. This act, which in effect shows that Ma Rainey is a black woman important enough to have a white man bribe a police officer on her behalf, also demonstrates that her ability to escape the law, her capacity to be the Mother of the Blues, depends on a white manager's ability to fix a legal problem.

The law, as in so many instances in Wilson's canon, does not comprise the objective rules that ensure justice but rather, facilitates the agents of class maintenance. Identifying African Americans as a class rather than a race, Wining Boy, in *The Piano Lesson*, explicitly states that "the difference between a white man and a colored man is that a colored man can't fix anything with the law" (*Piano*, 38).

The term "fix anything with the law" has more than one meaning. The colored man cannot use the law to redress a wrong or to claim a right. If one has been cheated or robbed or illegally arrested, he cannot use legal options to fix the problem. Nor can the colored man bend the law to his own devices, contrive the legal situation, or design the small print to his unfair advantage. Finally, he cannot get the legal system to turn a blind eye to his perceived transgressions. Thus, Ma Rainey is colored because her white manager can bribe the policeman, but she can't. The law is not statutory but instrumental, especially in regard to class rigidity and to the most rigidly policed class in American history, black people. In this sense, despite the class mobility that Harmond and Roosevelt ostensibly epitomize, African Americans remain an economic class, a class that continues, as it has since the first slave ship, to facilitate white wealth, even at a time when the process of exploiting that class enables, in fact sometimes requires, black dis-identification with its African American ethnicity.

From this perspective, Caesar Wilkes's grandson, Harmond, appears to have escaped his grandfather's explicitly articulated class, for clearly at the outset of *Radio Golf*, Harmond *can* fix things with the law. Early in the play, Old Joe enters Harmond's office to get legal assistance because Joe has been cited for vandalism for painting the house at 1839 Wylie, which used to belong to Aunt Ester. As a politically connected lawyer, Harmond gets the charges dropped with a quick, simple phone call. To Joe, however, the phone call is much more efficacious than it is just, in that Joe believes the house is his and that he has been unjustly cited for painting his own property. Because the house's history indicates that it was auctioned off to Harmond's real estate company, and because Joe appears extremely eccentric, Harmond seems to have done Joe a favor, that is, to have used the legal prerogative historically reserved for white people to fix Old Joe's situation. But the dramatic action of the play removes several historical layers, revealing that the house was auctioned illegally, that Old Joe, not Harmond, is the legal owner, that the taxes on the house had been paid throughout the bulk of the century by Harmond's grandfather, Caesar, and then by Harmond's father, that Aunt Ester was the role assumed by Black Mary, who was Old Joe's mother and Harmond's great-aunt, that he and Old Joe are cousins.

The most troubling discovery of all, however, is that when Harmond attempts to represent Joe's legal rights against the interests of the Bedford Hills Redevelopment Company and the banks and investors whose gentrification project stands to profit from destroying the house, Harmond not only fails terribly but also loses his chance to become mayor and is forced out of the Bedford Hills Development Company by Roosevelt's white backers. Harmond's most troubling discovery is that Joe's legal rights in no way affect Joe's claim. Being on the right side of the legal claim does not matter if he is on the wrong side of the color line. Because Harmond is *bought* out rather than *kicked* out, and because he still retains his other real estate interests, he will maintain a good level of financial security, but the fragility of his security has been made apparent by virtue of his having lost any ability to fix things with the law. At the end of the play, Harmond grabs the house paint—associated with the war paint of Native Americans, who have also been fixed by their alienation from legal power—to join the extralegal protest aimed at stopping the demolition of Aunt Ester's house.

The action of the play, in other words, is to compel Harmond to discover that he is a colored man, a wealthy colored man, like West, who owns the funeral parlor in *Two Trains Running*, but nonetheless and unmistakably colored. To put it another way, in discovering his African American (or, as Wining Boy would say, colored) history, Harmond has to accept or reject the realization that he is colored. This dramatic tension informs every moment of the play, as underscored by Harmond's growing conflict with his friend and partner, Roosevelt. That conflict arises from Harmond's embracing of the racial identity that Roosevelt is trying to reject. Roosevelt's picture of Tiger Woods, which initially decorates the office, makes this conflict graphic. Woods is Roosevelt's hero for several reasons, not least of which is his mastery of a traditionally white sport, one that at every historical turn emphasizes the idea that in America race, or at least blackness, is a class. Golf requires not only wealth—even one golf club in a set costs a lot more than a basketball, on top of which are the fees for using a golf course and the cost of getting to one, not to mention the cost of joining a country club— but also access. For the bulk of Wilson's century, black people had trouble joining country clubs, even those without explicitly or implicitly restrictive policies, in that a country club is a club first and a set of facilities second, so that in order to join a good country club one already had to be a member of the social club out of which that country club was constituted. But for many Americans the country club was another country, one delimited by social class, not simply by wealth. As Groucho Marx famously remarked at a time when the good country clubs barred Jews, "any club that would have me as a member, I wouldn't want to belong to."

In this context, *Radio Golf* extends the spirit of Groucho's comment by inverting it. When Harmond discovers the price of membership in a "post-racial" club, he doesn't want to be a member. Harmond thus differs with Roosevelt not over the nature of the post-racial club, but over the historical cost of joining it. In other words, the central issue in *Radio Golf* is the history of the African American lives that Wilson has described in the other nine plays.

The lessons of Wilson's American Century

That is why the play is a virtual compendium of the circumstances and lessons—call them blues lessons, call them piano lessons—learned in the other plays. The most didactic of these come from Sterling, who disrupts the 1969 world of *Two Trains Running* by infusing it with a logic that today would be described as critical race theory, with Sterling's idol, Malcolm X, as a proto-theorist.

In contrast to those who fix things with the law, Sterling fixes things with his hands. "Go up on Bedford and look where I fixed that porch," he tells Harmond. "I fixed up a house on Webster Street. 1615. Go look at that. Almost everything you see fixed up around here I did it."[6] But Sterling cannot fix the law, in this case the laws determining union membership, which functions both to protect and to exclude workers. The biggest exclusion is the right to create a union, that is, to create the body that sets the rules. Sterling, therefore, is not asserting the right to join a union but to form one. In relation to union membership, Harmond is on the side of the law, while Sterling is outside the law, from which perspective he can challenge its underlying assumptions.

When Roosevelt worries that he will not have any new business cards to pass out at the golf course—"Without them they'll think I'm the caddie" (*Radio*, 18)—he unwittingly replicates that moment when Ma Rainey enters the recording studio in police custody. Without white certification, Ma Rainey is no more significant to the cop than a caddie would be to people at a golf club.

Wilson makes this point again when Roosevelt, describing his visit to the golf club, takes pride in the fact that Bernie Smith covered all the expenses: "From the minute I set foot in the Cedar Oaks Golf Course it was made clear my money was no good there" (*Radio*, 35). Roosevelt does not realize, in the way those who remember early lessons of Wilson's cycle might, that when it came to fixing things with the cop, Ma Rainey's money was similarly no good. But Roosevelt, blind to this implication of his own assertion—that taking money from Smith diminished, rather than enhanced, Roosevelt's worth—rejects Harmond's claim that Smith is exploiting him to obtain a Minority Tax Certificate. "This is how you do it," Roosevelt explains, "This is how everybody do it. You don't think Mellon has ever been used?" (*Radio*, 33). Here, Roosevelt unwittingly echoes Ma Rainey's foil, Levee, who tells the band that he "don't need nobody messing with him about the white man" (*Ma Rainey*, 68). "You all just back up and leave Levee alone about the white man. I can smile and say yes sir to whoever I please. I got my time coming to me. You just all leave Levee alone about the white man" (*Ma Rainey*, 70).

Roosevelt's diatribes against lower-class blacks also uncannily paraphrase Caesar, who identifies with the law while praising the extralegal ways in which he achieved his wealth and his position as constable. Extolling a class position defined by wealth, Caesar nonetheless understands that class in racial terms. About the first rooming house that he buys, he says:

There was a fellow name Henry Bryant had a place on Colwell Street he sold me. They ran him out of town. Charged me three times what it was worth. Took the money and ran. They tried to kill him for selling to a Negro. I say all right I got me a little start. Niggers got mad at me. Said I must have thought I was a white man' cause I got hold to a little something. (*Gem*, 38)

Explaining the protests and riots at the mill following from the death of Garret Brown, Caesar regards the actions not as representing their common conditions as working men, but rather, as exemplifying the sensibility of a racial class:

You close down the mill you ain't got nothing. Them niggers can't see that . . . . You know whose fault it is. It's Abraham Lincoln's fault. He ain't had no idea what he was doing. He didn't know like I know. Some of these niggers was better off in slavery. They don't know how to act otherwise. You try to do something nice for niggers and it will backfire on you every time. You try to give them an opportunity by giving them a job and they take and throw it away. Talking about they ain't going to work. (*Gem*, 34)

Only because Caesar regards African Americans as a class can he see himself as rising above that class. When he recounts his thorny path to financial success, therefore, it is apt for us to interpret the word "race" as a pun inflected toward his ethnicity: "You look and see the race you got to run is different than somebody else's."[7] Because he is black, he has to buy the rooming house at three times its worth, but because he identifies with the laws that discriminate against blacks, he can produce the collateral that enabled him to pay the inequitable price. Each time Caesar broke the law—no matter how much his circumstances necessitated it—he went to jail, but on the county farm, "A couple [of niggers] tried to escape. I caught them" (*Gem*, 38), and when a fellow named John Hanson started a riot,

I took him on one-to-one, man-to-man . . . . He busted my eye but I put down the riot. They gave me a year. I did six months when the mayor called me in to see him. Say he wanted to put me in charge of the Third Ward. Told me say you fry the little fish and send the big ones to me. They give me a gun and a badge. I took my badge and gun and went down to the bank and laid it on the counter. Told them I wanted to borrow some money on that. (*Gem*, 38)

The irrevocable split between Caesar and his sister, Black Mary, that concludes *Gem of the Ocean* thus prefigures a century that will repeatedly represent the law as something that can or cannot be fixed. By so doing, Wilson will examine the multifarious meaning of the word "fix." To fix something with the law is to treat the law not as a set of rules but as an agent of power. Just as it has the power to classify Ma Rainey as having assaulted the cab driver when she opened the car door, it has the power to take away seven years of Herald Loomis's life by sentencing him to a work farm for simply walking down the road, or to send Lymon and Boy Willie to Parchman Farm for contrived reasons, or to charge Floyd Barton with attempted arson:

I asked one of the guards to show me the back door in case there was a fire. He said the jailhouse don't burn. I told him give me a gallon of gasoline and I'd prove him wrong. He told the judge I threatened to burn down the jailhouse. (*Seven Guitars*, 9)

Barton is not protected by the right to free speech but exempted from it for figuratively (and, since he is a character on stage, literally) crying fire in a crowded theatre. Unless one belongs to the class that can fix things with the law, free speech, as Holloway in *Two Trains Running* made clear, does not exist at all: "A nigger with a gun is bad news. You can't even say the word 'nigger' and 'gun' in the same sentence" (*Two Trains*, 77–78).

Class determines not only what words are permissible but also what deeds are doable. Because Mr. McKnight is a Gulf Oil executive, the law can classify his attack on Booster, recounted in *Jitney*, as rightful indignation, while at the same time classifying Booster's anger at having been wrongfully accused of rape as an irrational act of black violence against a white woman. In the world of Wilson's century, the law empowers the class it serves, and that class returns the favor. The problem of those who cannot fix things is concisely summarized when Floyd and Red Carter commiserate with each other:

Red Carter   One time they arrested me for having too much money. I had more money than the law allowed. Must have . . . cause the police arrested me, put me in jail. Told me if I had that much money I must have stole it somewhere.
Floyd   They got you coming and going. Put me in jail for not having enough money, and put you in jail for having too much money. (*Seven Guitars*, 42)

If *Radio Golf*, as I have argued, forces us to engage with Wilson's vision of progress, the opening of the play suggests that things have indeed changed since Wining Boy's pronouncement. An individual black man such as Roosevelt will never be *a priori* suspect for having too much money. Repeatedly throughout the cycle, the word "Mellon" is used as shorthand for white capital and the facility with which it can be deposited and withdrawn. It is shorthand for the source of white agency, as defined by Caesar. Sterling, explaining why he had gone to jail, says, "I robbed a bank. I was tired of waking up every day with no money. I figure I'd get my money where Mellon got his from" (*Two Trains*, 44). King echoes Sterling when he tells Tonya that he got his 500 dollars "from the same place Mellon got his. You don't ask him where he got it from" (*King Hedley II*, 76). Thus, when

Roosevelt becomes a vice president at the Mellon Bank, he seems to have transcended the confluence of legal and extralegal restrictions encapsulated by Wining Boy's distinction between the white and the colored man. This in part explains Roosevelt's identification with Tiger Woods, who signified in the public imaginary the fact that a black man could become rich and successful at a white man's game, and simultaneously that his self-designated "biracial" identity meant that his success could cast into doubt his "colored" identity.

Similarly, the fact that Harmond can fix things with the law, as much as, if not more than, the fact that he may be elected mayor of Pittsburgh, means that he has transcended class restrictions. Or perhaps it means that the *class* of African Americans has dissolved: if the colored man can fix things with the law, then there is no difference between colored and white.

This is not to say that Harmond is not of African American derivation, but rather, that in the 1990s that derivation seems to have lost its class distinctions. Unlike Troy Maxson, a Pittsburgh home-owner and civil servant of the 1950s, Harmond *can* enter the middle class. The perception of the play being about African Americans with middle-class aspirations, therefore, owes more to its evidencing that those aspirations are no longer restricted in the ways they were when race functioned as a class. But at the same time as Wilson demonstrates that Harmond is not confined to class, he also makes it clear that the class of African Americans has not dissolved. There is nothing, absolutely nothing, postracial about Harmond's world, as *Radio Golf* illustrates by systematically exposing his familial, legal, historical, and ethical connections to the class that he seems to have moved beyond.

The place of African Americans in America

To put it another way, the play forces Harmond to understand his *place* in the world, literally moving him from the office space that represents both his future (it is a campaign office) and the neighborhood's future (it is a construction office established for the renewal of the Hill District) to the protest at Aunt Ester's house, which represents his personal history and the neighborhood's past. If the process of moving in and out of this office provides the temporal parameters of the play, the retrospective engagement with the history of the century provides the temporal parameters of Wilson's century, which encapsulates the centuries of American inequity initiated by the arrival of the first shipload of Africans.

By implication, *Radio Golf* broadens the question of Harmond's place beyond the locales of Pittsburgh real estate to encompass his place in the social order, his place in history—being the first black mayor of Pittsburgh would "make" history—and, most important for this discussion, his place in Wilson's ten-play cycle. In so doing, it makes clear that the cycle is the story of the place history created for displaced people, people who, from the second they were sold on their home soil by their own chiefs to traders and captains, lost the capacity to fix things with the law. They were displaced not only on the global terrain and in the tortuous economic patterns of capitalist exchange, but in the mesh of legalities that form the fabric of American human rights. Nor is it possible to separate questions of law from questions of place from issues of identity. As the Invisible Man says to Mr. Norton at the end of Ellison's novel, "If you don't know *where* you are, you probably don't know *who* you are" (500).[8]

Not surprisingly, therefore, a very specific conflict over the kind of place that Harmond should occupy initiates *Radio Golf*. When Harmond and his wife, Mame, enter the new office of Bedford Hills Redevelopment, Inc., she expresses disappointment about its "raggedy" appearance, but Harmond tells her to "Look close" (*Radio*, 7) at the tin ceiling. Noting that it is "all hand tooled" (*Radio*, 7), Harmond demonstrates his concern with the process, that is, the history of production, the overlooked or taken-for-granted labor now visible only as artifacts, and only visible to someone who looks closely. This too can be taken as Wilson's cautionary note, a warning that if one does not look closely at *Radio Golf*, in the context of the cycle that it concludes, then one may miss a great deal about history and the craft of performing it. But if we do look closely, we can see that this is the first of the play's many allusions to *The Piano Lesson*, whose eponymous piano acquires its value not because of its instrumentality but by virtue of the labor and artistry that went into carving it.

In several other ways, the opening dialogue with Mame indicates Harmond's sense of racial identity, although his circumstances—wealth, political prominence, legal influence—might suggest a post-racial persona, exactly the image Mame, whose field is public relations, believes in. Thus, Harmond selects the campaign office for the same reason that Mame dislikes it: the location asserts Harmond's roots in the black Hill District.

In the first moments of the play, several small conflicts emerge, all of them relating to the neighborhood—what it means, how to change it, whether the ideas about change should come from the past or the present. Because the office is part of Harmond's campaign, it is about image, and because it is part of the urban renewal, it is about how people live. In other words, it represents the values ascribed to the piano in *The Piano Lesson*. Boy Willie wants to sell it to buy the land on which his ancestors were slaves, and Bernice wants to hold on to it because it represents the history of the family. For Harmond's partner, Roosevelt, the office represents a class of people from whom he wants to distance himself, no matter how anachronistic are his perceptions. He wants to be able to watch his car, for example, because he is afraid that the hubcaps will be stolen. "They quit making hubcaps in 1962," Harmond informs him, to which Roosevelt responds: "They'll get mad there aren't any hubcaps and steal the wheels" (*Radio*, 9).

Although a keen sense of the past informs both Harmond's and Roosevelt's values, the men view the meaning and impact of history in radically different ways. Because Roosevelt's ambitions are linked to distancing himself from the past, his anachronistic concerns about having his car damaged are symptomatic of his much more extensive fear that the neighborhood from which he came will damage him, his property, his dreams. Harmond's ambitions, to the contrary, are based on his appreciation of the past. Looking at the artist's rendering of the urban redevelopment project, Harmond notes that the name "Model Cities Health Center" has not been changed to Sarah Degree Health Center, after the first registered black nurse in Pittsburgh. To which Mame responds: "'Model Cities Health Center' has been around for twenty-two years. The organization has some history in the neighborhood. Nobody knows who Sarah Degree was" (*Radio*, 10). When Harmond argues: "That's why the Health Center needs to be named after her. So we remember," Mame counters: "I understand the sentiment, but it's not practical to throw all that history away" (*Radio*, 10).

This interchange succinctly indicates the contentious nature of history, which is never an objective reflection of the past but a value-inflected interpretation of it. Thus, the history Harmond wants to preserve belongs, for Mame, to the a historical realm of sentimentality, the power of which threatens to throw away all the history she favors. The values at stake in this historical dispute reflect those informing Boy Willie's dispute with Berniece in *The Piano Lesson*, where similarly, disentangling historical value from sentimental value reflects a struggle over power and ownership. In that play, however, the struggle is resolved, at least temporarily, through a deal between the warring siblings that invests both the piano's sentiment and history into its performative power; as long as it is played, it transcends the blood shed over it and legitimizes its ownership in the face of the white ghost who would reclaim it. In this regard, the piano is no different from Wilson's ten plays, which empower sentiment in the name of history through the power of performance.

The rightful ownership of the piano can never be resolved: it belonged to Sutter, but Sutter had purchased it with stolen goods, that is, with people stolen from Africa but "legally" purchased in the United States; the play, in the end, becomes a battle in which those who can marshal the spirit of history and the spirits of their family can, however temporarily, fend off those who can fix things with the law. In an inverse way, Sterling makes this point to Harmond when he sells Harmond back his own golf clubs (which were stolen from the trunk of Harmond's car), and then informs him "When you gave me that twenty dollars, you bought some stolen property. You can go to jail for that. You know how many niggers in jail for receiving stolen goods?" (*Radio*, 50). The original owner of the clubs, like the "original" owner of the piano, like the original "owner" of the slaves who were exchanged for the piano, muddies, rather than clarifies, the rights of possession. More importantly, in the process of confounding the issue, Sterling has shifted the term in dispute from the word *original* to the word *owner*, thereby making ownership not a right but rather the privilege of someone on the right side of the law. If *Radio Golf* thus restages the conflict over the nature of property and the legitimacy of ownership, it does so in a time when the spirit world is no longer active, and it remains to be seen whether the spirit of history is an adequate adversary for those who can fix the law.

Or, to put it another way, the play looks back over Wilson's century to ask "What can a colored man fix?" It does so by establishing a head-on collision between the meaning of "fix" and the meaning of "law." The previous black mayoral candidate, Mame points out, is now "fixing parking tickets" (*Radio*, 8). In this sense, "fix" means to rig or corrupt or circumvent the law, and at the most trivial level. A little while later, Old Joe compares America to a giant slot machine which spits back the black man's coin: "You look at it and sure enough it's an American quarter. But it don't spend for you. The machine spits it right back . . . . Is the problem with the quarter or with the machine?" (*Radio*, 22). Harmond responds:

> If it don't take all the quarters you *fix* it. Anybody with common sense will agree to that. What they don't agree on is how to *fix* it. Some people say you got to tear it down to *fix* it. Some people say you got to build it up to *fix* it. Some people say they don't know how to *fix* it. Some people say they don't want to be bothered with *fixing* it. You

mix them all in a pot and stir it up and you got America. That's what makes this country great. (*Radio*, 22, emphasis added)

Harmond's fixation with the ameliorative potential of democracy, indeed, aligns him with President Obama. As Harry Elam points out, the question Wilson poses for Harmond is "whether one can remain committed to a liberal paradigm of black empowerment and at the same time achieve economic or political success within the more conservative, white-dominated American mainstream."[9]

Harmond's faith in America and American justice is very a-typical of the characters in Wilson's century. Consider how this view of America contrasts with Toledo's description, in *Ma Rainey*, of the role of black people in America.

> Everybody come from different places in Africa, right? Come from different tribes and things. Soonawhile they began to make one big stew.
>
> . . .
>
> Now you take and eat the stew. You take and make your history with that stew. All right. Now it's over. Your history's over and you done ate the stew. But you look around and you see some carrots over here, some potatoes over there. That stew's still there. You done made your history and it's still there. You can't eat it all. So what you got? You got some leftovers. That's what it is. You got leftovers and you can't do nothing with it. You already machining you another history . . . cooking you another meal, and you don't need them leftovers no more. What to do?
>
> See, we're the leftovers. The colored man is the leftovers. Now, what's the colored man gonna do with himself? That's what we waiting to find out. But first we gotta know we the leftovers. (*Ma Rainey*, 57)

Or consider it in juxtaposition with Holloway, in *Two Trains Running*, explaining black unemployment in the 1960s: "The white man ain't stacking no more niggers" (*Two Trains*, 35).

From their perspective, the American slot machine is fixed, that is, rigged, and thus incapable of being fixed, that is, repaired. "I say get a new machine" (*Radio*, 22), Old Joe tells Harmond. Because he wields power with ease—consider the ease with which he fixed Joe's summons—the fact that the law is fixed, rigged, remains transparent to Harmond. This is why he can insist to Old Joe that "The law protects you when you pay your taxes. But the law protects the city when a property's abandoned" (*Radio*, 34), although Joe has not abandoned the house. "People act like I'm invisible" (*Radio*, 34), Joe says.

The place of history in Wilson's century

In this regard, Old Joe speaks for the entire cycle of African American history that Wilson has staged, a history that Harmond not only discovers but joins, trading his highly visible political profile for one among many in a community of protesters. Speaking on behalf of the law, Roosevelt reads from Old Joe's rap sheet: "Defendant states he wants to bring charges against the United States of America for harboring kidnappers" (*Radio*, 69). Although Joe's claim is more legitimate than Roosevelt's claim on 1839 Wylie, because of Old Joe's relationship to the law, Roosevelt can cite "evidence" that Old Joe is not in his right mind and, therefore, that his claims are insane rather than legal.

In discovering that Old Joe is his cousin, Harmond is recognizing his kinship with all the colored people of Wilson's century. He is recognizing exactly what Roosevelt refuses to: that he is legally empowered only to the extent that he represents the class of African Americans in such a way as benefits Bernie Smith, while Smith demonstrates his whiteness by fixing the law to his own advantage. By having Roosevelt as a minority partner, Smith can make his radio station eligible for special benefits. Similarly, by helping Roosevelt buy Harmond out of the Bedford Hills Redevelopment Corp., he can exploit the laws intended to help minority corporations restore minority neighborhoods.

Sterling's final exchanges with Roosevelt demonstrate another important way that *Radio Golf* is in dialogue with *Gem of the Ocean*. Using the mid-century perspective of Malcolm X to confront the strain of racial neoliberalism that started to coalesce at the beginning of the century, Sterling responds to Caesar's racial diatribes, as no one in *Gem* does. This rebuttal, a century in the making, shows that ideologically Roosevelt is more Caesar's heir than is Caesar's grandson, Harmond:

> You a Negro. White people will get confused and call you a nigger but they don't know like I know. I know the truth of it. I'm a nigger. Negroes are the worst thing in God's creation. Niggers got style. Negroes got blindyitis. A dog knows it's a dog. A cat knows it's a cat. But a Negro don't know he's a Negro. He thinks he's a white man. It's Negroes like you who hold us back. (*Radio*, 76)

In response, Roosevelt in fact confirms Sterling's charges by asserting his dis-identification: "Who's 'us'? Roosevelt Hicks is not part of any 'us,'"[10] demonstrating his "blindyitis": the only reason Smith is interested in him is his identity as black man, as one of "us" (which, for Smith, means "one of them"). Roosevelt is blind to the fact that Smith has just found another way to do what Holloway explained to Sterling in Memphis's restaurant, in 1969: stack niggers.

Another form, in the second half of the century, of stacking niggers has been their disproportionate use in war zones, a subtle point that informs the end of *Fences* when Cory attends Troy's funeral in a military uniform, indicating, as it did for most enlisted men in 1965 and especially most black soldiers, that his next stop would be Vietnam.[11] *Radio Golf* explicitly alludes to this moment through its reference to Harmond's twin brother, Raymond. Like Cory, Raymond was a talented football player, who, like Cory, was denied a career. In Raymond's case, it was because, like Cory, the military sent him to Vietnam, where Raymond was killed. While not in the same income bracket as Cory, Raymond shared with Cory membership in the same demographic class that served and died disproportionately in Vietnam.

In joining the act of civil disobedience that challenges the authority of the "legal" demolition, Harmond is confronting the legality of the law that, in its initial intervention, created the racial-economic class of African American, the law that enabled people to profit from selling stolen property—the human cargo brought to America by the boatload. The initial Aunt Ester was part of that cargo. Just as her kidnappers had illegally auctioned her off, the people who acquired her house illegally auctioned it to speculators, hoping, with the state's aid and blessing, to turn a profit. If, in *Gem of the Ocean*, Aunt Ester's house recreated the Middle Passage, in *Radio Golf* it recreates the slave auction. In so doing, it becomes a direct challenge to Harmond's faith in the law. "You have got to have the rule of law," he tells Mame, as he had earlier told Old Joe. "Otherwise it would be chaos. Nobody wants to live in chaos" (*Radio*, 70).

And with this declaration, Harmond provides dramatic unity to the Wilson cycle. As Harmond learns that he is a colored man, we conclude a unique and brilliant cycle of plays about a community, deprived of law, making art and comedy and tragedy out of their struggle to transcend the chaos into which the American legal system had tossed them, as though they were the leftovers of history.

CHAPTER 10
CRITICAL AND PERFORMANCE PERSPECTIVES

SEVEN GUITARS AND *KING HEDLEY II*: AUGUST WILSON'S LAZARUS COMPLEX

Donald E. Pease

Although *King Hedley II* is the eighth play in the Wilson cycle, it is the first play that Wilson created as a direct sequel to a previous play. *King Hedley II* repeats scenes, characters, and actions—preparation of a sacrificial animal, ritual murder, burial of the seed, robbing of a store—that Wilson's audience first came upon in *Seven Guitars*. In both plays, the core event centers on a violent confrontation that results in the death of one of the antagonists. In *Seven Guitars*, this violence culminates in a fatal encounter between a blues performer, Floyd Barton, and a West Indian immigrant, King Hedley, whose delusional paranoia induces him to murder Floyd. In *King Hedley II*, King Hedley's son feels compelled to repeat his father's violent actions as the sole means of inheriting his legacy. Instead of a beneficent patrimony, King Hedley II inherits this trauma as the deep truth of his own existence. The "only thing I know about the play," Wilson remarked in an interview about his baneful repetition, is that "his father killed a man. He killed a man. His surrogate father killed a man. He killed a man, and he has a seventeen-year-old son who's getting ready to kill a man" (*Conversations*, 202).

In *Seven Guitars*, the blues community transmuted the violent encounter between Hedley and Floyd into an object lesson in folk wisdom, into the subject of everyday gossip and rumor, and into the raw material for the surviving characters' blues performances. But the protagonist in *King Hedley II* becomes subsumed within a vertiginous cycle of violence that threatens to swallow the entire community. Wilson conveyed the potentially catastrophic consequences of King's way of inheriting his destructive patrimony by having it coincide with the death of Aunt Ester, the matriarchal wisdom figure who had accompanied the African community throughout its 366 years in America.

Indeed, the site of transition from *Seven Guitars* to *King Hedley II* locates what might be described as the primal scene of Wilson's dramatic epic. The symbolic event that was enacted at this site involved the communal effort to produce a vital cultural legacy for people disserved by the mainstreams of social life. That event also represents what Wilson described as the original motive for his dramatic project:

> I wanted to present the unique particulars of black America culture at the transformation of impulse and sensibility into codes of conduct and responses, into cultural rituals that defined and celebrated ourselves as men and women of highest purpose . . . . The field of manners and rituals of social intercourse—the music, speech, rhythms, eating habits, religious beliefs, gestures, notions of common sense, attitudes towards sex, and the responses to pleasure and pain—have enabled us to survive the loss of our political will and the disruption of our history. The culture's moral codes and the sanction of conduct offer a clear instruction as to the value of community and make clear that the preservation and promotion, the propagation and rehearsal of the value of one's ancestors in the surest way to a full and productive life. (viii–ix)

King Hedley II dramatizes actions under the aegis of a name that does not name the character responsible for the actions represented within it. King believes he is the son of a man named King, but in truth he is the son of a man who died before his mother had met Hedley. Wilson represents the meeting between King and Elmore, the man who killed King's biological father, as a repetitious flashback of two previous fatal encounters: between Floyd Barton and King Hedley I and between Elmore and King Hedley II's biological father, Leroy Slater. Overall, the play confronts King with the violence and the exploitation out of which he was begotten.[1] King's personal drama also allegorizes events that characters in his earlier plays were unable to work through, indicating that they must be worked through to secure the community's viable future.

The play's preface indicates the pivotal status that King Hedley II holds in Wilson's epic cycle:

> The cycle of plays I have been writing since 1979 is my attempt to represent that culture in dramatic art. . . . From *Joe Turner's Come and*

Gone (which is set in 1911) to *King Hedley II* (set in 1985), the cycle covers almost eighty years of American history. The plays are peopled with characters whose ancestors have been in the United States since the early seventeenth century. . . . From Herald Loomis' vision of the bones rising out of the Atlantic ocean (the largest unmarked graveyard in the world) in *Joe Turner's Come and Gone* to the pantheon of vengeful gods (The Ghosts of "Yellow Dog") in *The Piano Lesson*, to Aunt Ester, the then 349 year-old conjure woman who first surfaced in *Two Trains Running*, the metaphysical presence of a spirit world has become increasingly important to my work. It is the world they turn to when they are most in need. (vii–x)

If metaphysical presences have played important roles in all of the plays in the cycle (e.g., Toledo's instruction in how to conjure African gods in *Ma Rainey's Black Bottom*, Troy Maxson's rendezvous with Mr. Death in *Fences*, the confrontation with the Ghosts of the Yellow Dog in *The Piano Lesson*), *King Hedley II* marks a turning point in Wilson's relationship to the spiritual dimension of his dramatic project: the deadly struggle between King and his father's killer leads to overcoming the specter of black-on-black violence that haunted Africans in America from the period of the Middle Passage to the time of the play's setting in 1980s Pittsburgh. Like the bones Herald Loomis sees in *Joe Turner*, and the bones in the City of Bones that Barlow sees rise up from the sea, this specter positioned the characters in *King Hedley II* within the imperfect past of the Middle Passage. An action might be described as belonging to an imperfect past when the dimension of that past action that cannot be symbolized within available representations continues to haunt present activities.[2]

Hedley's father suffered a physical death without providing his son with the opportunity to acquit himself of his feelings of indebtedness. King inherited his father's inability to settle his paternal indebtedness. Because memory could not supplant the void made present by his father's absence and thus render it to the past, King remained stuck in the terrible spot where his father never stopped killing Floyd. Wilson has described this transgenerational structure of violence that eventuated there as having originated from African Americans' unconscious transference of the collective aggression aroused by an oppressive white supremacist social structure onto black surrogates. This cycle of violence overshadowed present events after the manner in which King's undead fathers haunted the actions of their son. Sharon Holland has persuasively argued that this transhistorical structure effected an uncanny propinquity between the living and the dead: "If black subjects are held in such isolation—first by a system of slavery and second by its imaginative replacement—then is not their relationship to the dead, those lodged in terms like heritage and ancestor, more intimate than historians and critics have articulated?" (Holland, 196).

In *Seven Guitars*, Hedley's biological death was preceded by his symbolic death, which resulted from his being shut up alive within his dead father's dream. In the final scene of his drama, King and his biological father's killer, Elmore, come face to face with apparitions who returned from the dead through their conflict. King imagined that by killing Elmore, the man who shot his biological father, Leroy, he would avenge his father's death. But as they reenacted this earlier scene of violence, the spectral presences of Floyd and Hedley arise from the dead to join the ghost of Leroy and the double of the Elmore who committed the murder.

Because the historical location for the reduction of Africans to the imagined conditions of death was the slave plantation, Hedley believed that he could become free only by opening up a slave plantation in downtown Pittsburgh, and his putative son, King, believed that his given name scripted him to repeat the role of the father who aspired to head a plantation. Whereas the undead Hedley had lingered in the realm between the living and the dead because he was denied his place in the social order, King's biological father, Leroy, returned to demand that his son render his death legible to a social order that had not taken notice of his life. King's discovery of the truth of his identity, in the form of the suppressed surname Slater, alienated him from every family member who had raised him. Their "son" became the conduit through which both fathers returned to the social order to relive the retributive violence responsible for their own deaths. The son both of a "King" and of a forgotten dead man, King was completely disseuered from the symbolic order resituated wholly within a cycle of fatal violence. Kinless and natally alienated, King exemplified the condition of social death that, Orlando Patterson explains, is the juridical fate that the white supremacist order had imposed upon the slave.

Patterson has famously diagnosed the feelings of kinlessness and natal alienation that haunt King as symptoms of what he calls the "social death" African Americans first experienced as slaves. Patterson defined "social death" as the imposition of a juridical and political condition originally intended to dispossess enslaved Africans of their knowledge of, or association with, history: "Slaves differed from other human beings in that they were not allowed freely to integrate the experience of their ancestors into their lives, to inform their understanding of social reality with their inherited meanings of their natural forbears, or to anchor the living present in any conscious community of memory."[3]

Variations of this motif—social death resulting from the unacted-upon will of a dead ancestor reliving itself through a descendant—appear in all of Wilson's plays. The psychosocial structures that compel these aggressive impulses derive from a self-destructive disposition that, for several reasons, I shall call the "Lazarus complex." Wilson frequently alludes to the biblical Lazarus to allegorize his characters' experiences within American culture, and the figure of Lazarus is explicitly invoked in both *Seven Guitars* and *King Hedley II* to refer to the deadly form of structural violence organizing American culture. Wilson's personification of the cultural memory of Africans' 366 years in America as the character of Aunt Ester, moreover, inspired me to employ "Lazarus" as the name of the allegorical figure who threatens violently to discontinue that memory.

In the New Testament, the name Lazarus identifies the character Jesus resurrected from the dead. When Canewell, a character in *Seven Guitars*, retells this parable, he describes Jesus as having raised Lazarus from the dead so that Lazarus would relive the painful conditions of his death. Canewell intended this redescription to reveal the much more pervasive structure of living death that I have named the Lazarus complex. The Lazarus complex performs the antithesis to Christ's resurrection from the dead. *Rather than lifting men up from what kills their spirits, the Lazarus complex represents the processes through which the dead oblige the living to relive their deaths.*

The Lazarus complex is social as well as psychological in that it operates through a relay of social, political, and juridical institutions that were set in place during the slave trade and that continued to structure the social order after Reconstruction. The white supremacist mentality on which this relay was founded identified Africans wholly with the social order's powers of subjection, such that the subjective "freedom" experienced by whites in taking up their socially mandated subject positions derived from their disidentification from black subjection.

This process of disavowal and subjection connected the psyches of Wilson's black characters with the entrenched relay of social structures that prevented their self-representations from appearing within the mirror of the dominant culture. The Lazarus complex thus names the structure of feeling that induces characters in Wilson's preceding plays to take the aggression that they should have directed against the white supremacist social structure and transfer it on to black surrogates.

Hedley's murder of Floyd displaced his aggression against the white supremacist culture that had demoralized his father: Elmore killed Leroy after Leroy threatened to kill Elmore for destroying his social credibility. Unable to embrace either man in his memory, King remains trapped by these traumatic events, so that the structure adjudicating Elmore's murder of King's father causes its repetitive reenactments. Because King refuses to consign punishment for this crime to the structural violence responsible for its enactment, he instead reperforms a substitute violence that made African Americans stand in both for the white power structure and for that power structure's victims.

King's confrontation with this structure of violence turns, within the same character, the continuity and the discontinuity of the Wilson cycle toward each other and in opposition to each other. In its efforts to produce an identity for a man who did not know his name and a future for a man who struggled to find the resources to work his way through his traumatizing past, *King Hedley II* is about the past and the future of Wilson's theatre. The traumatizing transgenerational memory to which King was a respondent constituted the deep truth of the African presence in the Americas. American history could not fill in the void that the historical trauma of the Middle Passage had opened up. The claims to universality of its historical paradigms and the exclusionary processes at work in its representational conventions were both part of the Lazarus complex that induced the trauma.

But Wilson's plays also ensure that his characters' actions and relationships are dramatized before the concerned regard of the blues community, whose culture inspired and whose members composed the ideal audience for Wilson's plays. The white supremacist structure had positioned a dominant white gaze that refused to allow black cultural achievements into the social order. In bearing witness to the profound spiritual significance of African American cultural representations, the blues community displaced this suppressed gaze by adding what was lacking in the visual field. Before they could truly see themselves, Wilson's characters had to learn how to behold the world through the eyes of the blues community that added this second sight. The blues community's second-sightedness ratified the worthiness of characters that the dominant culture had disqualified.

That blues community emerged out of the Great Migration, whose panoramic history supplied Wilson's cycle with its epic scope. The Great Migration is a documentable, historical representation of a mass movement that took place as African Americans migrated from the post-

Reconstruction South, from 1895 to the 1930s. But in Wilson's plays, the Great Migration also symbolizes a mythological exodus from slavery to freedom, making the events in Wilson's individual plays, in effect, all part of the collective drama of the Great Migration, which was made inevitable when the first African was forcibly transplanted to America. This is because the Great Migration, as the antithesis to the Middle Passage, names what mobilized the emancipatory aspirations of all of Wilson's characters.[4] In its largest sense, therefore, the Great Migration is both the emancipatory movement in which Wilson's characters participated and the historical force that is interrupted when Wilson's characters fall out of its flow.

As a collective movement, the Great Migration empowered its members to separate themselves from the cataclysmic violence of enslavement by replacing the compulsion to reenact this violence with forms of psychic, social, and spiritual mobility. Wilson's characters obtained access to the spiritual dimension of the Great Migration in moments when they felt as if they could not go on. The ongoing eventfulness of the Great Migration drew upon a repository of wisdom, lore, cultural practices, collective memories, prayers, role models, cooking instructions, conjurings, myths, symbolic rituals, chants, ancestral presences, and songs that have accompanied Africans throughout their 390 years in America. Wilson's characters deploy these spiritual resources to overcome the impediments to their social mobility imposed by the Lazarus complex. The individual and collective performances of music, song, celebration, resistance, backtracking, high-stepping, dance, recrimination, back-talking, and laughter through which Wilson's characters act upon these empowering resources materialize the freedom that the movement conveyed.[5]

The primary means of expression through which Wilson's characters recover their footing within this movement is the blues. The blues, the spirituals, and the folkways of the Great Migration mediate between Wilson's plays and the audiences they address. His blues performers overcome the conditions of kinlessness and social death by enacting improvisatory genealogies that construct surrogate family ties with ghosts from the immemorial past and with strangers from the unknowable future. The affinities the blues effect among performers, music, and the audience in large part presume a simultaneity of experience: the blues singer performs in the presence of and in response to the audience.[6]

In *King Hedley II*, Wilson gives the name Aunt Ester to that individual who embodies the restorative powers of the Great Migration. This 366-year-old matriarch is as old as the African presence in America. Because Aunt Ester personifies the collective memory of the Great Migration, her death renders the ordeal King undergoes in his face-off with Elmore a profound threat to the survival of the blues community. This threat is further evidenced by the fact that Ruby, King's mother, has lost the desire to perform the blues.

This highly condensed account of the actions that take place in the transition between *Seven Guitars* and *King Hedley II* may have induced confusion rather than a clarification of their significance. What follows constitutes an effort to accomplish this clarification by explaining the meta-drama connecting the two plays as the correlation of two profound symbolic actions: the dismantling of the Lazarus complex and the resurrection of Aunt Ester. In the course of this explanation, I shall take up several of the topics—the primal scene of retributive violence, the witness to the Lazarus complex, the destruction of the cycle of violence, and the resurrection of Aunt Ester—to which I have gestured in this compressed account of what took place at this turning point in Wilson's epic drama.

With the following exchange of refrains, Hedley and Floyd enter into the imaginary space in which Hedley believes that the blues singer Buddy Bolden will hand him his father's legacy:

Floyd   I thought I heard Buddy Bolden say . . .
Hedley   What he say?
Floyd   He said, "Wake up and give me the money."
Hedley   Naw. Naw. He say, "Come here. Here go the money."
Floyd   Well . . . what he give you?
Hedley   He give me the ashes.
Floyd   Tell him to give you the money. (*Seven Guitars*, 23–24)

Each time Hedley and Floyd ritualistically repeat these lines, they open a site within the symbolic order where Hedley reenters the dream space of his dying father's last will and testament:

It is my father's money. What he send to me. He come to me in a dream. He say, "Are you my son?" I say, "Yes Father I am your son." He say, "I kick you in the mouth?" I say, "Yes, Father, I ask you why you do nothing and you kick me." He say, "Do you forgive me?" I say, "Yes, Father, I forgive you." He say, "I am sorry I died without forgiving you your tongue. I will send Buddy Bolden with some money for you to buy a plantation so the white man not tell you what to do." Then I wait and I wait for a long time. Once Buddy Bolden come and he say, "Come here, here go the money." I go and take it and it all fall like ash. Ashes to ashes and dust to dust. Like that. It all come to nothing. (*Seven Guitars*, 70)[7]

Whereas Floyd hears Buddy Bolden say, "Wake up and give me the money," what Hedley hears is, "Naw! Naw! Here go the money." In between the money that Floyd has imagined hearing Buddy demand and the money Hedley has contrarily imagined seeing Bolden relinquish, the audience's field of audibility engages a cycle of retributive violence that cannot be restricted to the dimensions of this refrain. The contours of this cycle become starkly visible when King adds the following details about his relationship with his father: "I go home and my daddy he sitting there and he big and black and tired taking care of the white man's horses and I say how come you not like Toussaint L'Ouverture, why you do nothing? And he kick me with him boot in my mouth. I shut up that day, you know, and then when Marcus Garvey come he give me back my voice to speak" (*Seven Guitars*, 87).

On the day he stood at his father's deathbed, Hedley said:

> "I hope as God is with us now but a short time more that you forgive me my tongue." It was hard to say these things, but I confess my love for my father and Death standing there say, "I already cook him a half hour ago." And he cold as a boot, cold as a stone and hard like iron. I cried a river of tears but he was too heavy to float on them. So I dragged him with me these years across an ocean. (*Seven Guitars*, 87)

Hedley had wanted his father to emulate Toussaint L'Ouverture's power, which had overthrown the white power structure. But instead, Hedley's father redirected his rage against his son. This internalization of the violence initially perpetrated upon the members of the black community and then redirected at his own son constitutes the legacy of Hedley's father, a legacy that has already mandated Hedley's killing a man for refusing to call him "King." Hedley repeats this misdirected aggression when he cuts Floyd's throat with a machete after the blues performer refuses to give him the money he and Poochie Guillory have stolen from a white-owned department store.

If Hedley's father had suffered a physical death, he cannot undergo a symbolic death until his son, King Hedley, settles his debt to him. In the absence of that settling of accounts, Hedley's father disappears from the symbolic order, only to reappear within this dream space in which his son receives Buddy Bolden's money. But his father also reappears through Hedley's compulsive need to reenact the violence his father directed against him.

Hedley's oscillation back and forth between his experience of social death and his own self-destructive drives consigns him to this void in the social order, where the unacted-upon violence of his (un)dead father overtakes his psyche. When his undead father's violent behavior trespasses into the domain of his living son's body, Hedley imagines himself the head of a slave plantation where he can daily reenact the black-on-black aggression that his father has taught him: "Everything will fall to a new place. When I get my plantation I'm gonna walk around it . . . . I'm gonna be a big man on that day" (*King Hedley II*, 24).

When Floyd enters into the imagined space of Hedley's dream in the climactic scene of *Seven Guitars*, he collaborates in materializing the fatal environs of Hedley's imagined plantation. The refrain Hedley reenacts with Floyd there permits Hedley's father to trespass into the domain of his living son. Hedley imagines himself the head of a plantation through which the dead return from the City of Bones and demand the sacrifice of Floyd Barton.[8]

But the site at which Hedley kills Floyd and the social function of the man Hedley murders have violated the conditions of viability of the entire blues community. Wilson invests the scene of Hedley's crime with a quasi-sacred valuation. When Hedley kills Floyd on the plantation he imagines he had inherited from his father's dream, he transfers the death world of the antebellum South back to the material world of a twentieth-century Pittsburgh neighborhood backyard, killing the blues performer who personifies the spiritual resources necessary to liberate the community from that death world.[9]

Hedley's murder of Floyd may have been the climactic event of *Seven Guitars*, but the play is primarily concerned with the social processes through which the other members of the community cope with this tragedy. Individually and collectively, the characters in *Seven Guitars* searched for lyrics to express their intense grief.

In *Seven Guitars*, Floyd and Hedley enter into Hedley's father's Buddy Bolden blues song to perform the actions expressed in the lyrics. Hedley's killing of Floyd led the blues community to add new refrains to those lyrics so as to liberate themselves from their most self-destructive impulses. After they convert the terrible news of his death into a dozen blues lyrics and seven gospel songs, these performances translate the fatal give-and-take between Hedley and Floyd into the alternative structures of call-and-response, replacing the trauma of Floyd's death with ancillary cultural practices that convert its paralyzing effects into communally revitalizing energies.

In a splendid interview, Sandra Shannon inspired Wilson to articulate the following account of the significance of the blues to his dramatic vision:

I think that the music has a cultural response of black Americans to the world they find themselves in. Blues is the best literature we have. If you look at the singers, they actually follow a long line all the way back to Africa and various other parts of the world. They are people who are carriers of the culture, carriers of the ideas—the troubadours in Europe, etc. Except in black America—in this society they were not valued except among the black folk who understood. I've always thought of them as sacred because of the sacred tasks they had taken upon themselves to disseminate this information and carry these cultural values of the people. And I found that white America would very often abuse them. I don't think that it was without purpose in the sense that the blues and music have always been at the forefront in the development of character and consciousness of black America, and people have senselessly destroyed that or stopped that. Then you're taking away from the people their self-definition—in essence, their self-determination. These guys were arrested as vagrants and drunkards and whatever. They were never seen as valuable members of a society by whites. In fact, I'm writing a play that deals specifically with that. (*Conversations*, 121–22)

The blues constitute a way of passing along communal knowledge as sung stories that keep the knowledge memorable enough to be recirculated by successive listeners. Thus, the knowledge remains a vital resource in a system of cultural transmission—at work in the oral tradition—that sustains and is sustained by overlapping structures of response. The music provides emotional reference for stories that the community sanctions, and the singing of the song by other members of the community keeps the stories alive, while providing, as well, the means of understanding the significance of the stories to the community's survival.

Blues are not an autonomous idiom; they are interconnected with other idioms that exceed translation and lack definitive signification. The oral tradition includes these pluralized idioms, but without a single key that would supply their definitive translation. If blues performers work variations on their idioms' already-established meanings, every variation returns the blues performer to the sources of the idioms in the archival storehouse of the Great Migration. Through these variations, blues performers shift the direction of the idiom on which they are riffing so as to propagate transitions that advance the music's themes. These transitions pivot on the termination of totalizing melodies by embracing a multiplicity of different refrains.

The blues supply Wilson's community with a way of living within an alien symbolic order by providing the resources with which to transform it. The witness names the figure of freedom within the spectator who learns how to view the world from the perspective of the blues community. Wilson's plays add this unfamiliar figure of the witness to the symbolic field. A Wilson play takes hold when the playgoer, exposed to the finitude of his common sense—a set of limitations upheld by the symbolic order—becomes open to an alteration in the order of things.

One of the pieces of knowledge that the blues community of *Seven Guitars* communicates is that, by killing a blues performer, Hedley has destroyed one of the community's sacred regenerative figures. The surviving members of Barton's blues community perform riffs about its significance, which separates the community from what threatens to immobilize it. Wilson's next play represented the drama of Hedley's son in terms of his entrapment within the immobilizing structures. The transition between the two plays constitutes an impasse for the blues community, symptomatized by the fact that King's mother, Ruby, has lost her desire to sing the blues. Without the blues' power to reveal its devastating impact, the Lazarus complex threatens to engulf the community in tidal floods of violence.

In adding the figure of the Lazarus complex, whose structural role has not been allowed visible recognition, Wilson reveals the structures of perception that overdetermine the negation of black cultural representations within the dominant social order. The witness to this structural violence is not limited to African Americans; in its extensive form, Wilson's blues community includes the whites as well as the blacks in his audience. An audience member becomes a witness to this truth when he or she learns how to look at events from the position of this witness.

Because the Lazarus complex is structured in a racist way of looking at the world, Wilson's bearing witness *against* the oppressive visual structures that reproduce that way of looking aspires to annul racist ways of seeing. The witness adds a subjective viewpoint to the members of Wilson's audience. From that viewpoint, they can become cognizant of a framework of visual assumptions. The figure of the witness, furthermore, becomes an additional character, or meta-character, who frames the characters whom the audience re-sees through the perspective of this witness.

The witness produces two figures within the observer (the visualizer and the witness) and within the observed (the visualized participant and the witness). The witness, therefore, can annul the racist structures of visualization in the observer and can also destroy the figure of racial subjection from within the observed. When Stool Pigeon's witness takes hold of the visual positions that inform the audience's view of the world, this witness reveals the white supremacist gaze as that which blinds the observer to the truth of the blues community's perspectives.

Canewell, the one character in *Seven Guitars* who did not benefit from the blues community's restorative displacement of Floyd's murder, also plays a key role in *King Hedley II*. The harmonica player in Floyd Barton's blues band, Canewell brought Floyd's lover, Vera, the medicinal goldenseal plant under whose roots Floyd hid the stolen money. Canewell also accidentally dug up the money, forcing Floyd to reclaim it. Rather than using the blues to disassociate himself from the site of Hedley's violence, Canewell collaborates in the refrain with Hedley with which the play concludes:

Canewell   "I thought I heard Billy Bolden say . . ."
Hedley   What he say?
Canewell   He say, "Wake up and give me the money."
Hedley   Naw. Naw. He say, "Come here, here go the money."
Canewell   What he give you?
Hedley   He give me this.
Hedley (*holds up a handful of crumpled bills*)   They slip from his fingers and fall to the ground like ashes. (*Seven Guitars*, 107)

Canewell is also the character in *Seven Guitars* who invokes the figure of Lazarus to interpret Hedley's relationship with his father: "Jesus ain't had no business raising Lazarus from the dead. If it's God's will, then what he look like undoing it? If it's his father's work, then it's his father's business and he should have stayed out of it" (*Seven Guitars*, 25). "I'm talking about you ain't supposed to go against nature. Don't care whether you the Son of God or not. Everybody know that. Lazarus even know that" (*Seven Guitars*, 25–26). Canewell concludes that Christ's miracle is inappropriate because he believes in the justice of God the Father's law that irretrievably separates the living from the dead. Besides violating God's order, Christ's decision to raise Lazarus causes Lazarus to relive and thereby double the suffering that led to his first death: "When Lazarus was dying the second time—he was dying from pneumonia—somebody went up and got Jesus. Lazarus saw him coming and said, 'Oh no, not you again!' See, all Jesus had done by raising him from the dead was to cause him to go through that much more suffering. He was suffering the pain of living" (*Seven Guitars*, 26). According to Canewell, Christ had not resurrected Lazarus from the condition of death but resituated the dead Lazarus within the realm of the living.

Canewell is the sole character in *Seven Guitars* who bore the knowledge of the Lazarus complex that had induced Hedley to kill Floyd. But in the transition from *Seven Guitars* to *King Hedley II*, Canewell underwent a change in his nominal status from Canewell to Stool Pigeon. This change was the consequence of Canewell's having testified in court to Hedley's murder of Floyd. His given name "Canewell" was conferred upon him in honor of his slave ancestors, who had received the name as an indication of the efficiency with which they cut down the harvest on sugarcane plantations. But after Canewell turned into the state's star witness against Hedley, Ruby, the woman who told Hedley she was carrying his child, renames him "Stool Pigeon": "Ruby called me 'Stool Pigeon'. Somehow or another it stuck. I'll tell anybody I'm a Truth Sayer" (*King Hedley II*, 62).

In *Seven Guitars*, Canewell provides the state with the evidence it needs to punish Hedley for killing Floyd; in *King Hedley II*, Stool Pigeon becomes the Truth Sayer who bears witness against the structure of social death responsible for Hedley's commission of this deed. Canewell had criticized Christ for disrupting the order of God the Father by raising the historical figure of Lazarus from the death his father had ordained. But Stool Pigeon arrives at a revelation that leads him to reinterpret Lazarus as the figure God the Father had created to personify the relationship between the living and the dead. Stool Pigeon communicates this revelation in the following prophetic saying:

> The Mighty God
> Made the wind
> Mighty is His name
> Who made the water
> Called man out of the dust
> The Mighty God
> Made the firmament
> Called forth Lazarus. (*King Hedley II*, 80)

When he names Lazarus the figure God called forth after lifting man out of the dust, Stool Pigeon locates Lazarus within the firmament as the personification of death in life. Stool Pigeon also tells King that if he wants "eternal life," he must send Lazarus back to his grave: "For whosoever believeth, then shall I cause him to be raised into Eternal Life and magnify the Glory of My Father, the Lord God who made the firmament. Then shall Death flee and hide his face in darkness, For My Father ruleth over the things in his creation" (*King Hedley II*, 69). Stool Pigeon's role in causing the dead Lazarus to flee back into the darkness of his tomb requires that he stand in for the blues community, which the cycle of violence has threatened to destroy, and that he bear witness to the truth of the action that is about to take place.

Rather than continuing its processes, Stool Pigeon becomes the Truth Sayer who bears witness to the white supremacist structure of relations responsible for continuing the subjection and negation of African American culture. His witness culminates in the correlation of King's Lazarus complex with the iniquities of the fathers. To make certain that King understands the gravity of this revelation, Stool Pigeon hands him the machete with which Hedley killed Floyd:

> This is the machete Hedley used to kill Floyd Barton. This is the machete of the "Conquering Lion of Judea," I give that machete to you, and me and Hedley come full circle . . . . The Bible say, "Let him who knoweth duty redeem the house of his fathers from his iniquities against the Lord. And if he raise a cry saying he knoweth not the iniquities of his father then he knoweth not duty for even if the iniquities are great and his father's house be scattered to the numberless winds, if he shall gather it and raise it up then shall it stand even unto the end of time." Floyd was my friend. I give that to you and we can close the book on that chapter. I forgive. That's the Key to the mountain. God taught me how to do that. God can teach you a lot of things. He don't give you nothing you can't handle. God's a bad motherfucker. (*King Hedley II*, 62)

Although Hedley had imagined himself in the place of Abraham awaiting the birth of Isaac, Stool Pigeon saw that Hedley had called forth Lazarus. More importantly, Stool Pigeon understands that King can only banish this specter of living death by destroying the Lazarus complex that supports it. When Stool Pigeon hands King the sword with which his father had slain a sacred blues singer, he is challenging King to discover the resources that will end the retributive violence responsible for his father's iniquities. To dismantle the figure who made Hedley feel like Lazarus, therefore, King has to destroy the Lazarus complex within himself.

Stool Pigeon understands that the spiritual figure who can restore the blues community is not the Christ who caused Lazarus to relive his death, but Aunt Ester, whose death has threatened to destroy the repository of cultural resources that has accompanied the blues community throughout its 366 years within the Great Migration. Stool Pigeon's prophetic task also involves performing a ritual that will resurrect the spirit of Aunt Ester. Initially, Stool Pigeon believes that this work can be accomplished by sprinkling the blood of her dead cat over the sacred ground upon which Hedley had killed Floyd.

But Stool Pigeon's witness to the actions at the play's conclusion reveals that the killing of Lazarus is the sacred ritual the blues community must perform before it can reconnect to the spiritual resources of the Great Migration. This ritual sacrifice requires that King undergo an ordeal in which he successfully separates the portions of himself that belong to the Lazarus complex from those that descended from the Great Migration.

The blues community in *Seven Guitars* witnesses what the dominant order cannot; namely, the lyrical insights through which it reworks grim spectacle into restorative wisdom. In *King Hedley II*, Stool Pigeon witnesses the deadly cycle of violence to which Ruby had given birth, in her son, and he witnesses as well the threat that retributive violence poses to the entire community. After the horrific encounter, in *Seven Guitars*, between Floyd and Hedley, the blues community transfigures the scene into lessons in survival, but not even the blues community can transform the retributive violence that threatens to renew itself at the conclusion of *King Hedley II*.

The action at the heart of the play revolves around the return of Elmore, who eventually informs King of his true paternity and reveals his own role in Leroy's death. Elmore states that his motives for taking this action were based upon his desire to get King to agree to the justice of the rules of the game that led him to take the life of Leroy: "Tell King I am coming to see him. I know how he had some hard times, I want to see if he learned anything" (*King Hedley II*, 44). But Elmore has not, in fact, returned to find out what King has learned. He has come back to tell King something he could not otherwise have known:

> See, when you pulled that trigger you done something. You done something more than most other people. You know more about life 'cause you done been to that part of it. Most people don't never get over on that side . . . that part of life. They live on the safe side. But see . . . you done been God. Death is something he do. God decide when somebody ready. Not you. He decide when he want somebody. God don't like that, you thinking you him. He cut you loose. (*King Hedley II*, 73)

Beyond Elmore's ostensible motive for revealing the truth of King's paternity, he also feels obliged to confess his murder so that he can find peace. Instead of covering over the void he caused by taking another man's life, however, his disclosure opens up another void by depriving King of a representable identity.[10]

Elmore's revelation makes him responsible for the deaths of both of King's fathers. He killed King's biological father by shooting him in the face, and he killed King's symbolic father by telling King the secret of his origins. King felt doubly alienated by this news. After losing the name that renders him recognizable to himself, he is renamed after a man who lacks a place in his genealogy.

King discovers his true identity at this fatal crossroads, where the violent legacy of Leroy Slater converges with that of King Hedley I. The double of both fathers, King Hedley II has redoubled the loss of name. That redoubled loss signifies his exposure to the sheer contingency of radical anonymity. If the return of the suppressed name of his actual progenitor cost him one name, the name "Leroy Slater"—to which he is now forcibly bound—dissevers him from every known relation.

Hedley had killed Floyd to square his debt to his father; Elmore had killed Leroy for his failure to pay his debt to him. Because King feels compelled to reperform the violence that has led to the downfall of both fathers before he can live his own life, he has to settle his biological father's accounts within the symbolic order and to fulfill his symbolic father's wish to transform that order.

This felt need to fulfill their symbolic mandates thus positions King in between the deaths of both fathers in a domain resembling the death world of the Middle Passage, in that it opens up a space within the social order where death trespasses into the domain of life, and life crosses over into the region of death. There, life confronts its certain death, and death lives in anticipation of itself. This death world, which lies under the provenance of Lazarus, also names the place of the imaginary plantation on which Hedley had killed Floyd and the place of life in death where Elmore had killed Leroy. A sacred site, it also names the archaic ground on which the African ancestors of the blues community were violently uprooted from their families and their homeland and were thrown into the slave quarters of the Middle Passage.

Stepping into this domain, King yields his psyche to the Lazarus complex, which demands that he repeat the retributive violence in this cycle of living death. While King's compulsion to settle his father's debts may stir our pity, his drive toward annihilation arouses our deepest fears.

Elmore explains that his deep motive for killing Leroy originated out of a comparable death world. That world had encompassed Elmore's life when Leroy put a gun to his head before an audience of their friends in a crowded bar. When, instead of pulling the trigger, Leroy whispered, "Now you are a dead man," Elmore called forth Lazarus to take up Elmore's place in the social order, and, in keeping with the dictates of the Lazarus complex, Elmore proceeded to relive his own death in the displaced act of taking Leroy's life. Since Elmore had lost a place in the social order, he answered by opening up a void where Leroy once stood. In the concluding act of *King Hedley II*, Elmore returns figuratively to the scene of that crime, wanting King to agree to the justice of the rules that led him to take the life of King's biological father. King instead invents rules that induce the two men to reenact the scene in which Leroy had performed the symbolic killing of Elmore: "Elmore the way I see it . . . Leroy owed you fifty dollars. That was man to man. He should have paid you. You say he's my daddy . . . I'm gonna pay my daddy's debt. Here goes your fifty dollars. Now we straight on that. But see . . . my name ain't Leroy Slater, Jr. My name is King Hedley II, and we got some unfinished business to take care of" (*King Hedley II*, 99).

After repaying Leroy's debt, however, King reproduces the scenario in which his father had incurred the debt by refusing to give Elmore the betting money Elmore thought was owed to him:

Elmore   Twenty of this is mine. The bet was three to one.
King   When you play the lottery, do the state give you back what you played or do they just give you back what you won? Take that sixty dollars and get out of my face. Unless you want to make something of it. You can take it to the limit.
Elmore   All right. Those are your rules. Those are the rules you wanna play by. Come, let's play. Seven! (*King Hedley II*, 100–1)

After Elmore throws a seven, King knocks him to the ground and threatens to kill him with Hedley's machete. But upon taking up the machete that Stool Pigeon has handed down to him, King, rather than killing Elmore, repeats the phrase over the supine body of his father's killer: "Now you are a dead man twice." The repetition of this phrase, which Leroy had pronounced to Elmore before refusing to pull the trigger, gave expression to King's rationale for his decision not to kill Elmore. Holding up the machete with which Hedley had killed Floyd, King resurrects the memory of his symbolic father at the same instant as he refuses to slay the murderer of his biological father, thereby also declining to reenact his symbolic father's murder of Floyd. By feeling the compulsion to reperform both acts of vengeance yet declining to do so, King brings two cycles of violence to a close in a single act of rejection. Through the interruption of these cycles of violence, King atones for the "iniquities" of both fathers.

In accomplishing this reparation, King reenters the space where his symbolic father had murdered Floyd and the space where Elmore had killed Leroy, thus making a correlation between the archaic groves in Africa where blacks used machetes to force other blacks into the Middle Passage and the death worlds of white America's plantation slavery.

Ending the succession of violent actions that replenished these death worlds, King II destroys his Lazarus complex, in that the phrase "Now you are a dead man twice" finds its true addressee in the Lazarus complex that had taken possession of both Elmore and King. After Elmore hears the repetition in King's phrase, he recognizes that he has already been living his own death. When he fires his gun into the ground rather than at King, the audience knows that Elmore has sent Lazarus (who personifies the figure "dead man twice") back to his grave. Feeling his father's (and Elmore's) compulsion to kill but declining to act upon it, King disrupts the cycle of living death that originated during the time of the Middle Passage and continues to exact servitude to its destructive imperatives into the contemporary moment.

But King's refusal does not merely result in the sacrifice of Lazarus. In annulling the relay of violence that links his fate to the names of his fathers, King is no longer the son of either man. The settling of his fathers' symbolic debts squares the books and completes the circle that links his birth to their deaths. In de-creating the self who had been fated to repeat the cycle of violence, King can no longer be described as the son of man.[11] King has accomplished this transfiguration by dissevering himself from the cycle of retributive violence through which the Lazarus complex had taken hold of the African American community. King's transformation cannot be fully accomplished, however, until Ruby kills the Lazarus figure (the "you a dead man twice" figure) within King by accidentally shooting him in the throat. If King's emancipation has removed him from the social order, Ruby's shooting of her son opens up a space within that order through which Aunt Ester returns and restores Ruby's capacity to sing her favorite blues refrain:

Red sails in the sunset
Way out on the sea
Oh carry my loved one
Bring him home safely to me. (*King Hedley II*, 102)

In sacrificing Lazarus, the blues community brings about the dialectical separation between the deadening effects of the complex and what is eternally alive. As the mediator through whom the blues community's connection with the Great Migration is restored, Aunt Ester is the true beneficiary of this sacrificial rite. While alive, Aunt Ester names the medium through whom the blues community receives the spiritual resources of the Great Migration. After her death, Aunt Ester names the ancestor in whose name the Lazarus complex was sacrificed so that she could continue in her service as the blues community's intermediary.

King's ordeal must pass through the matrix of Aunt Ester before it can become transfigured into the unforgettable wisdom that promises to redeem the blues community. Ruby tells Stool Pigeon that Aunt Ester counseled her against an abortion before King's birth, and it is to Aunt Ester that Ruby consigns King's spirit after she brings about his death. The resurrection of Aunt Ester and the killing of Lazarus are co-constituting events. The figure who performs the murder is the blues performer, Ruby, whose voice has been silenced by the violence that had overtaken the community. Ruby's song delivers King to Aunt Ester, who has returned to the community to bear witness to the figure who had transformed it.

If the deep action of *King Hedley II* entails the displacing of a cataclysmic cycle of violence by a blues song through which the community has survived that violence, the figure who restores Ruby's voice is Aunt Ester, into whose body King is reborn. After Ruby sings her refrain, Stool Pigeon sees Isaac rise out of the body of Lazarus, from where he is carried into Abraham's bosom. It takes Stool Pigeon to recognize the fact that King's disruption of the cycle of violence has fulfilled Hedley's wish that his son become the Messiah.

> The fatted calf
> Told Abraham you wanted Isaac! Say I want your best!
> From the top of the mountain
> You sent the law!
> I want your best!
> I want Isaac!
> We give you our Glory.
> We give you our Glory.
> We give you our Glory. (*King Hedley II*, 103–4)

PERFORMANCE POLITICS AND AUTHENTICITY:
JOE TURNER'S COME AND GONE AND *JITNEY*

Harry J. Elam, Jr.

Introduction

August Wilson's history cycle takes on new meanings when lifted from the page onto the stage. To be sure, this is true for any playwright, because in performance the skills of the actors, the vision of the director, and the visual sensibilities of the designers all contribute to how we interpret the play. In her essay "Writing the Absent Potential: Drama, Performance and the Canon of African American Literature," Sandra Richards states that the "unwritten, or absence from the script is a potential presence implicit in performance."[12] The power of performance, for Richards, foregrounds the playwright's script as the space of absent potential, which the director, actors, and designers seek to engage productively. From his early career at the Eugene O'Neill Center, working on *Ma Rainey's Black Bottom* in 1982, to the debut of *Radio Golf* in 2005, Wilson traveled around the country, carefully observing how performers activated the absent potential, listening to audiences and their responses, talking with directors and designers about the staging of specific moments, adjusting the script along the way. Wilson, in fact, made specific alterations and even developed characters with certain actors in mind. For example, he created the role of Boy Willie in the *Piano Lesson* for Charles Dutton. Thus, as his singular playwriting process attests, Wilson invested deeply in the concept notion of theatre as a living art dependent on the mechanisms of production and empowered by performance.

What makes examining the production of Wilson's work particularly significant comes from analyzing how the dynamics of race and politics play out in a given performance. Each of Wilson's plays is set at a critical juncture in the African American past—*Ma Rainey* at the particular moment of 1927 when the interest in rural country blues transitions to more urban stylings and sound—and each work comments on the racial circumstances of those times. Most notably, however, the play in production as it unfolds in the "performative now"—the moment of performance, regardless of when it is set—simultaneously speaks to the present racial climate as well as to the past. Consequently, the context in which the performance takes place impacts how that particular mounting of Wilson speaks and how audiences and critics understand it.

I will discuss the potential racial and political dynamics of Wilsonian performance by examining two of the most important revivals of plays from Wilson's twentieth-century cycle, the Bartlett Sher staging of *Joe Turner's Come and Gone* at the Lincoln Center in 2009 and the Ruben Santiago-Hudson production of *Jitney* on Broadway in 2017. Sher's staging of *Joe Turner* marks the first major US production of a Wilson work by a white director. Considering how adamantly Wilson spoke out about wanting a black director for the film *Fences*, this posthumous production by Sher reverberates with racial meanings well beyond the show itself. Black director Ruben Santiago-Hudson's *Jitney* represents the last of Wilson's ten-play cycle to appear on Broadway, and, as a result, critics and audience met the show with some degree of overdue reverence for the late, great August Wilson. In addition, the actor-turned-director Santiago-Hudson, who helped lead the effort to get *Jitney* to Broadway, has become the leading Wilson interpreter. Sher and Santiago-Hudson take distinctly dissimilar approaches to detailing Wilson's black history and capturing racial and social truths of these plays. Staged eight years apart, early in the respective terms of two very different US presidents, these productions and their reception were impacted by the informing presidential politics. Context proves a vital element; although cultural experience and racial privilege figure prominently in the critical response to both productions, the political contexts of their moments of production are vital to understanding their reception.

Obama comes to the theatre

A watershed moment in the development of August Wilson's theatre occurred in June 2009 when President Barack Obama and his wife Michelle Obama went to see white director Bartlett Sher's production of August Wilson's *Joe Turner's Come and Gone* at Lincoln Center. *Joe Turner* had originally appeared on Broadway in 1988 under the direction of famed black director Lloyd Richards, and it won that year's New York Drama Critics' Circle Award for best play. Keith Herbert and Matthew Chase proclaimed in *New York Newsday*, "The nation's first black president was in town for a date night with his wife Saturday night that included a play about the sons and daughters of newly freed slaves."[13] Set in the progressive era of 1911, as blacks began the great migration from the South to the North,

Joe Turner is the most metaphysical and nonrealistic play in Wilson's cycle of twentieth-century plays. Accordingly, it is a challenge for any director. It was the author's favorite play, and scholars have repeatedly reexamined its assertion of the African presence in America, its articulations of the power of the spirit, and its representation of ritual observances and spiritual rebirth. Thus, the fact that the president of the United States and the First Lady went on a date night to a production of *Joe Turner* brought increased publicity and public awareness to this revival and to its celebrated African American playwright. After all, this was still the honeymoon period for America's first black president and the early height of his international popularity. Obama's attendance functioned, then, as an official affirmation of the value and vibrancy of Wilson's drama and of black theatre more generally.

Joe Turner, race, and culture

At the same time, even as Obama's date night at *Joe Turner* sanctioned the Lincoln Center revival, it also pointed to the complex nature of blackness, as well as the layered signification and often problematic ramifications of this production for black theatre. The play, the playwright, and the president represent an illuminating triad: Obama, the son of an African and white American, attending a play by the son of a white German baker and an African American woman, which attempts to foreground the Africanness still resonant in African American life. Both Wilson and Obama, despite their mixed heritage, have proudly identified as black. In so doing, they testify to blackness not as a fixed entity but as a product of social construction and lived experience. Yet, the fact that a white director mounted this particular production of *Joe Turner* raises important issues about the cultural transmission of blackness and the production of August Wilson. Notably, in the late 1980s, Wilson refused to let his Pulitzer Prize–winning play, *Fences* (1986), become a Hollywood film without a black director. He outlined his rationale for this decision in an essay entitled, "I Want a Black Director." "No wonder I had been greeted with incredulous looks when I suggested a black director for *Fences*. I sat in the office of Paramount Pictures suggesting that someone who was affected by an undesirable condition, who was a violator of public regulations, who was sullen, unqualified, and marked by a malignant influence, direct the film."[14] Wilson's ironic comments reflect his sense of the pejorative values attached to black people in Hollywood. He desired a black director who would have cultural familiarity with and sensitivity to the material, but who would also help to rebalance the unequal politics of representation in American film and media.[15] As Michael Awkward writes,

> Of preeminent importance to the playwright, I believe is whether, given the preeminence of caucacentric discourse and actions in our nation, Afro-Americans can afford to allow patterns of expressive cultural distribution to continue wherein blacks remain pawns to the whims and racialist will of white entrepreneurial forces interested primarily in economic bottom lines rather than in working to destroy the still-evident barriers to social, economic and cultural power for a large portion of the black population.[16]

Awkward maintains that Wilson's demand for a black director serves as an act of resistance against the dominant racial hierarchy that limits black social and cultural agency. Yet, some have argued that with the changing perceptions of race in the age of Obama, such political stands as Wilson's are no longer necessary. In the years since Wilson's death in 2005, the number of white directors who have staged his work has steadily increased. In fact, Wilson's white assistant directed Wilson's own final one-man show, *How I Learned What I Learned*, performed in 2004 at the Seattle Repertory Theatre. Still, the selection of Sher to mount the highly visible 2009 New York revival of *Joe Turner* caused considerable unrest in black theatre circles. Marion McClinton, who had directed New York productions of later Wilson works, such as *Jitney* in 2000 and *King Hedley II* in 2001, called the decision "straight up institutional racism."[17] McClinton's reaction points to the continuing system of white control over cultural production that determines access to directing opportunities for him and other black directors.

Sher, in accepting the assignment of directing *Joe Turner*, consciously sought to respond to the existing racial climate, as well as to the racial politics at play in his selection. Discussing the play with the *New York Times*, Sher—the 2008 Tony Award and Drama Desk Award winner for the Broadway revival of Rodgers and Hammerstein's *South Pacific*—asserted the relevance of Wilson's classic set in 1911 to the United States in 2009: "Every show I do has to speak to the times."[18] In fact, in the same interview, Sher relates his decision to direct *Joe Turner* to the election of Barack Obama. Journalist Mike Glitz writes, "The finale [of *Joe Turner*] is bloody and wrenching but somehow hopeful, with the characters stepping out of the darkness of slavery into an unknown future filled with danger, but at least the possibility of something better. After eight years of Bush, that's where Sher sees America: shaking off a terrible period and facing East."[19] Notably, this comment moves the question of meaning within *Joe Turner* from the cultural specificity of African American experiences to an overall concern for the United States emerging from the reputed failures of the Bush regime and into the age of Obama.

One of the enduring qualities of Wilson's twentieth-century cycle has been Wilson's ability to find cross-cultural commonality by exploring the specific details of his black characters at very particular historical moments. Throughout his all too brief career, Wilson fiercely sought to celebrate and explore artistically the cultural particularity of African American experiences. This desire drove his early demand for a black director for the film version of *Fences*, as well as his proclamations for black theatre made in his now-famous 1996 speech to the Theatre Communications Group. In this talk, "The Ground on Which I Stand," Wilson relates his own toils within the American theatre to the historic struggles of African Americans for freedom and equality:

> I have come here today to make a testimony, to talk about the ground on which I stand and all the many grounds on which I and my ancestors have toiled, and the ground of theatre on which my fellow artists and I have labored to bring forth its fruits, its daring and its sometimes liberating and healing truths.[20]

Reimagining the paradigms of cultural nationalism, Wilson links the ground of the American theatre with the ancestral ground of African American labor. It is this distinctive past, the efforts of his black forebears, that informs his dramaturgy.

And yet, Sher lacked the specificity of cultural experiences and cultural knowledge that Wilson championed. In order to compensate, Sher depended on the cultural knowledge of his black cast. Revealingly, he notes, "I've learned more from this cast than any group that I've ever worked with."[21] LaTanya Richardson Jackson, who played Bertha, remarks in an interview, "And from the start he was so collaborative. He would say, 'I know this,' and we would say, 'Yeah, but you don't know this . . .' As directors go, he was an amazing listener."[22] Sher sought the cast's assistance with moments such as the powerful spiritual Juba Dance, steeped in African American tradition and African retentions, that ends act one. Yet, is such dramaturgical advice enough? If listening functions as recompense for intimate cultural awareness, then what is potentially lost in this dramatic equation?

Sher and the critics

Interestingly, the New York critical establishment raved about Sher's interpretation. The play was nominated for six Tony awards, including best director, and won two. In a long, glowing review, Ben Brantley writes in the *New York Times*:

> Yet the revival of August Wilson's "Joe Turner's Come and Gone," a drama of indisputable greatness, feels positively airborne. Much of Bartlett Sher's splendid production, which opened Thursday night at the Belasco Theatre, moves with the engaging ease of lively, casual conversation. . . . It would be a shame if this production doesn't find a wide and enthusiastic audience. It's an (almost) unconditional pleasure to watch.[23]

Certainly, reviews such as this, coupled with the publicity that surrounded the Obamas' date night, helped the play to find "wide and enthusiastic audiences." Joe Dziemianowicz adds in the *New York Daily News*:

> Bartlett Sher seamlessly integrates realistic elements and the metaphoric, including the evocative set—fanciful floating windows with a so-real-you'd-pick-it vegetable garden. Sher has staged scenes that are dizzyingly powerful or beautiful (or both)—an ecstatic dance, a furious fit and a shimmering conclusion. But it's the compelling characters, superbly realized, that keep you rapt for 2 1/2 hours.[24]

Both Dziemianowicz and Brantley emphasize the collective appeal of Sher's production and of Wilson's text. They effusively place *Joe Turner* among the great works within the American dramatic canon. Brantley opines, "And, yes, in both soliloquies you hear Mr. Wilson's America lifting its voice in song." What does such strong praise portend for Wilson and black theatre more generally? To be sure, Wilson's work belongs among the celebrated works of American theatre history. Yet, such exalted status should not be at the expense of his drama's cultural particularity. Accordingly, Wilson, in his

Theatre Communications Group (TCG) speech, does not call for a separate black theatre, but rather, asserts: "We are not separatists. . . . We are artists who seek to develop our talents and give expression to our personalities. We bring advantage to the common ground that is American theatre" (TCG Speech, 73). The advantage to which Wilson refers comes to black artists not in spite of their black experiences and black specificity, but rather, because of it. Instead of essentializing black theatre and black artists, for Wilson, such assertions respond to the cultural particularity of the dominant culture that has delimited and devalued black cultural production.

The politics of representation

Evident in the selection of Sher to direct *Joe Turner* and the subsequent production are particularly racialized politics of representation. One could imagine celebrating the *Joe Turner* revival marked by the Obamas' attendance as a triumph for black theatre, opening it up to wider interpretation by an award-winning, critically acclaimed director, rather than limiting the possibility of directing Wilson only to blacks. Mike Glitz, in his interview with Sher, strikes a note seemingly for democracy and antidiscrimination in defending Sher's right to direct Wilson's work. "Aren't the plays just too good? Wouldn't any director bridle at NOT being allowed to tackle one of America's greatest playwrights?" "Exactly," he (Sher) says. Yet, present in Glitz's comment is a veiled white paternalism: Wilson is "too good" to be left just to the hands of black directors. Moreover, he ignores the fact that in the American theatre, it is not so much a matter of who would want to direct but who has access and agency to mount a production. Sher did ask and receive permission to direct the play from Wilson's widow, Costanza Romero. As executor of the Wilson estate, Romero believes her responsibility is to keep Wilson's work in the public eye. "My work is to get these stories out there . . . and to help ensure that audiences walk out of the plays with a deeper understanding for these American stories and for the ways our cultures intertwine."[25] Yet even more than Romero's consent, what enabled Sher to direct the revival was the fact that Andre Bishop, the producer of the Lincoln Center Theater, selected Sher, a resident director at Lincoln Center. The white-controlled theatrical hierarchy that Wilson railed against some fifteen years earlier was very much still in place. The Lincoln Center power structure determined how, when, and by whom *Joe Turner* would be reproduced.

And yet, in 2009 the dynamics of race in the United States most certainly had evolved. A black president had been only a dream just two years previously. Echoing such sentiment, Sher, in rationalizing his decision to direct the play, tells Glitz that while he respects Wilson's earlier position on a black director, "times [have] changed."[26] The idea he expresses is that because race is no longer of the same consequence, whites should have more license to direct black work. Romero voices similar sentiment in explaining her decision to grant Sher permission: "It's the quality of the work that matters now."[27] If the choice of Sher to direct *Joe Turner* truly serves as evidence that the racialized politics of representation in the United States have changed and white directors could, and should, now produce the plays of black playwrights, then logically, the converse should be equally true. Black directors should have more opportunities to stage the works of nonblack playwrights. Invariably, however, the only time that white theatre producers have called on black directors is to mount one black show in their season, often one of Wilson's plays. Kenny Leon, who directed the Broadway productions of Wilson's *Gem of the Ocean* and *Radio Golf* as well as the 2006 revival of Lorraine Hansberry's *A Raisin in the Sun*, laments that Broadway lacks "a level playing field." According to Leon, "I have to work with my agent to remind people that, yes, I direct comedies, I do musicals, I do plays about all races of people just like other directors do."[28] Leon's comments reflect an unequal distribution of power that is still operative within the American theatre.

My point here is not to suggest that white directors should never direct black theatre, just as I would not deny black, Asian, and Latino directors the opportunity to stage Henrik Ibsen or William Shakespeare. Rather, my point is to draw attention to the politics of representation and to consider how, within this equation, race in 2009 American theatre still matters.

Jitney in the times of Trump

While the attendance by the then president Barack Obama provides important context for interpreting the Sher production of *Joe Turner's Come and Gone*, the opening of the Broadway revival of *Jitney* just following the surprising 2016 election of Donald Trump provides for new understandings of the politics of performance present in the 2017 production directed by Ruben Santiago-Hudson. With bombast and bravado, Trump's campaign produced an atmosphere conducive to intensified racial stratification and unrest, and blacks and other people of color have felt more alienated from systems of power as a result. Only 8 percent of black voters voted for the new president, and the phrase and movement "Black Lives Matter" have continued to gain prominence under Trump's presidency. Notably, this racial resistance has prompted equally vocal opposition by some right-wing white observers, including some followers of the new president.

Evident in this production of *Jitney* under the reign of Trump is a championing of everyday black lives in the face of white racism and neglect. As Brantley astutely observes,

> The mantra "Black lives matter" seems addressed as much to obliviousness as to hostility within the white establishment. And it's hard not to flinch when, in "Jitney," an older taxi driver advises a young colleague: "You just have to shake off that 'white folks is against me' attitude. Hell, they don't even know you're alive."[29]

In this play set in the 1970s, Becker and his troupe of drivers operate out of an illegal gypsy cab stand in the Hill District of Pittsburgh outside of the immediate control and oppression of the white power structure, because the white-owned Yellow Cabs, which have a monopoly on legal transport in Pittsburgh, would not come to these black areas at that time. Thus, Becker's gritty determination to protect his black-owned business, as well as his stance against the city's plan for urban renewal, seems all the more relevant at a time when the president campaigned on a racially divisive platform.

The critical responses to the Broadway production of *Jitney* also suggest nostalgia for an earlier time, as did the campaign of Trump. Reflecting a racially insensitive longing for the past, President Trump proclaimed from the campaign trail onward that he would "Make America Great Again." His phrase evokes the memory of the late president Ronald Reagan's harkening back to the notion of "Morning in America." In both cases, the desire for a purportedly better past fails to recognize that for African Americans, these were not better times but times of segregation and greater inequality. The melancholy expressed around *Jitney* takes a rather different turn, as it reflects on the resilience of the characters in the face of racially charged times. According to Robert Khan of NBC,

> During the age in which "Jitney" transpires, legal racism may no longer be permitted, but city power brokers are indifferent to the idea of black prosperity. Wilson's vehicle is a group of men driving

second-class cars, but tired of being treated like second-class citizens. The MTC's [Manhattan Theatre Club] ensemble does a glorious job bringing home that message.[30]

Yet, there is not simply a critical appreciation of the characters' determined survival in the face of limited circumstances, but a celebration of and palpable longing for Wilson and a reverent posthumous praise not simply for the production, but also for the rightful place on Broadway of the only play from the twentieth-century cycle without a Broadway production. Thus, the title of Harry Haun's review in the *New York Observer* reads, "At Long Last, August Wilson's 'Jitney' Pulls into Broadway."[31]

Jitney and the critics

The revival of *Jitney* and its debut on Broadway earned virtually universal praise as a largely underappreciated gem from the Wilson canon. At a running time of only two-and-a-half hours, *Jitney* is decidedly shorter than other Wilson plays. His most naturalistic work, it flows with vibrant humor and readily accessible action. Accordingly, critics recognized that its entertainment value alone should easily make it one of the most crowd pleasing of the cycle. Notably, the *New York Times*'s Brantley responded quite differently to the Broadway debut in 2017 than to the off-Broadway production in 2000. In both the earlier and later reviews, Brantley praises Wilson's genius and acknowledges that *Jitney* was the work in which "Wilson said he found his voice as a dramatist." In fact, he uses virtually the same line in both reviews. Yet in the 2000 review, Brantley goes on to say that

> It [*Jitney*] still hasn't found its perfect shape. Its sentimental ending feels hammered on, with the nails showing, and a couple of the work's pivotal confrontations have a whiff of assembly-line melodrama. . . . By Wilson standards "Jitney" is slim on plot. It is a rare work from this author that introduces a loaded gun, as this one does, and then doesn't use it.[32]

Thus, in this review Brantley identifies *Jitney* as a minor early work from the master, written principally when Wilson was young and still developing his craft.

In contrast, Brantley writes in 2017:

> "Jitney" is also the work, Wilson said, in which he found his voice as a dramatist, one that borrowed from the musical traditions of blues and jazz, transliterated into spoken dialogue and monologues of Shakespearean eloquence. It is a language that makes lives perceived as marginal not only visible but monumental.[33]

Here, Brantley speaks in reverential terms, honoring Wilson's use of language and comparing him to Shakespeare. Later in the review, Brantley associates Wilson with another "great American dramatist," Arthur Miller. What has changed for Brantley in these seventeen years between *Jitney* viewings? Perhaps one difference is the quality of Santiago-Hudson's production versus Marion McClinton's, but Brantley is also clearly influenced by the context in which his viewing takes place. Brantley writes his later review after Wilson has completed the whole cycle, has become the first African American playwright to have a Broadway theatre named after him, and has passed away. These circumstances structure a very different atmosphere in which to appreciate and respond to this work by Wilson.

Ruben Santiago-Hudson and the real

The perceived authenticity of the production, and the fact that established Wilsonian director Ruben Santiago-Hudson staged the production, also impacted its reception. In contrast to Sher, Santiago-Hudson, in addition to having directed and acted in Wilson plays, had the blessing of the playwright himself. At the time of the Broadway production of *Jitney*, Santiago-Hudson had acted or directed nine of the ten plays in the cycle. As an actor, he won a Tony Award for his performance as Canewell in the 1996 production of Wilson's *Seven Guitars*, and he played Caesar in the original Broadway production of *Gem of the Ocean* in 2004, a role that Wilson even created with him in mind. Wilson's wife and executor, Costanza Romero, also selected him to play Wilson in the solo memoir production, *How I Learned What I Learned*, at the Signature Theatre in 2013. This role had previously been performed only by Wilson himself. It was first performed in 2003, and, notably, in 2004, Santiago-Hudson became a director at Wilson's insistence. "I turned director simply because he [Wilson] told me I needed to be directing his stuff. . . . That's why when

I closed in *Gem of the Ocean* [on Broadway], I went and directed a version of it for the McCarter."[34]

With this background, Santiago-Hudson now stands as perhaps the leading interpreter of Wilson's work. Moreover, as with the famous relationship between renowned director Jose Quintero and Nobel Prize–winning playwright Eugene O'Neill, Santiago-Hudson's directorial vision has been indelibly yoked to Wilson. To be sure, other directors have worked closely with Wilson after he and Lloyd Richards parted ways following *Seven Guitars* (1996), including Marion McClinton, who directed the Broadway production of *King Hedley II* (2001), and Kenny Leon, who directed the Broadway productions of *Gem of the Ocean* (2004) and *Radio Golf* (2007) as well as the revival of *Fences* with Denzel Washington 2010). Still, Santiago-Hudson seems to be the heir apparent.

His selection to direct *Jitney* did not evoke any backlash from other black directors as there was with the choice of Sher for *Joe Turner*. In his review, David Rooney notes of *Jitney*, "Actor-turned-director Ruben Santiago-Hudson's natural feel for the plays of August Wilson yields a superb production of this final work in the late dramatist's landmark ten-part cycle to make it to Broadway." But even as he tries to praise Santiago-Hudson's affinity for Wilson, Rooney's invocation of "natural feel" has a racialized tinge and patronizing quality to it—recalling how white sports announcers in the 1970s and 1980s often contrasted black inherent or "natural" abilities with white ingenuity and hard work. "Natural feel" suggests an instinctual, even blood connection to the work, denying the rigor of Santiago-Hudson's training and critical investment in interpreting the work. Rooney continues, "Since the passing of Wilson's longtime directing collaborator, Lloyd Richards, in 2006, Santiago-Hudson has taken impressive steps to continue the legacy."[35]

Santiago-Hudson and cultural affinity

Santiago-Hudson does, however, claim a racial and cultural affinity as an important foundation for directing *Jitney*. He said of the characters in the play:

I know these *Jitney* people intimately. . . . I know the textures of their clothes they wore. I know the smell that came from their lips after they put down a bottle of ginger flavored brandy. I know these guys. So to hear and feel and spend time with them is just a glorious thrill for me. That's what I love about the play—the familiarity, the warmth, the comfort these people bring me.[36]

Sher uses his distance to interpret the experience of the characters in *Joe Turner*, and he relies on the knowledge of his actors to shape his directorial approach. Santiago-Hudson, on the other hand, professes a profound and tactile intimacy with the characters in *Jitney* and their world. They are real to him, and this realness informs his choices and approach as a director. His comments sound not unlike those of Wilson, who often spoke of characters, such as Aunt Ester, as coming alive and speaking to him as he wrote. Notably, Santiago-Hudson's words suggest that directing the play for him is not about breathing life into the characters or enabling their work and meaning, but rather, that closely interacting with these people of the play is enabling and affirming for him.

Yet, even with this claim of kinship with the characters, for Santiago-Hudson as well as his cast, realness is actually constructed on and through the performance. Early in his career, in auditioning for Richards and Wilson, Santiago-Hudson came to understand that as a Wilsonian actor, in order to be "real" onstage, he needed to be artificial:

I auditioned for Lloyd and August four or five times, with no success. Then, right before auditioning for "Two Trains Running," I saw a show on public television about Wilson that had some clips of Charles Dutton, who had done a ton of Wilson's plays. When I saw those grand broad gestures he'd use, I realized there was a sort of theatricality that I wasn't doing.[37]

Santiago-Hudson discovered an important fundamental principle in acting Wilson, the realism, or perhaps authenticity, on stage upon capturing a certain theatricality. Thus, even as Wilson's characters speak in an "authentic" black dialogue, patterns of language and certain phrasings repeat and are particular to him. There is a rhythm and lyricism specific to Wilson that requires theatrical acumen. As evidenced by Santiago-Hudson's initial unsuccessful audition, not all black actors possessed this skill.

Interestingly, Santiago-Hudson selected the renowned, classically trained actor John Douglas Thompson to play the part of Becker in the revival of *Jitney*. Notably, handling iambic pentameter and making the dialogue both natural and theatrical were complimentary, not antithetical, to acting in Wilson. Critic Alexis Soloski proclaimed Thompson "a majestic actor, who viscerally absorbs the playwright's singular language."[38] Thompson himself articulates a difference he sees between his classical work and that of acting in Wilson:

> In some other plays—let's say *A Doll's* House—this writer didn't write it for me. I'm thankful I get to play those roles and I studied and trained to be a classical actor so that I could handle the breadth of the work. But when I encounter August Wilson, I'm assured he's saying, "I wrote this specifically for you. These words will fit you. This character will fit you. These are members of your community."[39]

Although Thompson's remarks evidence how Wilson's dramaturgy celebrates a specifically black reality, it must be noted that Wilson reaches this black reality through his penetrating art. Wilson's ability to paint African American experiences in his selectively distinct portraits in time validates and animates a resonant history of African Americans, a history that is at once personal and representative. Thus, Thompson's comments, as well as those of Santiago-Hudson, reflect the complex and continuous interaction of cultural history, racial identity, and personal identification in Wilson's work, and more specifically in *Jitney*. The characters are not literally members of Thompson's neighborhood, nor did Wilson write this play literally for him. Yet, in the powerful, figurative, space of representation, Wilson's construction of these characters, the "people" that Santiago-Hudson knows so well, can generate for those bearing witness not only racial pride but also identification with and even claims of racial privilege. For Santiago-Hudson and his cast, this racial connection serves their commitment and approach to the work.

David Gallo's set

The set designed by David Gallo, who also created the set for the 2000 off-Broadway production, equally foregrounds this relationship between the real and the representational. On the one hand, the backdrop of the set, the skyline of Pittsburgh's Hill District, functions as a pastiche of photographs inspired by the art work and cut-and-paste aesthetic of fellow Pittsburgh visual artist Romare Bearden. Bearden and his collages of black life served as a key influence on Wilson and his artistic creation. In a "Foreword" to a collection of Bearden's work, Wilson acknowledges, "In Bearden I found my artistic mentor and sought, and still aspire, to make my plays the equal of his canvases."[40] On the other hand, the backdrop of historical photos of the Pittsburgh Hill locates the play in time and place. The backdrop, therefore, is at once art and artifice. It does not mimetically reproduce the past, but rather, impressionistically captures the cultural climate of 1970s Pittsburgh.

The set design incorporates elements that are historically faithful but also fully employs the artistry of stagecraft to create an environment that evokes the period and also serves the needs of the story. With detail and dimensionality, large windows that wrap around the set to reveal the sloping Pittsburgh Hill District outside are the most important scenic element for Gallo. Gallo notes that in the actual Hill District, "there is no place that one can stand and claim it is level ground as it's always going up and down."[41] And Gallo's set mirrors this unevenness, as he positions the fictive jitney station on a slope and rakes the floor of the station to give the effect that this station is actually cut into the side of the hill.[42] Two beat-up old cars sit beyond the office doors, a 1966 Ford Falcon and a 1976 Chevy Nova. At once real and artificial, these two vehicles—created by craftsman Greg Merrigan, who purchased the actual cars, hollowed them out, and took them apart before putting them back together in an effort to make them stageworthy—serve the realistic detail of the setting as well as the action of the play. Gallo notes that both Wilson and Santiago-Hudson wanted "to see bits of cars and remind the audience what cars were like in the 1970s."[43] Santiago-Hudson also used the cars in the action of the play. The character Youngblood, a returned Vietnam veteran, works on these cars at different moments in the play. According to Gallo, "the cars reflect the reality of the situation for the residents of Pittsburgh back then."[44] Keeping their cars operational served as a critical element of survival.

In addition, the flyers and other objects that hang on the wall, as well as the wall paint, are all theatrically "distressed" to provide the illusion not simply of being of that time period but of signifying a building that has been in use and has served different occupants over time. As Gallo explains, "We would use different markers to age it depending upon how long we thought the object had been on the wall. Then we put another object and new vintage than that on top of that, and we put more paint . . . A lot of layers and a lot of history. Everything on the stage is about history."[45] Yet, this history is made present through the magic of theatre, as the set design is about not simply accurately recreating the past but also reflecting Gallo's aesthetic vision. Accordingly, the fleur-de-lis wallpaper selected by Gallo, while true to the period, is not so much true to the shop but particular to

David Gallo's artistic design. It is not the wallpaper's appropriateness but its uncommonness that attracts the designer. According to Gallo, "It's [the wallpaper] incredibly rare. I've seen it in real life once and in research twice, so that's good enough to use it."[46] Thus, the wallpaper, the sloping stage, the hollowed-out "stageworthy" cars and other scenic elements are all part of an artistic composition. At the same time, through their theatricality, through their representation, they remember the past and provide the audience with access to an earlier black reality.

The set design also directly assists the actors in their processes of representing the past. The set contains realistic detail that cannot be seen by the audience but rather, is visible only to the cast. Attached to the period refrigerator are a 1976 *Sports Illustrated* image of Pittsburgh Pirates pitcher Dock Ellis, two images of the Pirates' black star and emotional leader Willie Stargell, and a logo of Iron City Beer, a 156-year-old Pittsburgh icon, as well as one for the Red Bull Inn, a chain that once had more than twenty locations in Pennsylvania and surrounding environs.[47] These markers of historic time, unobserved by the audience, who are just too far away, help to situate the actors and to ground their performances. To support their ability to inhabit the historical past in the present, cast members, such as Andre Holland, who portrays Youngblood, also engage in preshow routines that stimulate their historical recuperation. Holland relates that before each show, "I have a playlist of music from the era, and we have a bunch of old *Ebony* and *Essence* magazines that I'll flip through. And I always carry James Baldwin's nonfiction *The Price of the Ticket* with me."[48] Notably, Baldwin's 1985 nonfiction collection of essays speaks with unapologetic determination, insight, and resolve to pressing issues of race and identity in the United States. Holland uses this text as his own personal mimetic prop to fuel and inspire his portrayal of Youngblood's tenacity and spirit of resistance.

Wilson and personal history

Jitney in performance operates also as a testament to the power of Wilson's own personal history. Inspired in the early 1980s by his wife at the time, Judy Oliver, and living in St. Paul, Minnesota, Wilson originally wrote *Jitney* to explain to her about jitney cabs in Pittsburgh and why he had not learned how to drive. When Wilson returned to the play in 1996 for a production at the Pittsburgh Public Theater, it was now different stylistically from the body of work he had amassed as he had evolved as a playwright. The actor

Anthony Chisolm, who performed in the play back then and also in the off-Broadway and Broadway productions, explains,

> It only ran an hour and a half, then, and during rehearsals, one of the actors—Willis Burk—said to August, "No one is going to recognize this as an August Wilson play." "Why's that?" August asked. "Because there are no monologs in it," Willis said. So August started writing another hour and 45 minutes on top of the hour and a half we started with.[49]

Interestingly, Willis challenged Wilson's own authenticity as a playwright: *Jitney* couldn't be a Wilson play because it didn't have any of his soaring monologues. So, Wilson added some to legitimize the work and make it more recognizably his own. Yet, in creating these monologues, Wilson disrupted the integrity of the singular playtext and the temporality of the cycle as he appropriated and redistributed monologues and stories that were initially in another play in the cycle and worked them into *Jitney*. According to Santiago-Hudson, "There are literally 30 to 40 minutes of this play taken directly from *Seven Guitars*—mostly from Canewell, the role I played. August split' em up with different actors. What he did by dissecting a couple of monologues and passing them around to give everyone a taste of the meal, I thought, was brilliant."[50] Certainly ingenious, Wilson's redeployment represents a form of signifying on himself, repeating and revising his own work. Yet, it disrupts the linearity of time; Wilson removes monologues from a play of 1946 and puts them in a play of the 1970s.

At the same time as this process seems to negate the integrity of the work, the singular narrative of *Jitney*, it reaffirms a collective history of the Hill District. As Chisholm explains,

> All these characters live in the Hill District, and they're interconnected in many ways. It's a neighborhood, so, as August would dramaturge his plays during city after city of rehearsals and performances, he would literally take stuff out and save it and stick it in another play.[51]

With such repurposing of monologues, Wilson keeps a consciousness of the cycle as a whole, the larger project behind the individual play. Moreover, Wilson ultimately reaffirms the interconnectedness of the characters in the completion of his history cycle, as the figures in *Radio Golf* in 1997 are actually related to those of *Gem of the Ocean* in 1904.

By way of conclusion

The Sher and Santiago-Hudson revivals of *Joe Turner* and *Jitney* evidence the lasting power of Wilson's art and ideas. In fact, Denzel Washington, with assistance from Santiago-Hudson and backing from HBO, plans to bring the entire ten-play cycle to television. In addition, as racial politics in this country evolve, they will have a continued impact on the staging of the pieces and their reception. Race will also affect how and where the cycle gets produced. While Wilson is coming to television, the space and places for black work at regional theatres across the country still remain limited. The mechanisms of production, the control over venues, budgets, and artistic selections, are, for the most part, not in black hands. The precarious situation that August Wilson decries for black theatre in "The Ground on Which I Stand" persists.

Such concerns have most certainly influenced both Sher's *Joe Turner* and Santiago-Hudson's *Jitney*, even as these directors and their design teams found decidedly different strategies for interpreting the truth and meaning in these plays. The realism and period detail of the *Jitney* set stand in sharp contrast to Michael Yeargan's design for Bartlett Sher's production of *Joe Turner*. Rather than creating a realistic environment for Seth and Bertha's 1911 boarding house, Yeargan removes all the walls and creates freestanding white windows and doors. This setting seeks to foreground the ethereal, otherworldly quality of *Joe Turner*, Wilson's most nonrealistic and spiritualistic play. In fact, at times, the settings disappear altogether, leaving a black empty space, reinforcing the existential qualities of Wilson's text and the questions that it raises about life. The design emphasizes the fact that the weary traveler Herald Loomis has suffered what Orlando Patterson terms "social death" at the hands of Joe Turner.[52] As Brantley describes it, Seth's boarding house in 1911, the environment for the action of the play, becomes "an island floating in mottled skies strobed by lightning."[53] The set becomes a metaphysical space rather than a realistic location.

To be sure, there is risk in such an approach, for the play's setting in 1911, a time just fifty years after slavery, is critical to situating the spiritual journey of the protagonist, Herald Loomis, and his vision of the Middle Passage—"Bones people walking on water." Similarly, by grounding their production too deeply in the specifics of Pittsburgh in the 1970s, Santiago-Hudson and Gallo would equally risk losing the enduring nature of the confrontation between father and son, Becker and Booster, at the center of the play. This play, like all those in the Wilson cycle, operates both inside and outside of time. Wilson's metaphysics are rooted in exploration of the real, firmly connected to the personal histories he details over each decade. As seen with the revivals of *Joe Turner* and *Jitney*, productions of Wilson's cycle can illuminate and explore this relationship between the real and the metaphysical, between art and social circumstance, all while still connecting to our present moment in profound ways.

NOTES

Introduction

1 Two Pulitzer Prizes, five New York Drama Critics Circle Awards, two Drama Desk Awards, and one Tony.

Chapter 1

1 Jackson R. Bryer and Mary C. Hartig, eds., *Conversations with August Wilson* (Jackson: University of Mississippi Press, 2006), 47. Subsequent citations in the text.

2 Christopher Bigsby, "An Interview with August Wilson," in *The Cambridge Companion to August Wilson,* edited by Christopher Bigsby (Cambridge: Cambridge University Press, 2007), 205–6. Subsequent citations in text.

Chapter 2

1 Alan Nadel, *Invisible Criticism: Ralph Ellison and the American Canon* (Iowa City, IA: University of Iowa Press, 1988), xiii.

2 J. L. Austin developed this distinction in *Speech Acts.*

3 John Timpane has explained exactly how details, circumstances, and perspectives enable Troy and Cory to construct inimical histories.

4 David LaCroix discussed at length the uses of time in *Radio Golf.*

5 Michel de Certeau, *The Practice of Everyday Life*, translated by Steven Rendell (Berkeley: University of California Press, 2002).

6 Ralph Ellison, *Invisible Man* (New York: Random House, 1983), 333.

7 Ibid.

8 Ibid.

9 Forum discussing the implications of this controversial speech can be found in *Theater* (vol. 27, 2 and 3), 5–41.

10 August Wilson, *The Ground on Which I Stand* (New York: Theatre Communications Group, 2001), 33.

11 Ibid., 16.

12 Ibid., 14.

Notes

13 Ibid., 17.

14 August Wilson, *Two Trains Running* (New York: Plume Books, 1993), 31.

15 Ibid, 34.

16 August Wilson, *The Piano Lesson* (New York: Plume Books, 1990).

Chapter 3

1 The extensive cross-play connections between characters and sites is extensively detailed by Mary Ellen Snodgrass. See also Glasco and Rawson.

2 See Glasco and Rawson.

3 Kim Pereira, *August Wilson and the African American Odyssey* (Champagne-Urbana: University of Illinois Press, 1995), 10.

4 Alan Nadel, "Introduction," in *May All Your Fences Have Gates: Essays on the Drama of August Wilson*, edited by Alan Nadel (Iowa City: University of Iowa Press, 1994), 5.

5 A passage from the Introduction to *May All Your Fences Have Gates* discussing the musical, rather than Aristotelean, understanding of resolution as informing Wilson's work was included in the program for the Goodman Theater production of *Seven Guitars*.

6 See Eileen Crawford, "The Bb Burden: The Invisibility of Ma Rainey's Black Bottom," in *August Wilson: A Casebook*, edited by Marilyn Elkins (New York: Garland, 1994), 31–48; Harry J. Elam, Jr., *The Past as Present in the Drama of August Wilson* (Ann Arbor: University of Michigan Press, 2004); Pereira, *August Wilson and the African American Odyssey*; John Timpane, "Filling the Time: Reading History in the Drama of August Wilson," in *May All Your Fences Have Gates: Essays on the Drama of August Wilson*, edited by Alan Nadel (Iowa City: University of Iowa Press, 1994); and Craig Werner, "August Wilson's Burden: The Function of Neo-Classical Jazz," in *May All Your Fences Have Gates: Essays on the Drama of August Wilson*, edited by Alan Nadel (Iowa City: University of Iowa Press, 1994), 21–50.

7 Sandra G. Shannon, "The Long Wait: August Wilson's *Ma Rainey's Black Bottom*," *Black American Literature Forum* 25, no. 1 (1991): 135–46, and Sandra Adell, "Speaking of Ma Rainey/Talking about the Blues," in *May All Your Fences Have Gates: Essays on the Drama of August Wilson*, edited by Alan Nadel (Iowa City: University of Iowa Press, 1994), 51–66.

Chapter 4

1 Edward Said, *Beginnings: Intention and Method* (New York: Columbia University Press, 1985), 6.

2 See Chapter 3.

3 August Wilson, *Fences* (New York: Plume, 1986), 9.

4 Thomas D. Morris, *Free Men All: The Personal Liberty Laws of the North, 1780–1861* (Union New Jersey: The Lawbook Exchange Ltd., 2001), 15.

5 Supreme Court, *Santa Clara County v. Southern Pac. r. Co.,* 118 U.S. 394 (1886).

6 One particularly ironic aspect of this legal trend is that the basis for treating a corporation, that is, property, as a person is the Fourteenth Amendment, which was designed to differentiate people from property. As David Korten points out: "The doctrine of corporate personhood creates an interesting legal contradiction. The corporation is owned by its shareholders and is therefore their property. If it is also a legal person, then it is a person owned by others and thus exists in a condition of slavery—a status explicitly forbidden by the Thirteenth Amendment to the Constitution. So is a corporation a person illegally held in servitude by its shareholders? Or is it a person who enjoys the rights of personhood that take precedence over the presumed ownership rights of its shareholders? So far as I have been able to determine, this contradiction has not been directly addressed by the courts." David Korten, *The Post-Corporate World: Life after Capitalism* (San Francisco, CA and West Hartford, CT: Berrett-Koehler Publishers and Kumarian Press, 1999), 268.

7 Mark Twain, *The Adventures of Huckleberry Finn*, ed. Guy Cardwell (New York: Penguin, 2002), 100.

8 David Krasner, "*Jitney*, Folklore and Responsibility," in *The Cambridge Companion to August Wilson*, ed. Christopher Bigsby (Cambridge: Cambridge University Press, 2007), 159.

9 See Eric Williams, *Capitalism and Slavery* (Chapel Hill, NC: University of North Carolina Press, 1944).

10 See also: Stephen Yafa, *Cotton: The Biography of a Revolutionary Fiber* (New York: Penguin Books, 2005); Gene Dattel, *Cotton and Race in the Making of America: The Human Costs of Economic Power* (Chicago: Ivan R. Dee, 2009); Walter Johnson, *River of Dark Dreams: Slavery and the Empire in the Cotton Kingdom* (Cambridge: Harvard University Press, 2013); Edward E. Baptist, *The Half That Has Never Been Told: Slavery and the Making of American Capitalism* (New York: Basic Books, 2014); Sven Beckert, *Empire of Cotton: A Global History* (New York: Alfred A. Knopf, 2015).

11 Krasner, "*Jitney*, Folklore and Responsibility," 160.

12 Harry Elam, Jr., *The Past as Present in the Drama of August Wilson* (Ann Arbor: University of Michigan Press, 2004), 84.

13 In chapter 1 of *Invisible Criticism* (Iowa City, IA: University of Iowa Press, 1991), I discuss the implications of the postbellum shift of surveillance and discipline of African Americans from the personal master to the impersonal state.

14 August Wilson, *Gem of the Ocean* (New York: Theater Communications Group, 2007), 33. Subsequent citations in text.

Notes

15 Sandra Adell, *Double Consciousness/Double Bind: Theoretical Issues in Twentieth-Century Black Literature* (Champagne-Urbana, IL: University of Illinois Press, 1994).

16 In actuality, the Lincoln penny was not minted until 1909, five years after the events of *Gem*. Nevertheless, it seems to me fruitful to read this as a Lincoln penny, making the reference to the penny one of Wilson's anachronisms, akin to his having the characters in *Seven Guitars* listen to the Joe Louis-Billy Conn fight, although neither of the two Louis-Conn fights took place in 1948.

17 August Wilson, *Jitney* (New York: Overlook, 2003), 11. Subsequent citations in text.

18 Ibid.

19 Ibid.

20 See Stephanie E. Smallwood, *Saltwater Slavery: The Middle Passage from Africa to American Diaspora* (Cambridge, MA: Harvard University Press, 2007).

Chapter 5

1 See Ira Berlin, *Slaves without Masters* (New York: Pantheon), 1970.

2 Michel de Certeau, *The Practice of Everyday Life*, translated by Steven Rendall (Berkeley: University of California Press, 1984), 186.

3 In *Ma Rainey*, in fact, Levee refers to it as the "Maxon-Dixon line" (82).

4 Wilson, *Fences*, 23. Subsequent citations in text.

5 Foucault examines the mental asylum (*Madness and Civilization*), the hospital (*The Birth of the Clinic*), and the prison (*Discipline and Punish*).

6 Wilson, *Joe Turner's Come and Gone* (New York: Plume Books, 1988), 5. Subsequent citations in text.

Chapter 6

1 Wilson, *The Piano Lesson*, 41. Subsequent citations in text.

2 To distinguish the Sutter who has just died (whose ghost haunts Berniece's home and from whom Boy Charles stole the piano) from his grandfather, Robert Sutter (who paid for the piano with Berniece's grandfather and great-grandmother), I will refer throughout to the younger Sutter as "Sutter" and the elder Sutter as "Robert Sutter."

3 Extensive scholarship on this issue, assembled generically under the rubric "critical race theory." See Patricia J. Williams, Richard Delgado and Jean Stefancic, and Kimberle Crenshaw et al.

4 Michelle Alexander demonstrates with convincing details how US penology replicates this process of forced black servitude in the post–Second World War period.

5 Douglas Blackmon, *Slavery by Another Name: The Re-Enslavement of Black Americans from the Civil War to World War II* (New York: Anchor Books, 2009), 7.

6 Ibid.

7 David Oshinsky. *Worse than Slavery: Parchman Farm and the Ordeal of Jim Crow Justice* (New York: Free Press, 1997), 2.

8 Elam (*Past*, 27–56) provides an extensive explanation of the role that music plays in Wilson's dramatic world. See also Werner.

9 This confusion/conflation is crucial to extensive debates about the origin and nature of the black church in America.

10 The same reason why the white man wants "to buy anything you can make music with" (35).

11 Michael Morales, "Ghosts on the Piano: August Wilson and the Representation of Black American History," in *May All Your Fences Have Gates: Essays on the Drama of August Wilson*, edited by Alan Nadel (Iowa City: University of Iowa Press, 1994), 109.

12 Tom Graves, *Crossroads: The Life and Afterlife of Blues Legend Robert Johnson* (Spokane: DeMers Books, 2008); see also Pete Welding, "Robert Johnson: Hell Hound on His Trail," in *Down Beat Music '66* (Chicago: Maher, 1966), 73–76, 103; Patricia R. Schroeder, *Robert Johnson, Mythmaking, and Contemporary American Culture* (Champaign-Urbana: University of Illinois Press, 2004).

13 This concept is crucial to understanding the structure of Wilson's drama. The reason why, out of all his plays, Wilson cared least for *Fences* was less a question of its quality than of its representing a notion of privilege inimical to the rest of the cycle. However much the community coalesces around Troy Maxson, and however much he is an agent of that coalition, Troy is the play's central figure. Its dramatic arc is the trajectory of his life from criminal and garbage man to the heroic figure who ascends dramatically from grave to heaven. Everywhere else in Wilson's cycle, communal energy derives from disparate goals, values, and beliefs, in the same way that a jazz jam session produces the kinds of resolution impossible to orchestrate in advance or dictate to members of the combo.

14 Morales, "Ghosts on the Piano," 110.

Chapter 7

1 James H. Cone, *Martin & Malcolm: A Dream or a Nightmare* (Maryknoll, NY: Orbis Books, 1991), 120. Subsequent citations in text.

2 See Glasco and Rowson; see also Tarr.

Notes

3 August Wilson, *Two Trains Running* (New York: Plume Books, 1993), 14. Subsequent citations in text.

4 Stephen Bottoms, "*Two Trains Running*: Blood on the Tracks," in *The Cambridge Companion to August Wilson*, edited by Christopher Bigsby (Cambridge: Cambridge University Press, 2007), 148.

5 Sandra G. Shannon, *The Dramatic Vision of August Wilson* (Washington, DC: Howard University Press, 1995), 190.

6 Sandra G. Shannon, "Turn Your Lamp Down Low!: Aunt Ester Dies in *King Hedley II*," in *August Wilson: Completing the Twentieth-Century Cycle*, edited by Alan Nadel (Iowa City: University of Iowa Press, 2010), 125.

7 Shannon, *Dramatic Vision*, 173.

8 See Mumford, Locke, and Herman.

9 See Chapter 4, footnotes 9 and 10.

10 Vivian Gist Spencer and Yvonne Chambers detail the ways in which Aunt Ester may be viewed as a Christ figure.

11 When he told me about these 1968 events, I asked him why he didn't set the play in 1968. He answered: "Too close."

12 As Bottoms notes: "There was a time when even Black Power radicals saw no equivalence between the struggles against racial and sexual oppression: Eldridge Cleaver spoke laughingly of women exercising 'pussy power', and [Stokely] Carmichael argued that the best position for women in the movement was 'prone'. For the scarred yet subtly defiant Risa, the feminist awakening of the 1970s cannot come too soon"; Christopher Bigsby, "An Interview with August Wilson," in *The Cambridge Companion to August* Wilson, edited by Christopher Bigsby (Cambridge: Cambridge University Press, 156).

13 Shannon, *Dramatic Vision*, 185.

Chapter 8

1 In light of Donald Pease's extensive reading of *Seven Guitars* and *King Hedley II* in the "Critical and Performance Perspectives" section of this book, this chapter, in order to avoid unnecessary repetition, is somewhat abbreviated.

2 August Wilson, *Seven Guitars* (New York: Plume Books, 1997), 13. Subsequent citations in the text.

3 This backyard is based on the backyard of the house at 1621 Bedford Avenue, in the Hill District of Pittsburgh. It was the last house in which Wilson's mother lived. See Glasco and Rowson, *August Wilson: Pittsburgh Places and His Life and Plays*, 68, 120.

4 August Wilson, *King Hedley II* (New York: Theater Communications Group, 2007), 85. Subsequent citations in text.

Chapter 9

1 The pioneering work on this topic is Jane Jacobs, *The Death and Life of Great American Cities* (New York: Random House, 1961). Gregory J. Crowley, *The Politics of Place: Contentious Urban Redevelopment in Pittsburgh* (Pittsburgh: University of Pittsburgh Press, 2005) focuses specifically on Pittsburgh; and Samuel Zipp's *Manhattan Projects: The Rise and Fall of Urban Renewal in Cold War New York* (New York and London: Oxford University Press, 2010), 157–252, discusses in detail the construction of the Lincoln Center. See also E. Michael Jones, *The Slaughter of Cities: Urban Renewal as Ethnic Cleansing* (South Bend, IN: St. Augustine Press, 2004).

2 Shannon notes that the two plays function as bookends, and in this context open up consideration of their connection to the other plays.

3 The term, which has been very widely written about, originates with Henry Luce's famous mid-century essay by that title; Henry Luce, "The American Century," *Life Magazine*, February 17, 1941: 61–65.

4 In *Television in Black-and-White America* (Lawrence, KS: Kansas University Press, 2006), I detail the crucial role that television played in creating a cohesive sense of place among the newly coalesced suburban population, for whom highways and driveways replaced common thoroughfares and public gathering places such as local shops, restaurants, bars, movie theatres, or town halls. In the 1950s and 1960s, for the only time in American history, those who owned television sets—the majority of the population—could simultaneously view the same image and hear the same news, creating a conceptual divide between the minority who did not own televisions as significant as the geographical divide between suburban and inner-city spaces.

5 Tom Lewis, *Divided Highways: Building the Interstate Highways, Transforming American Life* (New York: Penguin, 1997); Stephen B. Goddard, *Getting There: The Epic Struggle between Road and Rail in the American Century* (Chicago: University of Chicago Press, 1994).

6 August Wilson, *Radio Golf* (New York: Theater Communications Group, 2007), 16. Subsequent citations in text.

7 Ibid., 37.

8 Ellison, *Invisible Man*, 500.

9 Harry J. Elam, Jr., "*Radio Golf* in the Age of Obama," in *August Wilson: Completing the Twentieth-Century Cycle*, edited by Alan Nadel (Iowa City, IA: University of Iowa Press, 2010), 186–206, 189.

10 Ibid., 77.

11 Nothing in the text of *Fences* mentions Vietnam, but in the late 1990s I discussed this implication with Wilson, and he told me he would make the fact that Cory was Vietnam-bound more explicit in his planned screenplay.

Notes

Chapter 10

1 In order to distinguish King Hedley II from his father, King Hedley, throughout the chapter, I will refer, as is most commonly done in the scripts of the plays, to the father as Hedley and the son as King.

2 Sandra Shannon drew August Wilson into the following elaboration of the presences of the ancestors from the Middle Passage within the bodies of American Africans: "Loomis's connection with the ancestors—the Africans who were lost during the Middle Passage and were thrown overboard. They are walking around here now and they look like you because you are these very same people. This is who you are" (13). Shannon went on to explain the ghostly revenant of Joseph Sutter in *The Piano Lesson* as a manifestation of what I have called the Lazarus complex: "On another level his ghost exemplifies the looming threat of the white power structure."

3 Orlando Patterson, *Slavery and Social Death: A Comparative Study* (Cambridge, MA: Harvard University Press, 1982), 5.

4 Shannon supplied the emancipatory aspirations of Wilson's characters with historical warrant: "In the face of the South's changing status, many freedmen opted to start a new life in one of the several northern cities and thus escape their history as slaves" (13).

5 Wilson was careful to distinguish the poetic figures within his plays from the sociohistorical referents:

> From the beginning I decided not to write about historical events in the pathologies of the black community. The details of our struggle to survive and prosper in what has been a difficult and somewhat bitter relationship with the system of laws and practices that deny us access to the tools necessary for productive and industrious lives are available to any serious student of history or sociology. (*King Hedley II*, viii)

6 In an interview with Herbert Boyd, Wilson described the plot of *King Hedley II* in terms of the disintegration of the family: "So a community under assault begins to take care of itself. It's not so much a breakdown of the family in the play, but a break with the tradition of the extended family. It's the connection with the grandparents that is broken that causes many of the problems in the community" (*Conversations*, 237).

7 In a preceding passage, Hedley explained that his father named him King because that was his nickname for Buddy Bolden:

> My father play the trumpet and for him Buddy Bolden was a God, he was in New Orleans with the boats when he make them run back and forth. The trumpet was his first love. He never forgot that first night he heard Buddy Bolden play. He drink his rum, play his trumpet, and if you were lucky that night he would talk about Buddy Bolden. I say lucky cause you never see him like that with his face light up and something be driving him from the inside and it was a thing he love more than my mother. That is why he named me King . . . after King Buddy Bolden. (67)

8   Here is what Wilson has said about the misdirected aggression in this scene:

You see, if Buddy Bolden is bringing some money from Hedley's father, he represents his father's forgiveness. Also, Hedley is going to use the money to buy a plantation, not to get rich, but so the white man doesn't tell him what to do anymore, to become independent, land being the basis of independence. In a way, the play says that anyone who is standing in the way of a black man's independence needs to be dealt with. So it's very necessary that Hedley decides that Floyd, as Buddy Bolden, is the messenger, the courier who would like to keep the money, who will not give him the money so he can buy his plantation. It means it's a betrayal of Hedley's father. Of course the tragedy is he's not Buddy Bolden, that he's Floyd Barton. It's a mistake. It's an honorable mistake, but it is a mistake. (*Conversations*, 193–94)

9   Hedley's murder of Floyd Barton constituted a ritual reenactment of the rooster King Hedley had decapitated. King Hedley had earlier described the rooster as the sacred herald of the black Emancipation Day. Harry Elam has cited Wilson's description of the blues singers as sacred figures as evidence of this parallel: "I've always thought of them as sacred because of the sacred tasks they took upon themselves—to disseminate the information and carry those cultural values of the people" (Elam, 42).

10   King's mother, Ruby, recognized this aspect of Elmore:

Something always missing with him. There's always something he ain't got, he don't know what it is himself. If you gave it to him he wouldn't know he had it. I see him every four or five years, he come through and he always leave more trouble than when he came. Seem like he bring it with him and dump it off, he come and dump off that trouble and then he leave smelling sweet. (45)

11   I want to place my reading into dialogue with that of Harry Elam, who has written the most comprehensive analysis of the play: "Through presenting the machete to King, Stool Pigeon/Canewell closes the book on a cycle of black-on-black senseless violence and the personal trauma of suffering and blame that it causes them." I also agree with his claim that King is

literally the Chosen One who is sacrificed in order to prepare the way for the regeneration of the greater community, for the good of those who live on. His death is a repetition and revision of the sacrifice of the Christian Messiah on the cross who, according to doctrine, dies for the sins of mankind and whose blood is now ritualized as the Communion, blessing those who partake. King, too dies for our sins, and his death offers new life. As a ritualized act presided over by Stool Pigeon, King's sacrifice serves as a beacon of hope, promising a new tomorrow against the bleak backdrop of tragic loss and unfulfilled promise (87).

But I would not describe the figure who is sacrificed as Isaac. The Isaac in *King Hedley II* is liberated through Ruby's killing of the Lazarus figure in King.

12   Sandra L. Richards, "Writing the Absent Potential: Drama, Performance, and the Canon of African American Literature," in *Performance and Performativity*, edited by Andrew Parker and Eve Kosofsky Sedgwick (New York: Routledge, 1996), 83.

Notes

13 Keith Herbert and Matthew Chayes, "Obamas Come to New York to see Broadway Play," *New York Newsday*, May 30, 2009.

14 August Wilson, "I Want a Black Director," in *May All Your Fences Have Gates*, edited by Alan Nadel (Iowa City IO: University of Iowa Press, 1994), 203.

15 Ibid., 201.

16 Michael Awkward, "'The Crookeds with the Straights': *Fences*, Race and the Politics of Adaptation," in *May All Your Fences Have Gates*, edited by Alan Nadel (Iowa City IO: University of Iowa Press, 1994), 225.

17 Marion McClinton quoted by Patrick Healy, "Playwright's Race Adds to Drama for an August Wilson Revival," *New York Times*, April 23, 2009: A18.

18 Bartlett Sher quoted by Mike Glitz, "Theater: 'Joe Turner's Come . . .' to Broadway and Will Stay for a While," *Huffington Post*, April 22, 2008: www.huffingtonpost.com/michael-giltz/theater-joe-turners-come_b_189039.html

19 Glitz, "Theater: 'Joe Turner's Come . . .' to Broadway and Will Stay for a While."

20 August Wilson, "The Ground on Which I Stand," *American Theatre* (September 1996): 14.

21 Bartlett Sher quoted by Healy, "Playwright's Race Adds to Drama for an August Wilson Revival," A18.

22 LaTanya Jackson quoted by Healy, "Playwright's Race Adds to Drama for an August Wilson Revival," A18.

23 Ben Brantley, "Wilson's Wanderers, Searching for Home," *New York Times*, April 17, 2009: www.nytimes.com/2009/04/17/theater/reviews/17turn.html?pagewanted=all&_r=0

24 Joe Dziemianowicz, "Rich B'way Revival is August Occasion," *New York Daily News*, April 16, 2009.

25 Costanza Romero quoted by Healy, "Playwright's Race Adds to Drama for an August Wilson Revival," A18.

26 Glitz, "Theater: 'Joe Turner's Come . . .' to Broadway and Will Stay for a While."

27 Costanza Romero quoted by Healy, "Playwright's Race Adds to Drama for an August Wilson Revival," A18.

28 Kenny Leon quoted by Healy, "Playwright's Race Adds to Drama for an August Wilson Revival," A18.

29 Ben Brantley, "Finding Drama in Life, and Vice Versa," *New York Times*, April 26, 2000: www.nytimes.com/2000/04/26/theater/theater-review-finding-drama-in-life-and-vice-versa.html

30 Robert Khan, "With 'Fences' on Screen, August Wilson's 'Jitney' Makes a Broadway Debut" (January 19, 2017), NBC New York: www.nbcnewyork.

com/entertainment/the-scene/Review-Jitney-August-Wilson-411098745.
html#ixzz4fn1CLe6R

31 Harry Haun, "At Long Last, August Wilson's 'Jitney' Pulls into Broadway," *New York Observer*, January 19, 2017: http://observer.com/2017/01/august-wilson-jitney-broadway/

32 Brantley, "Finding Drama in Life, and Vice Versa."

33 Ibid.

34 Ruben Santiago-Hudson quoted by Harry Harlin, "How August Wilson Made Ruben Santiago's Career," *Playbill*, January 1, 2017: www.playbill.com/article/how-august-wilson-made-ruben-santiago-hudsons-career

35 David Rooney, "'Jitney': Theater Review," *Hollywood Reporter*, January 19, 2017: www.hollywoodreporter.com/print/964712

36 Ruben Santiago-Hudson quoted by Harlin, "How August Wilson Made Ruben Santiago's Career."

37 Ruben Santiago-Hudson quoted by Eric Grode, "From Nosebleed Seats to the Stage, Actors Discuss August Wilson," *New York Times*, January 11, 2017: www.nytimes.com/2017/01/11/theater/august-wilson-actors.html

38 Alexis Soloski, "'Jitney' Review—August Wilson's Playful and Poignant Drama is a Triumph," *The Guardian*, January 19, 2017: www.theguardian.com/stage/2017/jan/19/jitney-review-august-wilson-manhattan-theatre-club

39 John Douglas Thompson quoted by Alexis Soloski, "John Douglas Thompson 'Coming Home' to August Wilson's 'Jitney,'" *The Village Voice*, January 19, 2017: www.villagevoice.com/arts/john-douglas-thompson-on-coming-home-to-august-wilsons-jitney-9586580

40 August Wilson, "Foreword," in *Romare Bearden: His Life and Art*, edited by Myron Schwartzman (New York: Harry N. Abrams, Inc., 1990), 9.

41 David Gallo quoted by Bryan Reesman, "It's All in the Details: Scenic Designer David Gallo Brings 70's Pittsburgh to Life for August Wilson's *Jitney*," *Stage Directions*, March 8, 2017: http://stage-directions.com/current-issue/9329-it-s-all-in-the-details.html

42 Reesman, "It's All in the Details: Scenic Designer David Gallo Brings 70's Pittsburgh to Life for August Wilson's *Jitney*."

43 David Gallo quoted by Erik Piepenburg, "Inside the 'Jitney' Set: Picturing Pittsburgh Onstage," *New York Times*, February 9, 2017: www.nytimes.com/2017/02/09/theater/jitney-august-wilson-pittsburgh-set-design-david-gallo.html

44 Gallo quoted by Reesman, "It's All in the Details: Scenic Designer David Gallo Brings 70's Pittsburgh to Life for August Wilson's *Jitney*."

45 Gallo quoted by Reesman, "It's All in the Details: Scenic Designer David Gallo Brings 70's Pittsburgh to Life for August Wilson's *Jitney*."

Notes

46　Gallo quoted by Reesman, "It's All in the Details: Scenic Designer David Gallo Brings 70's Pittsburgh to Life for August Wilson's."

47　Piepenburg, "Inside the 'Jitney' Set: Picturing Pittsburgh Onstage."

48　Andre Holland quoted by Ashley Lee, "Off Script: Andre Holland Talks Broadway's 'Jitney' and 'Moonlight's' Impact on Oscar Diversity (Q&A)," *Hollywood Reporter*, February 14, 2017: www.hollywoodreporter.com/news/ andre-holland-broadways-jitney-moonlights-impact-oscars-diversity-q-a-970671

49　Anthony Chisholm quoted by Haun, "At Long Last, August Wilson's 'Jitney' Pulls into Broadway."

50　Ruben Santiago-Hudson quoted by Haun, "At Long Last, August Wilson's 'Jitney' Pulls into Broadway."

51　Chisholm quoted by Haun, "At Long Last, August Wilson's 'Jitney' Pulls into Broadway."

52　Orlando Patterson, *Slavery and Social Death* (Cambridge, MA: Harvard University Press, 1982), 38.

53　Brantley, "Wilson's Wanderers, Searching for Home."

REFERENCES

Adell, Sandra. *Double Consciousness/Double Bind: Theoretical Issues in Twentieth-Century Black Literature*. Champagne-Urbana, IL: University of Illinois Press, 1994.

Adell, Sandra. "Speaking of Ma Rainey/Talking about the Blues." In *May All Your Fences Have Gates: Essays on the Drama of August Wilson*, edited by Alan Nadel, 51–66. Iowa City: University of Iowa Press, 1994.

Alexander, Michelle. *The New Jim Crow: Mass Incarceration in the Age of Colorblindness*. New York: The New Press, 2012.

Austin, J. L. *How to Do Things with Words*, second ed. Cambridge, MA: Harvard University Press, 1975.

Baptist, Edward E. *The Half that Has Never Been Told: Slavery and the Making of American Capitalism*. New York: Basic Books, 2014.

Beckert, Sven. *Empire of Cotton: A Global History*. New York: Alfred A. Knopf, 2015.

Berlin, Ira. *Slaves without Masters: The Free Negro in the Antebellum South*. New York: The New Press, 1992.

Bigsby, Christopher. "An Interview with August Wilson." In *The Cambridge Companion to August Wilson*, edited by Christopher Bigsby. Cambridge: Cambridge University Press, 2007.

Blackmon, Douglas A. *Slavery by Another Name: The Re-Enslavement of Black Americans from the Civil War to World War II*. New York: Anchor Books, 2009.

Bottoms, Stephen. "*Two Trains Running*: Blood on the Tracks." In *The Cambridge Companion to August Wilson*, edited by Christopher Bigsby. Cambridge: Cambridge University Press, 2007.

Bryer, Jackson R., and Mary C. Hartig, eds. *Conversations with August Wilson*. Jackson: University of Mississippi Press, 2006.

Cone, James H. *Martin & Malcolm: A Dream or a Nightmare*. Maryknoll, NY: Orbis Books, 1991.

Crawford, Eileen. "The Bb Burden: The Invisibility of *Ma Rainey's Black Bottom*." In *August Wilson: A Casebook*, edited by Marilyn Elkins, 31–48. New York: Garland, 1994.

Crenshaw, Kimberle, Neil Gotanda, Gary Peller, and Kendall Thomas. *Critical Race Theory: The Key Writings that Formed the Movement*. New York: The New Press, 1996.

Crowley, Gregory J. *The Politics of Place: Contentious Urban Redevelopment in Pittsburgh*. Pittsburgh: University of Pittsburgh Press, 2005.

Dattel, Gene. *Cottoin and Race in the Making of America: The Human Costs of Economic Power*. New York: Ivan R. Dee, 2009.

References

de Certeau, Michel. *The Practice of Everyday Life*. Translated by Randall Stevenson. Berkeley: University of California Press, 1984.

Delgado, Richard, and Jean Stefancic, eds. *Critical Race Theory: The Cutting Edge*, second ed. Philadelphia: Temple University Press, 1999.

Elam, Harry J., Jr. *The Past as Present in the Drama of August Wilson*. Ann Arbor: University of Michigan Press, 2004.

Elam, Harry J., Jr. "*Radio Golf* in the Age of Obama." In *August Wilson: Completing the Twentieth-Century Cycle*, edited by Alan Nadel, 186–206. Iowa City: University of Iowa Press, 2010.

Ellison, Ralph. *Invisible Man*. New York: Random House, 1982.

Foucault, Michel. *The Birth of the Clinic: An Archeology of Medical Perception*. Translated by A. M. Sheridan Smith. New York: Vintage, 1975.

Foucault, Michel. *Discipline and Punish: The Birth of the Prison*. Translated by Alan Sheridan. New York: Vintage Books, 1979.

Foucault, Michel. *Madness and Civilization: A History of Insanity in the Age of Reason*. Translated by Richard Howard. New York: Vintage, 1973.

Glasco, Laurence A., and Christopher Rawson. *August Wilson: Pittsburgh Places and His Life and Plays*. Pittsburgh: Pittsburgh History & Landmarks Foundation, 2011.

Goddard, Stephen B. *Getting There: The Epic Struggle between Road and Rail in the American Century*. Chicago: University of Chicago Press, 1994.

Graves, Tom. *Crossroads: The Life and Afterlife of Blues Legend Robert Johnson*. Spokane: DeMers Books, 2008.

Herman, Max Arthur. *Summer of Rage: An Oral History of the 1967 Newark and Detroit Riots*. New York: Peter Lang, 2003.

Holland, Sharon Patricia. *Raising the Dead: Readings of Death and (Black) Subjectivity*. Durham, NC: Duke University Press, 2000.

Jacobs, Jane. *The Death and Life of Great American Cities*. New York: Random House, 1961.

Johnson, Walter. *River of Dark Dreams: Slavery and the Empire in the Cotton Kingdom*. Cambridge, MA: Harvard University Press, 2013.

Jones, E. Michael. *The Slaughter of Cities: Urban Renewal as Ethnic Cleansing*. South Bend, IN: St. Augustine Press, 2004.

King, Martin Luther. "Letter from a Birmingham City Jail." In *The Eyes on the Prize Civil Rights Reader*, edited by David J. Clayborne Carson, Gerald Gill Garrow, Vincent Harding, and Darlene Clark Hine, 153–58. New York: Penguin, 1991.

Korten, David. *The Post-Corporate World: Life after Capitalism*. San Francisco and West Hartford: Berrett-Koehler Publishers and Kumarian Press, 1999.

Krasner, David. "*Jitney*, Folklore and Responsibility." In *The Cambridge Companion to August Wilson*, edited by Christopher Bigsby, 158–68. Cambridge: Cambridge University Press, 2007.

LaCroix, David. "Finite and Final Interruptions: Using Time in *Radio Golf*." In *August Wilson: Completing the Twentieth-Century Cycle*, edited by Alan Nadel, 152–61. Iowa City: University of Iowa Press, 2010.

Lewis, Barbara. "Miss Tyler's Two Bodies: Aunt Ester and the Legacy of Time." In *August Wilson: Completing the Twentieth-Century Cycle*, edited by Alan Nadel, 134–44. Iowa City: University of Iowa Press, 2010.

Lewis, Tom. *Divided Highways: Building the Interstate Highways, Transforming American Life*. New York: Penguin, 1997.

Locke, Hubert G. *The Detroit Riot of 1967*. Detroit: Wayne State University Press, 2017.

Luce, Henry. "The American Century." *Life Magazine* 10, February 17, 1941: 61–65.

Morales, Michael. "Ghosts on the Piano: August Wilson and the Representation of Black American History." In *May All Your Fences Have Gates: Essays on the Drama of August Wilson*, edited by Alan Nadel, 105–15. Iowa City: University of Iowa Press, 1994.

Morris, Thomas D. *Free Men All: The Personal Liberty Laws of the North, 1780–1861*. Union New Jersey: The Lawbook Exchange Ltd., 2001.

Mumford, Kevin. *Newark: A History of Race, Rights and Riots in America*. New York: New York University Press, 2008.

Nadel, Alan, ed. *August Wilson: Completing the Twentieth-Century Cycle*. Iowa City: University of Iowa Press, 2010.

Nadel, Alan. "Introduction." In *May All Your Fences Have Gates: Essays on the Drama of August Wilson*, edited by Alan Nadel, 1–8. Iowa City: University of Iowa Press, 1994.

Nadel, Alan. *Invisible Criticism: Ralph Ellison and the American Canon*. Iowa City: University of Iowa Press, 1988.

Nadel, Alan, ed. *May All Your Fences Have Gates: Essays on the Drama of August Wilson*. Iowa City: University of Iowa Press, 1994.

Nadel, Alan. *Television in Black-and-White America*. Lawrence: Kansas University Press, 2006.

Nesmith, Eugene "Beyond the Wilson-Brustein Debate". *Theater* 27, no. 2 and 3 (1997): 5–41.

Oshinsky, David. *Worse than Slavery: Parchman Farm and the Ordeal of Jim Crow Justice*. New York: Free Press, 1997.

Patterson, Orlando. *Slavery and Social Death: A Comparative Study*. Cambridge, MA: Harvard University Press, 1982.

Pereira, Kim. *August Wilson and the African American Odyssey*. Champagne-Urbana: University of Illinois Press, 1995.

Said, Edward. *Beginnings: Intention and Method*. New York: Columbia University Press, 1985.

Schroeder, Patricia R. *Robert Johnson, Mythmaking, and Contemporary American Culture*. Champagne-Urbana: University of Illinois Press, 2004.

Shannon, Sandra. "A Transplant that Didi Not Take: August Wilson's Views on the Great Migration." *African American Review* 31, no. 4 (Winter 1997): 659–66.

Shannon, Sandra G. "The Long Wait: August Wilson's *Ma Rainey's Black Bottom*." *Black American Literature Forum* 25, no. 1 (1991): 135–46.

Shannon, Sandra G. "Framing African American Cultural Identity: The Bookends Plays in August Wilson's 10-Play Cycle." *College Literature* (Spring 2009): 26–39.

References

Shannon, Sandra G. "Turn Your Lamp Down Low! Aunt Ester Dies in *King Hedley II*." In *August Wilson: Completing the Twentieth-Century Cycle*, edited by Alan Nadel, 123–33. Iowa City: University of Iowa Press, 2010.

Shannon, Sandra G. *The Dramatic Vision of August Wilson*. Washington, DC: Howard University Press, 1995.

Snodgrass, Mary Ellen. *August Wilson: A Literary Companion*. Jefferson: McFarland, 2004.

Spencer, Vivian Gist, and Yvonne Chambers. "Ritual Death and Wilson's Female Christ." In *August Wilson: Completing the Twentieth-Century Cycle*, edited by Alan Nadel, 134–44. Iowa City: University of Iowa Press, 2010.

Tarr, Joel A. *Devastation and Renewal: An Environmental History of Pittsburgh and Its Region*. Pittsburgh: University of Pittsburgh Press, 2003.

Timpane, John. "Filling the Time: Reading History in the Drama of August Wilson." In *May All Your Fences Have Gates: Essays on the Drama of August Wilson*, edited by Alan Nadel, 67–85. Iowa City: University of Iowa Press, 1994.

Twain, Mark. *The Adventures of Huckleberry Finn*, edited by Guy Cardwell. New York: Penguin, 2002.

Welding, Pete. "Robert Johnson: Hell Hound on His Trail." In *Down Beat Music '66*, edited by Elmhurst, 73–76, 103. Illinois: Maher Publications, 1966.

Werner, Craig. "August Wilson's Burden: The Function of Neo-Classical Jazz." In *May All Your Fences Have Gates: Essays on the Drama of August Wilson*, edited by Alan Nadel, 21–50. Iowa City: University of Iowa Press, 1994.

Williams, Eric. *Capitalism and Slavery*. Chapel Hill: University of North Carolina Press, 1944.

Williams, Patricia J. *The Alchemy of Race and Rights*. Cambridge, MA: Harvard University Press, 1991.

Wilson, August. *Fences*. New York: Plume Books, 1986.

Wilson, August. *Gem of the Ocean*. New York: Theater Communications Group, 2007.

Wilson, August. *The Ground on Which I Stand*. New York: Theater Communications Group, 2001.

Wilson, August. *Jitney*. New York: Overlook Press, 2001.

Wilson, August. *Joe Turner's Come and Gone*. New York: Plume Books, 1988.

Wilson, August. *King Hedley II*. New York: Theater Communications Group, 2007.

Wilson, August. *Ma Rainey's Black Bottom*. New York: Plume Books, 1985.

Wilson, August. *The Piano Lesson*. New York: Plume Books, 1990.

Wilson, August. *Radio Golf*. New York: Theater Communications Group, 2007.

Wilson, August. *Seven Guitars*. New York: Plume Books, 1997.

Wilson, August. *Two Trains Running*. New York: Plume Books, 1993.

Yafa, Stephen. *Cotton: The Biography of a Revolutionary Fiber*. New York: Penguin Books, 2005.

Zipp, Samuel. *Manhattan Projects: The Rise and Fall of Urban Renewal in Cold War New York*. New York and London: Oxford University Press, 2010.

NOTES ON CONTRIBUTORS

Harry J. Elam, Jr., is Olive H. Palmer Professor in the Humanities at Stanford University, where he also serves as Senior Vice Provost for Education, Vice President for the Arts, and Freeman-Thornton Vice Provost for Undergraduate Education. He is the author of *The Past as Present in the Drama of August Wilson*, which won the Errol Hill Award. He is also author or editor of six other books, including *Taking It to the Streets: The Social Protest Theater of Luis Valdez and Amiri Baraka* and *Black Cultural Traffic: Crossroads in Performance and Popular Culture*. In 2006, he was inducted into the College of Fellows of the American Theatre.

Donald E. Pease is the Ted and Helen Geisel Third Century Professor in the Humanities at Dartmouth College, where he chairs the Master of Arts in Liberal Studies Program and directs the Futures of American Studies Institute. He is the author of several books, including, most recently, *Theodor Seuss Geisel* (2010) and *New American Exceptionalism* (2009). He is the editor of the Duke University Press New Americanist series, and has edited or co-edited more than a half-dozen volumes in American literature and American studies. His many awards include the 1987 Mark Ingraham Prize for Best New Book in the Humanities and Social Sciences and the 2012 American Studies Association's Bode-Pearson Prize for lifelong service in American Studies.

INDEX

Index

Index

Index

Index

CPSIA information can be obtained
at www.ICGtesting.com
Printed in the USA
LVHW022121270520
656688LV00003B/205